ROUTLEDGE LIBRARY EDITIONS: CONTINENTAL PHILOSOPHY

Volume 6

JACQUES DERRIDA

JACQUES DERRIDA
Critical Thought

Edited by
IAN MACLACHLAN

LONDON AND NEW YORK

First published in 2004 by Ashgate Publishing Limited

This edition first published in 2018
by Routledge
2 Park Square, Milton Park, Abingdon, Oxon OX14 4RN

and by Routledge
711 Third Avenue, New York, NY 10017

Routledge is an imprint of the Taylor & Francis Group, an informa business

© 2004 Introduction Ian Maclachlan. For copyright of individual articles refer to the acknowledgements.

All rights reserved. No part of this book may be reprinted or reproduced or utilised in any form or by any electronic, mechanical, or other means, now known or hereafter invented, including photocopying and recording, or in any information storage or retrieval system, without permission in writing from the publishers.

Trademark notice: Product or corporate names may be trademarks or registered trademarks, and are used only for identification and explanation without intent to infringe.

British Library Cataloguing in Publication Data
A catalogue record for this book is available from the British Library

ISBN: 978-1-138-06315-0 (Set)
ISBN: 978-1-315-10580-2 (Set) (ebk)
ISBN: 978-1-138-08640-1 (Volume 6) (hbk)
ISBN: 978-1-138-08805-4 (Volume 6) (pbk)
ISBN: 978-1-315-11098-1 (Volume 6) (ebk)

Publisher's Note
The publisher has gone to great lengths to ensure the quality of this reprint but points out that some imperfections in the original copies may be apparent.

Disclaimer
The publisher has made every effort to trace copyright holders and would welcome correspondence from those they have been unable to trace.

Jacques Derrida

Critical Thought

Edited by
IAN MACLACHLAN

ASHGATE

Introduction © Ian Maclachlan 2004. For copyright of individual articles refer to the acknowledgements.

All rights reserved. No part of this publication may be reproduced, stored in a retrieval system or transmitted in any form or by any means, electronic, mechanical, photocopying, recording or otherwise without the prior permission of the publisher.

Published by
Ashgate Publishing Limited
Gower House
Croft Road
Aldershot
Hampshire GU11 3HR
England

Ashgate Publishing Company
Suite 420
101 Cherry Street
Burlington, VT 05401-4405
USA

Ashgate website: http://www.ashgate.com

British Library Cataloguing in Publication Data
Jacques Derrida : critical thought
  1.Derrida, Jacques
  I.Maclachlan, Ian, 1960-
  194

Library of Congress Cataloguing-in-Publication Data
Jacques Derrida : critical thought / compiled by Ian Maclachlan.
  p. cm.
  Includes bibliographical references and index.
  ISBN 0-7546-0806-9 (alk. paper)
  1. Derrida, Jacques. I. Maclachlan, Ian, 1960-

BT2430.D484J335 2004
194--dc22

2003062880

ISBN 0 7546 0806 9

Printed and bound in Great Britain by MPG Books Ltd, Bodmin, Cornwall

Contents

Preface		vii
Acknowledgements		ix
Abbreviations		x
1	Introduction: Deconstruction, Critical Thought, Literature Ian Maclachlan	1
2	'Literature'/Literature Alan Bass	14
3	Household Words: Alterity, the Unconscious and the Text Ann Wordsworth	24
4	Skepticism and Deconstruction A.J. Cascardi	36
5	Un dialogue de sourds? Some Implications of the Austin–Searle–Derrida Debate Ian Maclean	49
6	Autobiography and the Case of the Signature: Reading Derrida's *Glas* Jane Marie Todd	67
7	Metaphorics and Metaphysics: Derrida's Analysis of Aristotle Irene E. Harvey	86
8	Time after Time: Temporality, Temporalization Timothy Clark	110
9	Circumcising Confession: Derrida, Autobiography, Judaism Jill Robbins	126
10	Memento Mori Robert Smith	146
Index		162

Preface

In assembling the present selection of essays from the vast corpus of writings which Derrida's work has elicited, I have adopted two simple principles: that the essays included should not previously have been collected in book form, and that they should be substantial pieces illuminating important and potentially difficult aspects of Derrida's work. Thus, although the selection cannot claim to offer a comprehensive view of that work – that would have not only been impossible within the confines of one volume, but would also imply the possibility of a totalizing perspective which sits uneasily with Derrida's thought – the reader will find that the essays range over most of Derrida's published output, and that they focus on a number of crucial topics (some if not all of which, one might add, overflow the containing spatial figure of the *topos*): these include literature, iterability, the signature, time, alterity, Judaism, metaphor and death.

I have made no systematic attempt to choose essays highlighting the various debates or controversies provoked by Derrida's work, except where an essay seemed to me to recommend itself on the grounds of an especially lucid exposition of a thorny area, as was the case with those by A.J. Cascardi and Ian Maclean. Many of these 'debates' have emerged from hasty readings of Derrida's work and consequently have generated more heat than light. In the case of certain important encounters between Derrida's work and other modes of thought, such as Marxism and feminism, there already exist helpful collections of essays dealing with those points of contact.[1]

The essays are reprinted here in chronological order of their first publication. The final paragraph of the original version of Timothy Clark's essay has been omitted at the author's request. Otherwise, the texts are unchanged in substance; the only editorial interventions I have made are to correct obvious typographical errors and to achieve a degree of uniformity in presentation. Thus, a system of abbreviated references to English translations of Derrida's texts has been adopted. Where the essays included references to, or quotations from, the original French texts, English references and quotations have been added. Any otherwise unattributed translations from French texts are mine, and are marked as such.

I should like just to comment briefly on the first and last essays collected here. In kindly consenting to the inclusion of his early essay '"Literature"/Literature' in this collection, Alan Bass was at pains to point out that this piece was written to a tight deadline at the request of Richard Macksey for a special issue of *MLN* in 1972, at a time when the major translations of Derrida (including Bass's own) were yet to appear and when, in his words to me, Bass himself was a graduate student and 'a novice in this area'. For my part, I have no doubt about the value of Bass's essay as an opening to the present collection, both for its clear exposition of aspects of Derrida's work of the late 1960s and early 1970s, particularly in relation to the status of writing, and for its suggestive insights into the precarious, aporetic ontology of 'literature'. At first sight, the inclusion of Robert Smith's article 'Memento Mori' may seem surprising, given that Derrida's name only appears in one of its epigraphs and in a few references in the latter part of the essay. However, it seems to me that the thinking of death which Smith eloquently explores will be an invaluable aid to anyone seeking to grasp the significance of terms such as death, mourning, the event, the promise or the future in so many of Derrida's texts, and not only in those, such as *Aporias*, which feature death as an explicit theme.

Note

[1] Reactions to Derrida's *Specters of Marx* have been collected in Michael Sprinker (ed.), *Ghostly Demarcations: A Symposium on Jacques Derrida's 'Specters of Marx'* (London and New York: Verso, 1999). Two edited volumes have traced the relationship between Derrida's work and feminism: Ellen K. Feder, Mary C. Rawlinson and Emily Zakin (eds), *Derrida and Feminism: Recasting the Question of Woman* (London and New York: Routledge, 1997), and Nancy J. Holland (ed.), *Feminist Interpretations of Jacques Derrida* (University Park, PA: Pennsylvania State University Press, 1997).

Acknowledgements

My thanks go firstly to Philip Shaw, who initially invited me to edit this volume. Frances Britain and Rachel Lynch of Ashgate Publishing were instrumental in seeing it through to its completion. I am grateful and indebted to the authors of these essays for kindly consenting to their inclusion here. I am further grateful to the following copyright holders for permission to reproduce the articles which comprise this volume:

Alan Bass, '"Literature"/Literature', *MLN*, 87 (1972), 852–64, © 1972 The Johns Hopkins University Press; A.J. Cascardi, 'Skepticism and Deconstruction', *Philosophy and Literature*, 8 (1984), 1–14, © 1984 The Johns Hopkins University Press; Jill Robbins, 'Circumcising Confession: Derrida, Autobiography, Judaism', *Diacritics*, 25, 4 (1995), 20–38, © 1996 The Johns Hopkins University Press. All of these reprinted by permission of the Johns Hopkins University Press.

Ann Wordsworth, 'Household Words: Alterity, the Unconscious and the Text', *Oxford Literary Review*, 5 (1982), 80–95, © 1982 *The Oxford Literary Review*; Timothy Clark, 'Time after Time: Temporality, Temporalization', *Oxford Literary Review*, 9 (1987), 119–35, © 1987 *The Oxford Literary Review*. Both reprinted by permission of the editors of *The Oxford Literary Review*.

Ian Maclean, 'Un dialogue de sourds? Some Implications of the Austin-Searle-Derrida Debate', *Paragraph*, 5 (1985), 1–26, © 1985 Ian Maclean. Reprinted by permission of the author.

Jane Marie Todd, 'Autobiography and the Case of the Signature: Reading Derrida's *Glas*', *Comparative Literature*, 38, 1 (1986), 1–19, © 1986 Jane Marie Todd. Reprinted by permission of the author.

Irene E. Harvey, 'Metaphorics and Metaphysics: Derrida's Analysis of Aristotle', *Journal of the British Society for Phenomenology*, 17, 3 (1986), 308–30, © 1986 The British Society for Phenomenology. Reprinted by permission of the British Society for Phenomenology and Jackson Publishing.

Robert Smith, 'Memento Mori', *Angelaki*, 3, 3 (1998), 45–57, © 1998 Carfax Publishing Ltd and the Editors of *Angelaki*. Reprinted by permission of the editors of *Angelaki* and Taylor & Francis Ltd, PO Box 25, Abingdon, Oxfordshire, UK.

Abbreviations

Abbreviations used in reference to English translations of Derrida's work are given here in alphabetical order.

A	*Aporias: Dying – Awaiting (One Another at) the 'Limits of Truth'*, trans. Thomas Dutoit, Stanford, CA: Stanford University Press, 1993.
ATM	'At This Very Moment in This Work Here I Am', trans. Ruben Berezdivin, in *Re-Reading Levinas*, ed. Robert Bernasconi and Simon Critchley, London: Athlone Press; Bloomington: Indiana University Press, 1991, pp. 11–48.
BL	'Before the Law', trans. Avital Ronell and Christine Roulston, in Jacques Derrida, *Acts of Literature*, ed. Derek Attridge, London and New York: Routledge, 1992, pp. 183–220.
C	'Circumfession', trans. Geoffrey Bennington, in Geoffrey Bennington and Jacques Derrida, *Jacques Derrida*, Chicago and London: University of Chicago Press, 1993.
Com	'Coming into One's Own', trans. James Hulbert, in *Psychoanalysis and the Question of the Text*, ed. Geoffrey Hartman, Baltimore and London: Johns Hopkins University Press, 1978, pp. 114–48.
D	*Dissemination*, trans. and intro. Barbara Johnson, London: Athlone Press; Chicago: University of Chicago Press, 1981.
F	'Fors: The Anglish Words of Nicolas Abraham and Maria Torok', trans. Barbara Johnson, *The Georgia Review*, 31, 1 (1977), 64–116.
FL	'Force of Law: The "Mystical Foundation of Authority"', trans. Mary Quaintance, in *Deconstruction and the Possibility of Justice*, ed. Drucilla Cornell, Michel Rosenfeld and David Gray Carlson, London and New York: Routledge, 1992, pp. 3–67.
G	*Glas*, trans. John P. Leavey, Jr and Richard Rand, Lincoln and London: University of Nebraska Press, 1986.
HAS	'How to Avoid Speaking: Denials', trans. Ken Frieden, in *Languages of the Unsayable: The Play of Negativity in Literature and Literary Theory*, ed. Sanford Budick and Wolfgang Iser, New York: Columbia University Press, 1989, pp. 3–70.
LG	'The Law of Genre', trans. Avital Ronell, in *Acts of Literature*, pp. 223–52.
LI	*Limited Inc*, ed. Gerald Graff, trans. Samuel Weber and Jeffrey Mehlman, Evanston: Northwestern University Press, 1988.

LJF	'Letter to a Japanese Friend', trans. David Wood and Andrew Benjamin, in *A Derrida Reader: Between the Blinds*, ed. Peggy Kamuf, London and New York: Harvester Wheatsheaf, 1991, pp. 270–76.
LO	'Living On: Border Lines', trans. James Hulbert, in Harold Bloom *et al.*, *Deconstruction and Criticism*, London: Routledge and Kegan Paul; New York: Seabury Press, 1979, pp. 75–176.
MB	*Memoirs of the Blind: The Self-Portrait and Other Ruins*, trans. Pascale-Anne Brault and Michael Naas, Chicago and London: University of Chicago Press, 1993.
Me	'Me – Psychoanalysis: An Introduction to the Translation of "The Shell and the Kernel" by Nicolas Abraham', trans. Richard Klein, *Diacritics*, 9, 1 (1979), 4–12.
MP	*Margins of Philosophy*, trans. Alan Bass, Brighton: Harvester Press; Chicago: University of Chicago Press, 1982.
MPDM	*Mémoires: for Paul de Man*, trans. Cecile Lindsay, Jonathan Culler and Eduardo Cadava, New York: Columbia University Press, 1986.
OAT	'Of an Apocalyptic Tone Recently Adopted in Philosophy', trans. John P. Leavey, Jr, *Oxford Literary Review*, 6, 2 (1984), 3–37.
OG	*Of Grammatology*, trans. and intro. Gayatri Chakravorty Spivak, Baltimore and London: Johns Hopkins University Press, 1976.
P	*Positions*, trans. Alan Bass, London: Athlone Press; Chicago: University of Chicago Press, 1981.
PC	*The Post Card: From Socrates to Freud and Beyond*, trans. and intro. Alan Bass, Chicago and London: University of Chicago Press, 1987.
PI	*Points . . . Interviews 1974–1994*, ed. Elisabeth Weber, trans. Peggy Kamuf *et al.*, Stanford, CA: Stanford University Press, 1995.
PM	'Perhaps or Maybe', in 'Responsibilities of Deconstruction', ed. Jonathon Dronsfield and Nick Midgley, *PLI: Warwick Journal of Philosophy*, 6 (1997), 1–18.
PR	'The Principle of Reason: The University in the Eyes of its Pupils', trans. Catherine Porter and Edward P. Morris, *Diacritics*, 13, 3 (1983), 3–20.
Psy	'Psyche: Inventions of the Other' [extract], trans. Catherine Porter, in *Acts of Literature*, pp. 311–43.
RDP	'Remarks on Deconstruction and Pragmatism', trans. Simon Critchley, in Simon Critchley *et al.*, *Deconstruction and Pragmatism*, ed. Chantal Mouffe, London and New York: Routledge, 1996, pp. 77–88.
SM	*Specters of Marx: The State of the Debt, the Work of Mourning, and the New International*, trans. Peggy Kamuf, London and New York: Routledge, 1994.
SNS	*Spurs: Nietzsche's Styles*, trans. Barbara Harlow, Chicago and London: University of Chicago Press, 1979.
SP	*Speech and Phenomena, and Other Essays on Husserl's Theory of Signs*,

	trans. and intro. David B. Allison, Evanston, IL: Northwestern University Press, 1973.
SST	'Some Statements and Truisms about Neologisms, Newisms, Postisms, Parasitisms, and Other Small Seismisms', trans. Anne Tomiche, in *The States of 'Theory': History, Art, and Critical Discourse*, ed. David Carroll, Stanford, CA: Stanford University Press, 1994, pp. 63–94.
TOJ	'The Time is Out of Joint', trans. Peggy Kamuf, in *Deconstruction is/in America*, ed. Anselm Haverkamp, New York and London: New York University Press, 1995, pp. 14–38.
TP	*The Truth in Painting*, trans. Geoff Bennington and Ian McLeod, Chicago and London: University of Chicago Press, 1987.
TSICL	'"This Strange Institution Called Literature": An Interview with Jacques Derrida', trans. Geoffrey Bennington and Rachel Bowlby, in *Acts of Literature*, pp. 33–75.
TTP	'The Time of a Thesis: Punctuations', trans. Kathleen McLaughlin, in *Philosophy in France Today*, ed. Alan Montefiore, Cambridge: Cambridge University Press, 1983, pp. 34–50.
WD	*Writing and Difference*, trans. and intro. Alan Bass, London: Routledge and Kegan Paul; Chicago: University of Chicago Press, 1978.

CHAPTER 1

Introduction: Deconstruction, Critical Thought, Literature

Ian Maclachlan

More than 40 years after the publication of Derrida's first article, and about 30 years after his work first began to have an impact on literary studies in the anglophone world, deconstruction still seems to sit uneasily in that same field in which it was first hailed as a new theoretical approach. Or, rather, it might be more accurate to say that, at a time when the term 'deconstruction' is more widely used than ever, whether its demise is being heralded by proponents of other critical approaches or whether it is being deployed more or less as a synonym for 'critique' or 'refutation' by academics or journalists, the significance of Derrida's work for our critical thinking about literature still calls for elucidation. In my introduction to this collection of essays on Derrida, which themselves range over a period of some 30 years, I propose to examine why it is that Derrida's work unsettles what we understand by each term in a phrase such as 'critical thinking about literature'.

In the now well-known text entitled 'Letter to a Japanese Friend', where Derrida addresses the problem of translating the term 'deconstruction' which has become inescapably associated with his name, he insists that:

> ... deconstruction is neither an *analysis* nor a *critique* ... It is not an analysis in particular because the dismantling of a structure is not a regression toward a *simple element*, toward an *indissoluble origin*. These values, like that of analysis, are themselves philosophemes subject to deconstruction. No more is it a critique, in a general sense or in a Kantian sense. The instance of *krinein* or of *krisis* (decision, choice, judgment, discernment) is itself, as is all the apparatus of transcendental critique, one of the essential 'themes' or 'objects' of deconstruction. (LJF 273)

I intend to examine this differentiation of deconstruction from critique in general terms, but since Derrida alludes to Kant and transcendental critique here, let us briefly pursue that path.[1] Deconstruction would disturb the distinctions which are necessary to the Kantian project of establishing the conditions of possibility of knowledge, beginning, for example, with the distinction between the transcendental and the empirical, but not in order to suggest that we can simply do without such distinctions, that we can collapse, bypass or dialectically transcend them, nor that we can simply replace them with better ones. Rather, deconstruction would involve provisionally embracing such distinctions in order to pursue them to the point at which the necessary co-implication of the distinguished terms manifests itself: the transcendental, for instance, never quite managing to pull itself clear of the empirical, and the empirical never quite free of traces of the transcendental. It is because of this constitutive impurity and incompletion of any would-be foundational dimension, such as the transcendental, that the conditions of possibility which might be sought on such a dimension turn out, at the same time, to be conditions of impossibility, as we shall see later in relation to the notion of decision.[2]

Thus, while deconstruction may loosely be said to share with Kantian critique a process of desedimentation, exposing the aprioristic grounds for what various forms of philosophical idealism and materialism have to assume as simply given, this can no longer be in view of establishing an ultimate, secure ground, and thus can no longer properly be termed critique; if we were to insist on retaining the term, it would have to be a neologized, 'improper' critique. As Geoffrey Bennington observes of Irene Harvey's provisional suggestion that deconstruction be considered a critique of critique, 'this can only be a first move, in so far as critique is always a digging for foundations, a search for firm ground on which the edifice of metaphysics might subsequently be (re)built, and the point is that deconstruction is not even a metacritique in this sense.'[3] However, if deconstruction renounces the ambition of positing an ultimate epistemological ground, this does not entail simply abandoning the transcendental movement of critique, for such a gesture would ultimately amount to a return to a pre-critical empiricism or to a scepticism which simply leaves the symmetrical poles of would-be rational or empirical certainty in place.[4] Thus, in his 'Remarks on Deconstruction and Pragmatism', commenting on his use of the term 'quasi-transcendental', Derrida affirms 'the necessity of posing transcendental questions in order not to be held within the fragility of an incompetent empiricist discourse, and thus it is in order to avoid empiricism, positivism and psychologism that it is endlessly necessary to renew transcendental questioning' (RDP 81).[5]

Turning to the relationship between deconstruction and critique in the context of contemporary literary and cultural criticism, one would have to observe that, by and large, the term 'critique', as it is deployed in that field, seems to have rather more to do with Marx than with Kant. Resisting the assimilation of deconstruction to critique, Geoffrey Bennington remarks of the latter term that it is 'notoriously slippery between a Kantian sense and a Marxist inflexion of that sense',[6] and goes on to cite a passage from Barbara Johnson's introduction to her translation of *Dissemination* which neatly illustrates this slipperiness. Immediately after describing critique as an 'analysis that focuses on the grounds of [a] system's possibility', Johnson allows this roughly Kantian sense to merge into what appears to owe more to a Marxist notion of critique when she continues: 'The critique reads backwards from what seems natural, obvious, self-evident, or universal, in order to show that these things have their history . . . and that the starting-point is not a (natural) given but a (cultural) construct, usually blind to itself' (D xv).[7] The widespread use of the term 'critique' in the sense of a demystification of what is taken to be natural or universal doubtless betrays some sort of debt, however indirect, to the ideological critique of Marxism. None the less, the use of 'critique' in the former sense presents far too diffuse a category to enable a useful point of comparison with deconstruction. Ideological critique would present some significant parallels and contrasts with deconstruction, but a thorough account would require a detailed examination of various strands of Marxist thought and cannot therefore be properly undertaken here.

However, sketching the picture with broad brush-strokes, one could say that deconstruction shares with Marxist critique the gesture of uncovering the material, historical moorings of what is given as ideal and universal, and the exploitation, for the purposes of critical intervention, of contradictory fissures in what is given as natural or self-evident. Such parallels would then have to be qualified by the observation that deconstruction would part company with Marxism to the extent that the latter posited an ultimate, self-present ground for its critique, this ground in effect circularly reappearing as a dialectically projected *telos*, and also to the extent that Marxism relied on determinate moments of *krinein* which deconstruction would put in question: the material and the ideal, base and superstructure, use-value and exchange-value, sensuous thing and commodity, and so on. But this picture already risks confronting deconstruction, falsely conceived as a theory, a method or simply even as an activity with a monolithic Marxism. For one thing, one would already have to note that such conceptions of ground and determinate oppositions are already put into question in the texts that constitute the Marxist 'tradition'. In fact, one might say that the texts of this tradition are already 'in deconstruction' (and therefore not simply in a single tradition), but not in order to effect an assimilation or subordination of an entity called 'Marxism' to one called 'deconstruction'. There is perhaps one point of confluence which we may briefly adduce without being unduly reductive, namely that neither deconstruction nor Marxism pretends to effect a transcendental critique of a system from the outside and in such a way as to leave it intact[8] (although any Marxism which sought to establish itself as a positivist science would be unable to avoid such a transcendentalizing movement): both may be described, in terms which are familiar from more than one Marxist tradition, as transformative and emancipatory critiques. In *Specters of Marx*, Derrida proclaims that:

> ... if there is a spirit of Marxism which I will never be ready to renounce, it is not only the critical idea or the questioning stance (a consistent deconstruction must insist on them even as it also learns that this is not the last or first word). It is even more a certain emancipatory and *messianic* affirmation, a certain experience of the promise that one can try to liberate from any dogmatics and even from any metaphysico-religious determination, from any *messianism*. And a promise must promise to be kept, that is, not to remain 'spiritual' or 'abstract', but to produce events, new effective forms of action, practice, organization, and so forth. (SM 89)[9]

We shall return later to another guise of this affirmation as an unfulfillable and therefore ineradicable promise when we consider the significance of literature for Derrida. But first, having sketched the relationship between deconstruction and critique in Kantian and Marxist senses of the latter, let us consider in more general terms what both makes possible and marks the limit of any *rapprochement* between deconstruction and the *krinein* of the critical moment. In response to an interviewer's question about the relationship between deconstruction and critique, Derrida first asserts the necessity of the critical idea, as we saw him do in relation to 'a spirit of Marxism' a moment ago, before going on to observe that '[i]n the style of the Enlightenment, of Kant, or of Marx, but also in the sense of evaluation (esthetic or literary), *critique* supposes judgment, voluntary judgment between two terms; it attaches to the idea of *krinein* or of *krisis* a certain negativity' (PI 357). To locate the divergence of deconstruction and critique at the moment of decision (*krinein*) is not at all to imply that deconstruction entails, for example, the annulment of that moment. Instead, deconstruction reveals that a decision can only come about through an experience of undecidability, and that this undecidability is at once the condition of possibility and of impossibility of the decision. It is the condition of possibility in as much as the moment of decision exceeds what is decidable in terms of the following of already determined rules, conventions or codes: 'A decision that would be taken otherwise than on the border of this undecidable would not be a decision' (PI 147). Thus, this possibility of the decision already exceeds the possible in terms of what falls simply within the ambit of such established rules, of prior knowledge or competence: 'The only decision possible is the impossible decision. It is when it is not possible to *know* what must be done, when knowledge is not and cannot be determining that a decision is possible as such' (PI 147).

But we should take care not to conclude from this that a decision takes place in the absence of any regulatory or conventional framework, for a decision would equally no longer be a decision if it were ineffective, if it did not effect a moment of *krinein* within a given system. Indeed, the experience of undecidability or *aporia* which we have described as the condition of (im)possibility of the decision is inconceivable without reference to such a framework or system. Thus, the moment of decision which appears to issue from such systemic undecidability cannot be said to break entirely free of that undecidability, lest it become an absolutely disassociated and therefore ineffective event, without purchase on any system, or, in definitively resolving the undecidability, it reveal itself to have been no more than the simple application of a rule after all. A passage in which Derrida delineates this situation in respect of the relation of law to justice is worth citing at length here:

> There is apparently no moment in which a decision can be called presently and fully just: either it has not yet been made according to a rule, and nothing allows us to call it just, or it has already followed a rule – whether received, confirmed, conserved or reinvented – which in its turn is not absolutely guaranteed by anything; and, moreover, if it were guaranteed, the decision

would be reduced to calculation and we couldn't call it just. That is why the ordeal of the undecidable that I just said must be gone through by any decision worthy of the name is never past or passed, it is not a surmounted or sublated (*aufgehoben*) moment in the decision. The undecidable remains caught, lodged, at least as a ghost – but an essential ghost – in every decision, in every event of decision. (FL 24)

The persistent undecidability that haunts decision is what weakens the negativity which, as we saw Derrida remark earlier, accompanies the notion of critique. Thus, the negative interval which the decisive moment of *krinein* would seek to establish between the terms of a distinction is never once and for all complete. At the same time, such terms would themselves be constitutively haunted by an undecidability which would undermine their self-identity, reinscribing *within* them the negative interval which critique would have sought to pose *between* them. This last observation indicates why deconstruction cannot simply renounce the negation effected by *krinein*, for to do so would only be to return to a pre-critical thinking of ideal or empirical self-identity. We might say, then, that deconstruction involves a passage through critique, but a transformative passage that does not leave critique intact. In weakening the negativity of critique, deconstruction disables the decisive movement beyond a given system which is necessary for a transcendental critique, and likewise impairs the self-contained interiority of a system which an immanent critique must suppose. In more general terms, this weakened negativity disturbs the demarcating boundaries of any supposed critical object.

If deconstruction cannot be said to have a determinate object, then neither can it be conceived as an operation effected by an autonomous agency. In the 'Letter to a Japanese Friend', Derrida stipulates:

> It must also be made clear that deconstruction is not even an *act* or an *operation*. Not only because there would be something 'patient' or 'passive' about it . . . . Not only because it does not return to an individual or collective *subject* who would take the initiative and apply it to an object, a text, a theme, etc. Deconstruction takes place, it is an event that does not await the deliberation, consciousness, or organization of a subject, or even of modernity. (LJF 274–5)

To cast this in terms of the undecidability and decision which we have been exploring, the undecidability which is the condition of (im)possibility of the decision also disrupts the self-identity of the subject and makes the decision something other than the voluntaristic act of a self-possessed agent:

> There is something passive in the most radical decision. If a decision is wholly under my control, if it is predicated of a subjectivity, if I am the one who decides for the decision, and it is totally active in that sense, then what follows as an effect of the decision is programmed. (PM 14)

In a sense, it is only in the moment of decision that subjectivity is decided, but since I never entirely decide for myself, then, in deciding, I never quite decide myself either, for 'my' decision, if it is to be one, must continue to be haunted by a constitutive undecidability, an alterity which is always at play in my identity:

> However paradoxical it may sound I must be affected by my own decision. To the extent that my decision is the other's, my decision is passive, it is affected by itself (as the other's) – which is I hope consistent with what I say about alterity constituting my own identity. (PM 14)[10]

The undecidability which is the only chance for the effectivity of a decision also precludes the punctual self-identity of the deciding agent, and thus, in issuing the promise of a decision, at the same time I promise myself, indefinitely.

Returning to the phrase 'critical thinking about literature' with which we began, it will already be apparent from what we have said about the grounds and decisions of critique, and indeed about the critical object and subjectivity, that Derrida's work raises questions about what we mean by 'thinking'. To say that Derrida's work challenges the principles or categories of thought risks corroborating the charge of irrationalism which has from time to time been made against him. In this respect, it is worth noting a passing remark in the essay 'The Principle of Reason: The University in the Eyes of its Pupils', where Derrida suggests that 'irrationalism, like nihilism, is a posture that is completely symmetrical to, thus dependent on, the principle of reason' (PR 14–15). Thus, in the same essay, the challenge posed to the principle of reason does not emerge from a position supposedly outside of reason. Instead, Derrida is interested in what it might mean to apply the principle of reason to itself:

> Are we to use reason to account for the principle of reason? Is the reason for reason rational? Is it rational to worry about reason and its principle? ... Who is more faithful to reason's call, who hears it with a keener ear, who better sees the difference, the one who offers questions in return and tries to think through the possibility of that summons, or the one who does not want to hear any question about the reason of reason? (PR 9)

One could pursue Derrida's challenge to thought through his many readings of key texts in the Western philosophical tradition, but to underline the contention that such a challenge does not constitute a recourse to irrationalism, let us briefly refer to the early essay on 'Cogito and the History of Madness' (WD 31–63). There, it is above all not a question of taking the side of the irrational against that of reason; indeed, the incoherence of such a gesture is what, for Derrida, undermines the Foucauldian project of a history of madness. Rather, in Derrida's reading of Descartes, the madness that is included in the test of hyperbolic doubt from which Descartes derives the certainty of the *cogito* continues to haunt the *cogito*. If the *cogito* is what survives hyperbolic doubt – survives the possibility, for example, of insane delusion – then that possibility of madness remains secretly lodged in the *cogito* as a constitutive condition which the *cogito* can never entirely dispel.[11]

In terms of foundationalist thought more generally, we can say that whichever ground we would give to thought, that ground, if it is to be ultimate, would have to be able to account for itself as a ground, to ground itself. Now, the point of applying the principle of reason to itself, for instance, would be to effect that opening of itself which would permit any ground to address itself, and thereby to reveal that, if a ground of thought may thus open itself to address itself, it must already be more or less than itself, already *other* than itself to be *itself*.[12] Of course, deconstruction would not be alone in posing a challenge to foundationalist thought, but to seek to locate deconstruction on one side or the other of a divide between foundationalist and anti-foundationalist thought would be to encounter essentially the same scenario which we glimpsed in respect of transcendental and immanent critiques. Thus, deconstruction would again part company with anti-foundationalist thought, such as pragmatism, to the extent that the latter is obliged to suppose a given context or community as a self-present totality, whereas, for Derrida, the limiting decision which would stake out such a context is only possible on the basis of a persistent undecidability which would open that same context in the very gesture which defined it.[13]

Everything we have said thus far about the relation of deconstruction to critique will have repercussions for the notion of critical thought within the literary field. Thus, we would find the effects of the weakening of the critical moment repeated variously across the range of literary critical theories and methodologies, such that deconstruction, although it may at times appear to accompany such theories or methodologies, would do so only to repeat them otherwise, turning the law which governs them back upon itself to disclose the difference from itself which lifts the law even as it imposes it. So, for example, when Derrida challenges Jean-Pierre Richard's thematic reading of Mallarmé in 'The Double Session', he does so by seeming to imitate such a reading, a key part of his discussion taking as its apparent theme the word 'hymen' which appears in Mallarmé's text *Mimique*. However, Derrida pursues the deconstructive logic of the hymen to the point where the oppositions between theme and form, signified and signifier, or semantics and syntax can no longer hold, and indeed to the point where the word 'hymen' no longer appears to be simply 'in' Mallarmé's text, nor to exercise a determining semantic function there, nor *a fortiori* a thematic one.[14] However, it is not merely a matter of advocating a formalist approach over thematic criticism. The thrust of Derrida's argument in 'Force and Signification' (WD 3–30), for example, is that any formalist criticism which deploys essentially spatializing structures in its analysis cannot account for the differing and deferring movement of *différance* which is the condition of (im)possibility of such determinate structures. More generally, formalist criticism is, for Derrida, entirely symmetrical with thematic criticism in its reliance on a form/content opposition which is also susceptible to the weakening of the moment of *krinein* which we described earlier.[15]

We can account for the divergence of deconstruction from various critical methodologies, and indeed from the notion of literary theory *tout court*, in terms of the blurring of the boundaries of any supposed critical object which we noted earlier. If the 'object-text' can no longer be conceived as a self-contained entity, and to conceive it as such would be to conceive of it as closed to any reading, then reading can no longer be said to find its purchase either inside or outside of the text, but must instead be subject to a tension between interiority and exteriority, between immanent and transcendental critique, between what used to be called 'practical criticism' and so-called theoretical abstraction. The constitutive opening of a text to its outside means that reading cannot entirely avoid the move into the metalinguistic space of theory, but equally cannot situate itself once and for all in that space, hence Derrida's remark in *Glas*: 'I do not cease to decapitate metalanguage, or rather to replunge its head into the text in order to extract it from the text, regularly, the interval of a respiration' (G 115, right column).[16] It may be that 'literature' names the situation in which this tension of reading is at its most acute, and so, at this point, let us turn to some of Derrida's remarks about literature.

A well-known moment in Derrida's thesis defence for his *doctorat d'Etat* signals his long-standing fascination with the literary, whilst already adumbrating the difficulty in giving a Derridean definition of literature:

> What is literature? And first of all what is it 'to write'? How is it that the fact of writing can disturb the very question 'what is?' and even 'what does it mean?' To say this in other words – and here is the *saying otherwise* that was of importance to me – when and how does an inscription become literature and what takes place when it does? (TTP 37–8)

If the peculiar ontology of literature is such that it poses a challenge to the question 'what is?', then it is not surprising that, when we attempt none the less to trace answers to this question in Derrida's texts, we are likely to find ourselves confronted by a series of qualified negatives. Thus, for example, 'there is no essence of literature, no truth of literature, no literary-being or being-literary of literature' (D 223), or again, 'there is no text which is literary *in itself*', but, Derrida adds in the same interview:

> ... this does not mean that literarity is merely projective or subjective – in the sense of the empirical subjectivity or caprice of each reader. The literary character of the text is inscribed on the side of the intentional object, in its noematic structure, one could say, and not only on the subjective side of the noetic act. There are 'in' the text features which call for the literary reading and recall the convention, institution, or history of literature. (TSICL 44).[17]

This last sentence appears to offer us something of a foothold in our investigation of Derrida's conception of literature. First of all, literature is an institution, albeit a 'strange' one, as is indicated by the remark which gives this interview its title. Elsewhere in that interview, Derrida observes that literature 'is an institution which tends to overflow the institution' (TSICL 36), and, in another interview, that 'it is at once institution and counter-institution, placed at a *distance* from the institution, at the angle that the institution makes with itself in order to *take a distance from itself, by itself [s'écarter d'elle-même]*' (PI 346).[18] The second potentially helpful indication is that 'there are "in" the text features which call for the literary reading', and we have already touched on what necessitates the scare quotes around the word 'in'. We may shed some light both on this call for, or call of, the literary and on the 'strange' institution of literature – its quasi-institutionality we might say – by considering what Derrida has to say about the sort of literary texts to which he is drawn.

In the same interview, Derrida says of these texts – by the likes of Mallarmé, Joyce, Celan, Bataille, Artaud and Blanchot – that:

> ... [they] all have in common that they are inscribed in a *critical* experience of literature. They bear within themselves, or we could also say in their literary act they put to work, a question, the same one, but each time singular and put to work otherwise: 'What is literature?' or 'Where does literature come from?' 'What shall we do with literature?' These texts operate a sort of turning back, they *are* themselves a sort of turning back on the literary institution. Not that they are only reflexive, specular or speculative, not that they suspend reference to something else, as is so often suggested by stupid and uninformed rumour. (TSICL 41)

Derrida's highlighting of the *critical* moment of such texts, their turning back on the literary institution, combined with his insistence that this is not simply a matter of reflexivity, can help us understand the quasi-institutionality of the literary to which we referred a moment ago. Rather than reflexivity, it would be better to say that such texts exhibit the structure of the re-mark – that is, a sort of supplementary mark which is always already double, marking the relation of the text to a set of norms, rules or conventions, to an institution in short, without which it would not be readable, but at the same time marking itself in its singularity.[19] The fact that this re-mark is not simply reflexive, but rather, in effecting a disjunction or failure of self-reflection, marks an opening to reading, is what gives a chance to the uncertain moment of the literary. The text at once re-marks itself *and* re-marks itself as a particular type of text: that is, it at once signals its own uniqueness – its idiom or signature – and its relation to a shared institutionality without which it could not even be recognized for the unique text it aspires to be. It marks itself, therefore, as at once *same* (the identity of this particular text) and *other* (relying for that identity on a relation with other texts) or, alternatively, as *other* (unlike any other text) and *same* (bearing a likeness to a set of similar texts). The *differantial* instability which the re-mark brings about prohibits the text from being 'only reflexive', since it always marks itself otherwise, and entails that the literary is neither simply 'in' nor 'outside of' the text. The literary is not therefore a property, but is better envisaged as a ceaseless shuttling between idiom and law, event and structure, inscription and reception, signature and counter-signature.[20]

In order to situate this notion of the re-mark in relation to more familiar conceptions of literary reflexivity, it may be helpful to draw a brief comparison with a highly influential model of reflexivity, namely Roman Jakobson's definition of the poetic function of language.[21] Before attempting to recast Derrida's notion of literature in the terms proposed by Jakobson, I should like to cite another passage from the interview '"This Strange Institution Called Literature"', where Derrida has just been addressing the question of the literary in relation to referentiality, to self-referentiality and to other discourses to which, he claims, literature is irreducible, even though it must still 'open onto' them: 'There is no literature without a *suspended* relation to meaning and reference. *Suspended* means *suspense*, but also *dependence*, condition, conditionality. In its suspended condition, literature can only exceed itself. No doubt all language refers to something other than itself or to language as something other' (TSICL 48). It is with the aid of this notion of a suspended-dependent relation to reference, of a reference that involves self-reference and a self-reference that involves hetero-reference – this *differeferentiality*, as Derrida puts it elsewhere (TOJ 24)[22] – that I propose to adapt Jakobson's model.

It will be recalled that Jakobson identifies the poetic function as operative when, of the six factors necessarily involved in any act of verbal communication (addresser, addressee, context, message, contact, code), the orientation of the communication is towards the message itself. A full exploration of this model in the light of Derrida's work would entail, amongst other things, questioning the 'presence' of the six communicative factors and their decidability for any given utterance, but for present purposes I want just to focus on the foregrounding of the utterance itself in the poetic function. Where Jakobson posits a hierarchical coexistence of functions within a given utterance, with one function being predominant,[23] I want to suggest the undecidability of such predominance, whereby the other communicative functions would be suspended by the poetic function, but at the same time dependent on it, and the poetic function dependent on them. In terms of the poetic function, if the utterance is to foreground itself, it must also foreground itself *as* fulfilling one or more of the other functions, since to foreground itself as itself, so to speak, in a perfect self-referentiality, would be to erase itself as language. Similarly, to fulfil any of the other functions, an utterance must still foreground itself as an utterance, as *this particular utterance* fulfilling such and such a function, so that the poetic function would operate as a sort of ghostly condition of any of the other functions. Considered in this light, Jakobson's poetic function would name that self-reference which is at once impossibility and inevitability for all language, that 'property of language', as Derrida remarks, 'whereby it always can and cannot speak of itself' (Psy 325). In contrast, Derrida's conception of literature may be regarded as maintaining the tension of that impossible, inevitable self-reference, of that undecidable oscillation of auto- and hetero-reference.

To come to a critical decision about literature, in terms of its essence, its property, its 'being-literary' or whatever, would be to arrest the undecidability which gives literature its chance, the chance of always again saying (itself) otherwise. Even though it may appear more propitious, we should also be wary of the decision that, rather than *being* something, literature *does* something, that it is a question of performativity or of an event. The sticking-point here would be the presumed unity of such an event in any account which held the literary text to *enact* itself. If the text is supposed to accomplish such an enactment, this can only be on the basis of the institution of an opposition within the text, between form and content for example, this opposition then being resolved in the accomplishment of the textual event of self-enactment. To conceive of literature as an event in this sense would, in Derrida's terms, be to conceive of the text as saturating its own context and thus closing itself to reading, thereby denying itself the very purchase necessary for the effectivity of an event. To identify literature as such an event is, in other words, precisely to lose it as an event, to arrest the undecidable oscillation described earlier. If literature is an event, it is one which is persistently inactual, surviving each inescapable actualization of reading and, moreover, doing so as the very condition of its 'availability' to reading: a ghostly event which ceaselessly promises itself as yet to come.[24] In his introduction to *Parages*, a volume which gathers his writings on Maurice Blanchot, Derrida describes this impossible event in the following passage, with which I should like to conclude as an opening to further reading:

> But the event – meeting, decision, appeal, nomination, initial incision of a mark – can only come about [*advenir*] from an experience of undecidability. Not that undecidability which still belongs to the order of calculation, but the other one, which no calculation could anticipate. Without this experience, would there ever be the chance of taking a step [*pas*], an appeal for the event *(come)*, a gift, a responsibility? Would there be anything other, any other cause than causality? Would not everything be at the mercy of programming?[25]

Notes

[1] On deconstruction and critique (especially in Kant's sense), see Geoffrey Bennington's 'Almost the end' in his *Interrupting Derrida* (London and New York: Routledge, 2000), pp. 141–52; a version of Bennington's paper was first delivered at a conference on 'Critique and Deconstruction' held at the Centre for Modern French Thought, University of Sussex.

[2] For extended accounts of Derrida's relation to the Kantian tradition, see Rodolphe Gasché's *The Tain of the Mirror: Derrida and the Philosophy of Reflection* (Cambridge, MA and London: Harvard University Press, 1986) and Irene E. Harvey's *Derrida and the Economy of 'Différance'* (Bloomington: Indiana University Press, 1986). Christopher Norris has been at pains to emphasize the elements of continuity between Derrida's work and the Kantian Enlightenment project; for a helpful overview see his review article on Harvey's book, reprinted as 'Derrida and Kant' in his *What's Wrong with Postmodernism: Critical Theory and the Ends of Philosophy* (London and New York: Harvester Wheatsheaf, 1990), pp. 194–207. For a remarkable deconstructive reading of Kant's accounts of the transcendental object, to which my own brief remarks are indebted, see Geoffrey Bennington's 'X', in John Brannigan, Ruth Robbins and Julian Wolfreys (eds), *Applying: To Derrida* (London: Macmillan Press; New York: St Martin's Press, 1996), pp. 1–20.

[3] Geoffrey Bennington, 'Deconstruction and the Philosophers (The Very Idea)', in his *Legislations: The Politics of Deconstruction* (London and New York: Verso, 1994), pp. 11–60 (26).

[4] For an account of what distinguishes deconstruction from such a scepticism, see A.J. Cascardi's essay in this volume (Chapter 4).

⁵ As for the relation between the terms 'deconstruction' and 'pragmatism', I would just observe very summarily that the extent to which deconstruction continues to work with a version of or, as Derrida suggests in the same text, something like a parody of transcendental critique, even though it must remain irreducible to the latter, would constitute the limit to the assimilation of deconstruction to pragmatism which has been proposed most notably and robustly by Richard Rorty. On this issue, besides the volume containing this text by Derrida, see, for example, Rorty's 'Philosophy as a Kind of Writing: An Essay on Derrida' in his *Consequences of Pragmatism* (Brighton: Harvester Press; Minneapolis: University of Minnesota Press, 1982), pp. 90–109, and his 'Is Derrida a Transcendental Philosopher?', in David Wood (ed.), *Derrida: A Critical Reader* (Oxford and Cambridge, MA: Blackwell, 1992), pp. 235–46. Almost anything Christopher Norris has written on Derrida, such as his *Derrida* (London: Fontana, 1987), could be read as an exemplary counterpoint to Rorty's position.

⁶ Bennington, *Legislations*, p. 24.

⁷ Cited in ibid., p. 24.

⁸ In this regard, let us note Derrida's remarks about the philosophical institution in France in the essay 'Parergon': 'Following the consistency of its logic, [deconstruction] attacks not only the internal edifice, both semantic and formal, of philosophemes, but also what one would be wrong to assign to it as its external housing, its extrinsic conditions of practice: the historical forms of its pedagogy, the social, economic or political structures of this pedagogical institution. It is because deconstruction interferes with solid structures, "material" institutions, and not only with discourses or signifying representations, that it is always distinct from an analysis or a "critique"' (TP 19).

⁹ More generally, the relationship between deconstruction and Marxism has been helpfully explored by Michael Ryan in his *Marxism and Deconstruction: A Critical Articulation* (Baltimore and London: Johns Hopkins University Press, 1982), although one would have to signal the recurring problem of Ryan's tendency to present deconstruction in instrumental terms. Geoffrey Bennington's review of Ryan's book, 'Outside Story', is very illuminating (reprinted in *Legislations*, pp. 88–98), as are his other essays on Marxist responses to deconstruction ('Demanding History' and 'Not Yet', ibid., pp. 61–73 and 74–87). For an examination of the political stakes of deconstruction, see Richard Beardsworth's *Derrida and the Political* (London and New York: Routledge, 1997).

¹⁰ Another name for this constitutive alterity might be the unconscious, but for an account of the ways in which Derrida's thinking of alterity exceeds the categories of psychoanalysis, particularly as a method of literary criticism, see the essay by Ann Wordsworth in Chapter 3 of this volume.

¹¹ For a more detailed account, see A.J. Cascardi's essay in Chapter 4 of this volume.

¹² See Irene E. Harvey's essay in Chapter 7 for an account of Derrida's treatment of the founding metaphors of philosophy as just such a ground.

¹³ This argument about the necessary opening of a given context could be recast in terms of iterability, according to which it is the structural possibility of limitless recontextualization that makes a given context possible. Derrida's clearest account of iterability is to be found in the essay 'Signature Event Context' (MP 307–30; LI 1–23). See also Ian Maclean's essay in Chapter 5 of this volume.

¹⁴ 'This word, this syllepsis, is not indispensable; philology and etymology interest us only secondarily, and the loss of the "hymen" would not be irreparable for *Mimique*. It produces its effects first and foremost through the syntax, which disposes the "*entre*" in such a way that the suspense is due only to the placement and not to the content of words' (D 220).

¹⁵ On the symmetry of these critical approaches, see P 63–4. Alan Bass's essay (Chapter 2 of this volume) should also be consulted for a discussion of 'formalism' and 'thematism' in relation to literary criticism and the moment of *krinein*, as well as for an account of the peculiar ontology of literature, to which I turn in the latter part of this Introduction.

¹⁶ On the relationship between deconstruction and literary theory or theories (including 'deconstructionism'), see SST.

¹⁷ In the volume containing this interview, see also Derek Attridge's helpful Introduction, 'Derrida and the Questioning of Literature' (pp. 1–29).

¹⁸ On literature, institutionality, and the law, see especially BL.

[19] On the re-mark, particularly in relation to the question of literary genre, see LG. A helpful exposition and illustration of the re-mark may be found in Timothy Clark's *Derrida, Heidegger, Blanchot: Sources of Derrida's Notion and Practice of Literature* (Cambridge: Cambridge University Press, 1992), pp. 119–23.

[20] See Jane Marie Todd's essay in Chapter 6 of this volume for a discussion of the unstable relations between signature and text. The strange singularity of the signature is also implicitly at issue in other guises (for instance, the mark of circumcision) in the essay by Jill Robbins (Chapter 9).

[21] See Roman Jakobson, 'Closing Statement: Linguistics and Poetics' in Thomas A. Sebeok (ed.), *Style in Language* (New York and London: The Technology Press of the Massachusetts Institute of Technology and John Wiley and Sons, 1960), pp. 350–77.

[22] See also Geoffrey Bennington's essay 'Index' in his *Legislations* (pp. 274–95) for an account of what he there describes as the 'constitutive undecidability between auto- and hetero-reference' (p. 293).

[23] Jakobson, 'Closing Statement', p. 353.

[24] That the experience of such a promise is also the aporetic experience of mortal existence as infinite finitude (see A 81) is elegantly demonstrated by Robert Smith in the essay which closes this volume.

[25] *Parages* (Paris: Galilée, 1986), p. 15; my translation. The insertion of the word 'come' [*viens*] in this passage alludes to the *viens* which appears in Blanchot's narrative *L'Arrêt de mort* (Paris: Gallimard, 1948), and which Derrida explores in the essay 'Pas', in *Parages* (pp. 19–116). The essay by Timothy Clark (Chapter 8) concludes with a discussion of 'come' as a summons beyond any temporality construed in terms of presence.

CHAPTER 2

'Literature'/Literature

Alan Bass

> . . . pourquoi 'littérature' nommerait encore ce qui déjà se soustrait à la littérature – à ce qu'on a toujours conçu et signifié sous ce nom – ou, ne s'y dérobant pas seulement, la détruit implacablement? (*La Dissémination*)
>
> La littérature s'annule dans son illimitation. (*La Dissémination*)[1]

If the question 'What is literature?' has never satisfactorily been answered, it may be time to scrutinize the question itself. Does 'literature' have any status as an 'object', as something about which the question 'what is it?' can be asked? Or if the question cannot be answered, how does literature affect the rest of what is, everything – excluding, perhaps, literature – which the question 'what is it?' is pertinent to? And in what discipline can these questions be situated? Science? Philosophy? Literature itself? Our traditions tell us that science has the most immediate, the most potentially 'truthful' relationship to the question 'what is it?', that is, to an object outside itself. Philosophy, we know, aspires to 'scientific' truthfulness, often constituting itself as the path from naïve non-scientificity to science itself.[2] Literature is seemingly excluded from answering this most basic of questions, because it never gets beyond its own textuality, is not concerned with determining the 'essence' or 'truth' of objects outside itself. This framework could even be recapitulated as degrees of textual transparency: accepted values indicate that the text of science should be totally transparent in relation to the 'reality' it deals with; that philosophy, in quest of 'truth', proceeds from an opaque to a transparent text, or is a 'transparent' text insofar as it is scientific; and that literature is all opaque textuality, somehow in relation to 'reality' only through its use or disregard of the imitative techniques that always imply a distance from reality.[3] The analysis, and possible breakdown, of this traditional framework would have to have as its focus the possibility of the *presence* of truth in science and its *non-presence* in literature. In other words, is there a text (for science is as textual, as written-down as literature) in which truth can be made present? What is the relationship between truth, presence, and textuality? This question is the brunt of the work of Jacques Derrida, a 'philosopher' whose texts are 'literary' because they have attacked the fundamental notion of 'scientific' truth. As Derrida has written, the question 'what is literature?' can make the authority of the question 'what is – ?' tremble, because the question is 'located' between literature and truth, between literature and the presence of anything that is.[4] The possible subversion of the oppositions truth/non-truth or presence/absence is to be sought between each term of the opposition, and the question of literature has always been the question of the 'between'.[5]

The first question that would have to be examined in the analysis of the relation between text and truth is that of the sign. All texts – scientific, philosophical, literary – are apparently made of signs, linguistic signs which have two faces: the *signifier*, the acoustic material making up the sign, and the *signified*, the conceptualization of the referent, the thing outside language. That which makes a text a text, distinguishing it from spoken discourse, is writing, and in the case of Occidental culture, phonetic writing; the function of writing, the 'analysis' and fixing of the (acoustic) signifier, would apparently make it the signifier of the signifier, the sign of the sign. At least since the *Cratylus* of Plato, philosophy has grappled with the relationship between the signifier and the signified, the question usually bearing on whether or not they are intrinsically related; and also, at least since Plato, writing has been defined as exterior to the sign itself, precisely because it is the signifier of the signifier, the sign of the sign. Spoken discourse is always associated with presence – it is 'alive'. Its written 'representation' signals non-presence – the author of the discourse is silent, or even dead insofar as his text is concerned.

This valuation of spoken discourse over the written text, the association of writing with exteriority, is at work in one of the most influential texts of modern linguistics, *le Cours de linguistique générale* of Ferdinand de Saussure. The essence of Saussure's work in linguistics is his doctrine of the arbitrary or unmotivated relationship between the signifier and the signified. According to Saussure, there is no intrinsic relationship between signifier and signified because of the differential character of language: the concept signified by the signifier is never present in and of itself because signs are made possible through the *differences* between sounds. That is, there is nothing to link any particular sound to any particular concept, but the perception of differences between combinations of sounds permits one group of sounds (signifier) to stand for, or take the place of a thing, which itself is engaged in a system of differences.[6]

It can be inferred then (although Saussure does not state so explicitly) that the possibility of conceptuality depends upon a *silent* system of differential references: one concept refers to another in their difference; one signifier refers to another in their difference.[7] If, as Saussure says, language is a classificatory system that did not fall from the sky, these silent differences were somewhere produced, have somewhere a point of origin: that which makes speech possible – a system of differential reference – must obviously precede speech and speakers, what Saussure calls '*le sujet parlant*' (which has the larger signification of being consciousness in general). But this immediately leads to a logical contradiction, a contradiction that contradicts logic itself, for the concepts of 'cause' and 'effect', 'before' and 'after' here become confused. If all causes are localized points of presence, if every 'after' is preceded by a 'present' that came before it, how can the pre-requisite for speech – difference, which is never present itself, but is always *between* two 'presences' – be its origin? How can the *sujet parlant*, the consciousness of presence, be constituted by what never was or will be present? Further, this concept of 'original difference' (how can a difference be original?) has a fundamental bearing on the (metaphysical) concepts used to determine being (what is): time and space. First, the possibility of the sign itself, the substitution of the sign for the thing in a system of differences, depends upon the temporal concept of *deferral*, the putting-off into the future of the present grasping of the thing itself. That a system of differences permits a sign to stand for a thing, to replace it, always implies a future relationship to an element from the past. Which brings us to the second point, and the significance of the fact that etymologically *defer* and *differ* are the same word: this temporal *interval*, which separates the thing present from itself in time, also irreducibly divides all 'spatial' presence; for the system of differential reference requires that each present element refers to an element *other* than itself, the perception of objects depending upon the perception of their differences. The sign is thus constituted by the *trace* of a past element that was never fully present, because it must always refer to something other than itself; and this trace refers to a future that will never become present, because the interval separating sign from thing must always reconstitute itself. Any other alternative, any attempt to save the value of full presence would lead to the postulation of a point of origin not different from itself (an in-different origin), thus destroying the essentially differential quality of language. This concept of the *trace* is the production of intervals in both time and space, 'is' a kind of writing before writing as we know it, for writing has never been concerned with anything but tracing and leaving the trace of speech. 'Is' must be in quotation marks because the trace, the original difference, the writing before speech, destroys the idea of a simple presence, of the presence of a being as the simple origin of beings.

Thus, the origin of 'alive' spoken discourse 'is' an enlarged conception of 'dead' silent writing. Silence is not exterior to speech, writing is not the signifier of the signifier, the sign is neither motivated nor arbitrary. The philosophical gesture which devalues writing, because speech always implies presence, can be construed as the principle common to all metaphysics, the system that always prefers presence to non-presence. Derrida has named this epoch of metaphysics (our own) 'logocentrism', and one could say that it always writes to devalue writing.[8] Speaking of the philosophical desire to devalue writing that always leads to this contradictory logic, Derrida says, in *De la grammatologie*:

> To what zone of discourse does this strange functioning or argumentation belong . . . ? How is this functioning articulated with the ensemble of theoretical discourse, throughout the history of science? Rather, how does it work upon the concept of science from within it? . . . this index and several others (generally speaking, the treatment of the concept of writing), provide us with an assured means of commencing the de-construction of the *greatest totality* – the concept of *epistémè* and logocentric metaphysics – in which were produced all Occidental methods of analysis, explication, reading or interpretation without ever posing the radical question of writing. What must now be thought is that writing is simultaneously more exterior to speech, because it is not the 'image' or 'symbol' of speech, and that it is more interior to speech which in and of itself

is already writing. Before even being linked to a . . . signifier referring in general to a signifier signified by it, the concept of *graphie* implies, as the possibility common to all systems of signification, an *instituted trace* . . . The instituted trace cannot be conceived without conceiving the retention of difference in a referential structure in which difference appears *as such* and permits a certain freedom of variation between full terms. The absence of an *other* here and now, of another transcendental present, of an *other origin* of the world appearing as such, presenting itself as irreducible absence in the presence of the trace is not a metaphysical formulation substituted for a scientific conception of writing. This formulation, besides being *the* objection to metaphysics itself, describes the structure implied by the 'arbitrariness' of the sign. The 'unmotivated' quality of the sign requires a synthesis in which the completely other is announced as such – without any simplicity, identity, resemblance or continuity – in that which is not itself . . . . The trace, in which the relationship to the other is marked, articulates its possibility on the entire field of being that metaphysics has determined on the basis of the occulted movement of the trace. The trace must be conceived as coming before being. But the movement of the trace is necessarily occulted, produces itself as its own occultation. When the other is announced as such, it presents itself as a dissimulation of itself. (pp. 67–9: OG 46–7; trans. modified)

The essential notion to be grasped from this analysis of Saussure (who represents only one moment of the valuation of presence, of the equivalence between truth and presence) is that all speculation on the origin of being can always be deconstructed to show that the point of origin is different from itself. Origin is always *other* than itself, for the idea of origin depends upon the production of 'spatial' and 'temporal' difference that must *precede* any origin. Since writing, throughout the history of philosophy, has been associated with the values 'non-origin', 'secondariness', 'exteriority' – in short, 'otherness' – the treatment of writing by philosophy is a means of taking apart the fundamental oppositions upon which our thought is based – presence/non-presence, truth/non-truth, interior/exterior. The concept of 'trace' forces us to think in ways proscribed by metaphysics, making us 'conceptualize' an exterior within an interior, a presence constituted by non-presence, etc. Which is not to say that an anti-metaphysics that would assert non-presence as an absolute origin would escape the contradictions of metaphysics. It must be emphasized that this notion of an origin other than itself, here called 'trace', makes it impossible to locate any origin, ever to constitute a full presence. The movement of the trace can never be stopped, or pinned down to a *point* of absence or presence.

The disappearance of an origin implied in this enlarged conception of writing (writing as *différance*, the word invented by Derrida to connote production of spatial and temporal difference), also entails an enlarging of the concept of repetition. In his analysis of Plato, Derrida comes to associate writing, the disappearance of a present origin of presence, with the Platonic concept of *epekeina tes ousias* (the beyond of all presence).[9] Derrida demonstrates that the presence of the *eidos*, the thing itself, the unity of the signified and the referent, cannot be separated from the concept of (grammatical) difference, since Plato defines the origin of the visible as that which cannot be viewed directly (the sun). If the invisible 'beyond' of all presence is the origin of the thing itself, the thing itself can never be present. Derrida further proceeds to demonstrate the link between writing and the idea of that which is in excess of being, is 'beyond' being, is *epekeina tes ousias*. Again, a generalized concept of writing can be shown to be the (non) origin of being. And if 'truth' is absolute presence, the presence of the *eidos*, the disappearance of an original presence would simultaneously make truth possible and impossible. This simultaneity amounts to postulating that the thing itself, in its identical presence, is 'duplicitous' (true and not-true), is doubled, doubles itself, as soon as it appears, or rather it appears as the possibility of its own duplication: it *repeats* itself, its origin is its repetition. The menace that Plato ascribed to the Sophists – that, in their preoccupation with combining signifiers they mechanically *repeat* things without any real knowledge of them – is what makes truth possible, thereby destroying truth. Truth and non-truth derive from repetition.

If, then, repetition is the production of unity, there can be no 'full' unity, no unity without something missing, something that calls for the production of a supplementary 'unity' that is similar enough to and different enough from the 'faulty' original (which is thus *not* the original) to be added to it, as that which it is missing, *or* to replace it, as its double. Be added to *or* replace: this contradictory assertion is included in another of Derrida's 'concepts', that of *supplementarity*. The verb *suppléer* in French has the double sense of adding for the sake of completion and of replacement – how can a *missing* element replace (take the place of, stand for) that from which it is missing? And the word *supplément* has a necessary link to writing: as Rousseau defines it, writing is the *supplément* of speech, completing it and standing for it. Derrida has used the supplementary status of writing – the addition that replaces, the part bigger than the whole – to deconstruct one of Rousseau's major contributions to thought, the opposition nature/culture, as well as to deal, once more, with the strange phenomenon of the philosopher who writes to attack writing. The philosophical attack upon writing is perhaps always motivated by the danger of mechanical repetition that Plato first associated with writing, the fear of the machine gone out of control, producing double after double of the same thing with no attempt to master its product.[10] But it is obvious that philosophy needs this machine as much as it fears it, and thus the incessant attempts to circumscribe it, to make writing a simple *means* for the presentation of truth. Philosophy has even provided itself with an adjunct whose job is to keep watch over the machine, to keep the means in control by separating good writing from bad so that it can express the truth as *adequately* as possible: rhetoric.[11] But these attempts, which inevitably link writing with difference, repetition, supplementarity allow us to turn them against themselves.

What then does one call the writing, the text in which philosophical concepts turn against themselves, explode themselves in order to demonstrate their own (im)possibility, their irreducible doubleness? Since they obey no philosophical regulations of truth, these texts have a certain 'fictive' or 'literary' quality; but since they must rigorously explode the truths by which philosophy aspires to scientificity, they have an intimate relationship with what philosophy has construed as 'science'. Thus, Derrida proposes to elaborate a 'double science',[12] a 'science' in which each concept, each term carries within it the principle of its own death. Once one has determined the totality of what is as 'having been' made possible by the institution of the trace, 'textuality', the system of traces, becomes the most global term, encompassing all that is and that which exceeds it. The 'double science' is then the 'science of textuality', giving a privileged place to what was formerly called 'literature', but can no longer be called such when the relationship to truth and reality that allegedly distinguished literary, scientific and philosophical texts from each other breaks down as we are forced to rethink the metaphysical concept of 'reality' in terms of textuality. What becomes particularly revelatory for the 'double science' are the ways of reading 'literary' texts that are governed by the classical, metaphysical concepts of interpretation. In other words, the deconstruction of 'literary criticism' and the explosion of some of its key concepts play a crucial role in this 'double science'.

The word 'criticism' derives directly from the Greek verb *krinein* and its adjectival form *kritikos*, meaning 'able to discern or to judge'. In other words, criticism *decides* (discerns, judges), and what it decides is the meaning of a text. 'Meaning' is a value intrinsically associated with those of 'truth' and 'presence' – a text's meaning is the truth that is present 'behind' or 'under' its textual surface that criticism makes fully present by placing it before us. Since 'truth', 'presence', or meaning are made (im)possible by textuality, by writing as trace, we can foresee that a text is precisely always that which cannot be decided upon, and that the project of criticism is linked to the project of philosophy by its drive to efface writing before single *or* multiple meanings implicitly (immanently) 'present' in it. Whether it falls under the rubric of 'formalism' (attention to that which makes literature literature, the attempt to determine a specificity of 'literariness'), or of 'thematism' (attention to the combinations, juxtapositions, and recurrences of meaningful units within a text, usually stopping at the level of the word), all criticism as we know it depends upon the notion of the sign, of a signified (a meaning) behind the signifier and the pertinence of their opposition;[13] criticism is thus engaged in the system of values attached to the sign. The 'double science', founded upon the incompatability of the notions 'sign' and text, must explore the consequences of this incompatability as it deconstructs the project of deciding, of criticism.

For a text to be 'undecidable' it must resist being consumed or exhausted by its semantic relationships, that is, it can never be fully 'saturated' with meaning.[14] At some point its syntax – syntax being that which philosophically is always subordinated to semantics, because it is not concerned with the presentation of meaning – must overflow its apparent meanings. This hypothesis is a direct result of the demonstration that the sign is dependent for its existence upon the production of (temporal and spatial) difference, for syntax is the principle of textual arrangement, that is, of differentiation. The most obvious 'index' of syntax is the space *between* words, what Mallarmé called the *blanc*; and it is upon the Mallarmean example of the *blanc* that Derrida has articulated some of his most important deconstructions of literary criticism. It is by now apparent that for Derrida words with irreducibly double meanings (such as *supplément, différance* and others not mentioned here),[15] which are always connected to the concept of textuality, have a certain privilege. A crucial aspect of this privilege is that these words are dependent upon syntax for their meaning. These words (and the *hymen* in Mallarmé: either wedding or hymen, that which is between consummation and non-consummation, signifying both) have no intrinsic meanings, there is always the *space*, *veil* or *blanc* of syntax between them and their meanings. To simplify greatly, since all texts are dependent upon the silent, blank intervention of space between words in order to make meaning possible (similar to the way in which the supposedly acoustic sign is dependent upon silent differentiation), these 'duplicitous' words, marking the points at which syntax overflows semantics, destroy the possibility of semantic saturation, of a text's meaning or meanings being greater than its syntax. And since what these words mark is the *necessary* intervention of blank space in a text (*'indéfectiblement le blanc revient . . .'* – Mallarmé), we can postulate that a text's meaning or meanings are destroyed *and* produced by the principle of spacing – *espacement*. One immediate consequence of this essential openness of texts is the destruction of the idea of literature, if by 'idea of' is meant something that has an essence, a truth, a particular state of being, for all these values by definition exclude the openness of the undecidable. There is no quality, no assignable 'literariness' that makes literature literature, rendering not pertinent the question 'what is literature?', which was our point of departure.[16] This too, is the 'basis' upon which formalist or thematic criticism, which never accounts for the plus/minus of the space *between* words (that is, that which is *less* than meaningful, since it is by definition non-meaning, and is *more* than meaningful since it includes within it the possibility of meaning) can be taken apart.[17]

That a text is undecidedly open does not mean that there is nothing to say about it. Rather, a 'system' of textuality must be elaborated that does not rely upon reducing a text to its 'meaning'. Again, to undertake this task rigorously one would have to depend upon concepts that destroy themselves, that lead not to the presence of the singular, but to division and silence of the differences that constitute the multiplicity that is textuality (one could say: the multiplicity that 'is'). All that 'is' has as its *supplément* – the part that makes it whole, the part that replaces the whole – text*s*, the 'appearance' of difference as such, that divides every 'thing' from itself, *doubling* it, *repeating* it, *citing* it. The *supplément*, the part bigger than the whole, can be construed as a citation, a double that is not the thing itself, always referring backwards and forwards to an impossible present. Citation itself is the textual form of doubling, of transplanting or inserting part of another text into a text, making the citation slightly different from itself. And citations ultimately have no source or origin: they always refer to another text which refers to another text, etc.[18] Since any exhaustive attempt to find the source or origin of a text will always lead to another text, (or to other text*s*, since a single text as a punctual source would reinstate the metaphysical notions of textuality as secondary and derivative, as for instance in the theories of all books having their source in *the* Book – the Bible) all the theories of *mimesis*, of imitation, that have governed interpretation break down, for all these theories interpret a text according to its relationship to a referent outside textuality. Derrida has demonstrated that criticism has always been programmed by two propositions (and their consequences) concerning *mimesis* – it either produces the double of the thing, and is not qualitatively different from its model, or resembling its model or not, the vehicle of imitation exists, because there is *mimesis* – and that in either case *mimesis* is governed by a truth outside textuality.[19] The major acquisition of the 'double science' is that there is nothing outside textuality, outside '. . . the temporalization of an *experience* which is neither *in* the world nor in an "other world" . . . no more *in* time than *in* space, [in which] differences appear between elements or rather produce them, making them emerge as such and constitute *texts*, chains and systems of traces . . .'.[20]

The old name for textuality, 'literature', is then the possibility of science, as it is the possibility of science's objects – being, in time and space. Because of its illimitability, literature must be seen as annihilating itself, exploding itself and thereby implacably subverting the metaphysical system that has *named* it such in order to confine the *letter*, which, as Rousseau has taught us, *kills*.

Notes

[1] Jacques Derrida *La Dissémination* (Paris: Seuil, 1972), p. 9 and p. 252: '. . . why is "literature" still the name for that which already withdraws itself from literature – withdraws itself from what has always been conceived and signified by this name – or, not only eluding it, implacably destroys it?' (D 3; trans. modified); 'Literature annihilates itself through its illimitability' (D 223; trans. modified).

[2] This description has Hegel most specifically in mind, at very least because of his powerful treatment of the progression from intuitive, naïve certitude to scientific truth. The 'vehicle' upon which Hegel proposes to take us from certitude to truth is the *Aufhebung*, the idealization of a given stage of mental development through its negation and conservation that permits us to go on to the next stage. Derrida has defined the 'deconstruction of metaphysics' as 'indefinite explications with Hegel'. Cf. *L'Ecriture et la différence* (Paris: Seuil, 1967), p. 371 (WD 253).

[3] There is an obvious similarity between the hierarchy 'science'–'philosophy'–'literature' and 'Plato's' paradigm (in *The Republic*) god–artisan–painter as degrees of direct relationship to Forms, specifically the form of the bed. (God creates the form, the artisan manufactures the object, approximating the form, and the painter imitates the object. The painter is thus the furthest from the original truth.) However, it is not my intention to assimilate one scheme to the other, disregarding all specificity. The point to be made is that there is a correspondence between the theories of imitation regarding painting and those regarding literature. Cf. *La Dissémination*, pp. 158–60 (D 137–40).

[4] *La Dissémination*, p. 203 (D 177).

[5] Again, an anticipation, another philosophical example, may be of assistance. Artistic creations, literature included, are often deemed creations of the 'imagination', the faculty that produces works that are neither in nature, nor in some other world, mediating *between* 'intelligence' and nature. This particular articulation of what might be called *between-ness* belongs at least to Kant and to Jean Rousset, a contemporary French critic. Derrida discusses this formulation of Kant's in an essay on Rousset; cf.

L'Ecriture et la différence, p. 16 (WD 7). The underlying question is the relationship of form and content, specifically of the imagination which can 'fill' mental 'forms' with 'content' from the world because it mediates between them. For a further discussion of the possibility of confining a text to the realm of the imagination cf. *La Dissémination*, p. 266 (D 235–6), where the text in question is precisely *L'Univers imaginaire de Mallarmé* by Jean-Pierre Richard.

⁶ It goes without saying that within the field of linguistics Saussure does not represent the final word on the problem of the motivation of the sign. Saussure's disciples themselves have modified his original conceptions. The obvious stumbling blocks are imitative words, e.g. onomatopoeias, which are not arbitrarily connected to their referent.

⁷ This implication of Saussure's work, and the discussion of it to follow are taken from Derrida's essay 'La différance' in *Théorie d'ensemble* (Paris: Seuil, 1968) [also in MP 1–27]; the reference here is to pp. 49–54 (MP 10–13). This question is covered more fully, with reference to many linguistic thinkers in *De la grammatologie* (Paris: Minuit, 1967), pp. 42–108 (OG 27–73).

⁸ Derrida has often used the Freudian concepts of denegation and the logic of dreams, which 'illogically' ignores negation, as indices of this evidently contradictory logic of writing so that writing may be devalued (or presence constituted as an ultimate value). Cf. *La Dissémination*, p. 126 (D 110–11). In *The Interpretation of Dreams* (Standard Edition, Vol. IV, p. 120) Freud uses the case of the kettle as an analogue to dream-logic; the man charged by his neighbour with having returned a borrowed kettle in damaged condition retorts 1. that he gave back the kettle undamaged; 2. that the kettle had a hole in it when he borrowed it; 3. that he never borrowed the kettle at all.

⁹ For what is to follow, cf. *La Dissémination*, pp. 192–5 (D 166–9). The status of *epekeina tes ousias* was one of Derrida's first preoccupations: cf. *L'Ecriture et la différence*, pp. 86–8 and 126–8 (WD 56–7 and 85–6).

¹⁰ The analysis of the fear of automatic mechanical repetition is one of the richest strata of Derrida's thought. For one, it opens new perspectives in charting what might crudely be called the 'philosophic unconscious', which would first require a systematic confrontation of the Freudian and philosophical (Hegelian) concepts of negativity, as already implied in note 8, above. For the machine in Hegel, Cf. 'Le puits et la pyramide', in *Hegel et la pensée moderne* (Paris: PUF, 1970), p. 82 (MP 107–8), where what is in question is again the relationship of signified to signifier. The machine in Freud – an automaton – concerns the relationship of fiction to reality and the concept of castration in an essay called 'Das Unheimliche' ('The Uncanny' — Standard Edition, Vol. XVII). Derrida has written that his essay on Mallarmé, 'La double séance' constitutes a rereading of this essay of Freud's. Cf. *La Dissémination*, p. 300 n. 56 (D 268 n. 67).

¹¹ Ever since Aristotle, in the *Poetics*, distinguished good metaphors from bad on the basis of adequation (*homoiosis*), similarity to a natural model, rhetoric has been concerned with keeping discourse truthful. For an analysis of the Aristotelian concept of metaphor and the role of metaphor in science and in the creation of negative concepts, cf. 'La mythologie blanche' in *Poétique*, 5 (1971), 1–52 (MP 209–71).

¹² Elsewhere, Derrida has proposed the name 'économie générale' for this science, cf. 'De l'économie restreinte à l'économie générale', in *L'Ecriture et la différence*, pp. 369–407 (WD 251–77). In note 2, above, reference was already made to this essay which concerns the relationship of Bataille to Hegel. This is perhaps the place to cite the guiding question of the general economy or the double science, the question that involves it in indefinite explications with Hegel: '. . . after having exhausted the discourse of philosophy, how can we inscribe, in the lexicon and syntax of a language, *our* language, which was also the language of philosophy, that which nevertheless exceeds the oppositions of concepts governed by its communal logic?' (WD 252–3).

¹³ The opposition form/theme has been treated at length by Freud in his analyses of the *pleasure* to be taken from literature: the work of art obeys the pleasure principle, its 'form' being the enticement to the release of tension found in the 'theme' behind the form. For a brief discussion of this and the essential references to Freud, cf. *La Dissémination*, p. 279 n. 44 (D 248 n. 52). The question of formalism cannot be raised without reference to Hegel, whose treatment of the complicity between

formalism and empiricism is crucial to Derrida. Cf., among other places, *La Dissémination*, p. 17 (D 11–12).

[14] It is this resistance of the text to semantic saturation, the fact that something always remains behind after every attempt to idealize a text into its meaning, that is the key to the deconstruction of the concept of *Aufhebung*, for the process of negation-and-conservation always implies an idealization so complete that no *trace* of that which is idealized is left behind. Cf. *La Dissémination*, pp. 15–37 (D 9–31). Thus, Derrida has called the concept of *Aufhebung* the 'decisive target' in the deconstruction of metaphysics (p. 280 n. 45; D 248 n. 53). To say, then, that Derrida has interpreted Heidegger's destruction of humanism as 'a strategy that allows for both a transcendence and a conservation of the inherited concepts [of metaphysics], in line with the Hegelian principle of *Aufhebung*', or that the 'chief lesson' that Derrida's work offers to criticism 'is that it seeks to balance in scrupulous fashion both the conserving and the negating forces involved in the activities of reading and of interpretation' is to profoundly misconstrue the import of everything that Derrida has had to say about Hegel. (Cf. Alexander Gelley, 'Form as Force' in *Diacritics*, 2, 1 (1972), 9 and 13 respectively.)

[15] Two other particularly important examples: *pharmakon*, the Greek word which simultaneously means poison and remedy and is systematically associated with writing by Plato, especially in the *Phaedrus* (cf. *La Dissémination*, pp. 108–33; D 95–117); and *usure*, the word implying both a process of impoverishment, using up, and of profit-taking, the too-large profits made by lending (usury). *Usure* covers the entire history of metaphor, the 'lending' of a name to something other than itself (as it is defined by Aristotle in the *Poetics*), for the concept of metaphor always implies 1. that a word can etymologically be traced back to a primitive sense of which we no longer think in using the word, which thus has been impoverished through constant circulation, and 2. that the passage from a primitive sense of the word to a more abstract one corresponds to the passage from the physical to the metaphysical, the acquiring of a richer sense. This double sense of *usure* guides the analysis of the metaphoricity of science in 'La mythologie blanche'. Further, Freud's essay on 'Das Unheimliche' concerns the conversion of one sense of a word to another (here, the 'familiar' to the 'unfamiliar') through the concept of castration. Derrida's concept that covers irreducible doubleness – *la dissémination* – has important ties to the Freudian concept of castration, the cutting off of the ultimate model of unicity and presence – the phallus –, although the two are not interchangeable. Cf. *La Dissémination*, pp. 32 and 300 n. 56 (D 25–6 and 268 n. 67).

[16] This is an over-simplification of the arguments found in *La Dissémination*, pp. 249–53 (D 220–22).

[17] Reasons of space and the necessary *closeness* to particular texts upon which these arguments are articulated prevent even a cursory summary of them. For the argument concerning thematic criticism, cf. *La Dissémination*, pp. 276ff. (D 245ff.), and for those on formalist criticism, *De la grammatologie*, pp. 86–8 (OG 59–60) and *L'Ecriture et la différence*, pp. 9–49 (WD 3–30 – the essay on Rousset).

[18] Again, an over-simplification. Cf. *La Dissémination*, pp. 350–52 (D 314–17).

[19] For the dissection of mimetology, cf. *La Dissémination*, pp. 209–21 (D 183–95).

[20] *De la grammatologie*, p. 95 (OG 65; trans. modified).

CHAPTER 3

Household Words: Alterity, the Unconscious and the Text

Ann Wordsworth

Geoffrey Hill quotes the painter Francis Bacon as saying somewhere that he 'tried to paint the track left by human beings like the slime left by a snail'.

One can imagine this track in quite familiar ways: man's secret sharer, his phantasmagorical or antithetical other, the inner self revealed to creative vision. But it could also be seen as an effect, the relation between writing or painting, and what passes as its subject, what Derrida calls in another context, 'a certain foreign body working over our household words' (F 83). A track or trace, perhaps, but not one that can be submitted to an aesthetic survey or a critical restoration. Not, therefore, a derivative or secondary sign whose purpose is to recall a true full presence; rather a deconstructed and inassimilable movement which itself sets up the staging of presence, and which sets up also in the same double sense (provides means for, dissembles) literary production; thereby unsettling contexts, conceptual relations, genre-identity, all the many guarantees of closure, and indeed closure itself – 'the indefinable therapeutic element in art', as Geoffrey Hartman describes it, heroically resisting its deconstruction in his recent book called *Saving the Text* and dedicated 'For the Subject'.

The relation of alterity, the unconscious, and the text are what perhaps make up this tracing; but to investigate this at all involves exposing both literature and psychoanalysis to deconstructive effects. This implies the sort of irrecuperable processes that Derrida finds in Blanchot's title *Arrêt de mort*:

> *Arrêter*, in the sense of suspending, is suspending the *arrêt* in the sense of decision. *Arrêter*, in the sense of deciding, arrests the *arrêt*, in the sense of suspension. They are ahead of or lag behind one another .... The indecision of the *arrêt intervenes* not *between* the two senses of the word *arrêt* but *within* each sense, so to speak .... It stands (but gets no foothold), stays (within no mainstay) on this unstable line, this ridge [*arête*] that relates it to itself ... without being able to constitute it in self-reflection and reappropriation of self. It remains [*reste*] on the *arête* of itself without remaining to itself, in itself, for itself .... No consciousness, no perception, no watchfulness can gather up this remnance, this *restance*; no attentiveness can make it present, no 'I', no ego. (LO 114–16)

No consciousness as organizing principle of a deciding taste or judgment, no Ego as the synthesizing power of the reading or writing self – the 'arrhythmic pulsations' of the title refuse both.

It is clear that psychoanalytical discourse in its relation to literature is not so radical. Freud demonstrates that 'the conscious ego' cannot be taken as fully identical with the self as a whole; but despite posing a category alien to all the assumptions of an author-based criticism (criteria of consciousness, intelligibility, aesthetic investment), Freud links psyche and textual content by the recognitions of intersubjectivity. The philosophical category of the subject – hero, author and reader – remains unquestioned and Freudian criticism reverts to biographical studies, dubiously extended by the activities of the unconscious. In using Freud, Derrida distinguishes between a therapeutic practice, a regional science and theoretical writings which institute certain breakthroughs: work on the originary constitution of the subject and its value, a radical recognition of trace structure, oblique and not fully understood implications for writing and language – effects that escape binarism and open up the possibility of a work that Derrida identifies as a 'psychoanalysis of literature respectful of the *originality of the literary signifier*' (WD 230).

Psychobiographical critics are not concerned with the originality of the literary signifier; their work is simply and often crudely diagnostic. Problem plays and poems like *Hamlet* and Tennyson's *Maud* are charged with an incoherence which certain missing facts would repair. T.S. Eliot claims that 'artistic "inevitability" lies in the complete adequacy of the external to the emotion'.[1] Regrettably, this adequacy is not found in *Hamlet* or *Maud* and there are two possible explanations – biographical or clinical. If the latter, then as Eliot discreetly observes, 'we should have to understand things [the poet] did not understand himself'.[2]

The diagnosis which permits the linking of textual content and psychic affairs has only a limited usefulness however. It can account for the presence of obscurities and offer clinical explanations but it cannot claim aesthetic significance for a work that has eluded conscious control. Aesthetic theory protects art from any continuous and constitutive relation to unconscious processes but, on occasion, it will offer up ravaged words for a clinical study. Its claim is that the pleasure of art – the satisfaction of recognizing 'artistic inevitability' – is the response of the conscious ego; however, the notion of intersubjectivity has an implication in Freud's aesthetics which disregards the requirements of intentionality and consciousness. Psychic economy permits the recognition of pain as pleasure: Freud claims that tragic pleasure is masochistic and closely bound up with narcissism. Aristotelian 'recognition', the conscious mind's assent to a given position, is translated by Freud as identification and this allows for the return of the repressed: playwright and spectator are both involved in a sort of averted attention, indirectly permitting pleasure, otherwise screened by the conscious mind.

This sating of unconscious desire is the subject of Ernest Jones's essay on Hamlet; but it shows too how dependence on the category of the subject keeps Freudian interpretation within the perimeters of classical aesthetics even as it reformulates the terms of aesthetic pleasure. The intention of Jones's essay is impeccably straightforward: to find the reason for Hamlet's 'vacillation', a problem that will seem insuperable to Eliot because of Shakespeare's failure to find representation for his emotions. No correlative objectifies the emotion – to use Eliot's jargon; the madness merely doubles as a tactic for both character and writer. For Hamlet it acts as 'the buffoonery of an emotion which can find no outlet in action' and for Shakespeare it acts as 'the buffoonery of an emotion he cannot express in art'.[3] The failure of causality that baffles Eliot, and seemingly Shakespeare too, is not, however, too baffling for psychoanalysis with its vocabulary of displacements, condensation, defence mechanisms, etc. The enigma of the vacillation can be understood if it is explained as repression: vacillation is adequate to the fact of repression. Clarification comes simply through the privileging of the unconscious, a transindividual domain whose processes are not reducible to experience. The play is not a confused glimpse into an individual dilemma but an averted acknowledgement of constitutive psychic processes underlying consciousness in all human subjects. Obviously, the grounds of explanation are not Johnsonian or Bradleyan, but the aesthetics are not radically changed. Hamlet's burden is not the knowledge of his uncle's crime nor his mother's passion, but the unconscious relation of these events: they provoke the repressed, the infant's phantasy of incest and patricide. Because the unconscious processes are transindividual and constitutive, oedipal desire and repression must be present in Shakespeare and the audience as in Hamlet himself. Jones concludes, 'we reach the apparent paradox that the hero, the poet and the audience are all profoundly moved by feelings due to a conflict – the source of which all are unaware'.[4] *Hamlet* affords pleasure even though its sources are not identifiable and are presented as pain, and through it we share a clinical intersubjectivity that it was Shakespeare's power to intuit, in Jones's words, 'three centuries before the advent of psychoanalysis'.

The satisfactions of this reading are warm and innocent, preserving recognitions in the structure of the interpretation even if not in the material. To move from Jones's *Hamlet* to Lacan's[5] is to have all literary and critical familiarities obliterated by an insistence on the articulations of the unconscious. So *uncontexted* are the structures Lacan describes – 'human desire as it appears in psychoanalysis', the subject's submission to the signifier, the crossing into the imaginary and from the imaginary into the symbolic, 'the charting of subject and Other', 'the relation of mourning and the object in desire' – that no connection can be felt between this substratum and the manifest content of the play. This disassociation is quite proper given Lacan's account of the Freudian unconscious, which is

> ... not at all the romantic unconscious of the imaginative creation. It is not the locus of divinities of the night.... To all these forms of unconscious, ever more or less linked to some obscure will regarded as primordial, to something preconscious, what Freud opposes is the revelation that at the level of the unconscious there is something at all points homologous to what occurs at the level of the subject – this thing speaks and functions in a way quite as elaborate as at the level of the conscious which thus loses what seems to be its privilege.[6]

Lacan's *Hamlet* demands a systematic under-reading that can reach the activity of this thing that speaks and functions, and of necessity this bypasses all sense of the writing itself. Even Hamlet's punning is without privilege: it functions abstractly as 'the play of signifiers in the dimension of meaning'. Writing is no more than an involuntary act of conveyance: not of course the means of matching emotion to the external as in Eliot's recipe for artistic inevitability or of intuitively sharing oedipal desire, but no less the passive vehicle via which unconscious desire is satisfied in a text.

This effacement of writing, disrespect for 'the originality of the literary signifier', is the effect of one mode of relating psychoanalysis and the text; another mode, its direct opposite, takes unconscious processes into language, aligning a specific kind of expression, figural writing, with 'the very organization of the mind'. There is a benign agreement of literary effects and psychoanalytic description in Lionel Trilling's work: 'it was left to Freud', he says, 'to discover how in a scientific age we still feel and think in figurative formations and to create what psychoanalysis is, a science of tropes, of metaphor and its variants, synecdoche and metonymy'.[7] This adequation continues in the far more dramatic and conflictual processes that organize Harold Bloom's staging of poetry as 'an anxiety of influence'. 'To discuss the poetic will,' Bloom says, 'without referring to the ego's defences, becomes less and less interesting'.[8] Just as Trilling relates figural language to the very organization of the mind, Bloom relates it to the poetic drive which in his most recent work he sees as itself putting in question the Freudian drives. 'What begins to be clear', he says, 'is that the drives and the defences are modelled upon poetic rhetoric . . . . Eros or libido *is* figurative meaning; the death drive *is* literal meaning. The defences *are* tropes . . . Eros and Thanatos take the shape of a chiasmus, but this is because the relation between figurative and literal meaning in language is always a crossing-over'.[9] In this description consciousness and writing alike take us back to the will. The conscious ego becomes the narcissistic ego, psychically driven – a poetic will bent on a quest for priority and for resistance against time and death; a will that collects meanings, locates them and can be read through a learning of its defensive patternings and its disjunctive but meaningful negative moments that Bloom calls the three crossings. These rhythms of figured defences and crossings make, says Bloom, 'a more certain link between rhetoric and psychology' than has been made in his own earlier identification of tropes and defences in the revisionary ratios.

This complex new scheme makes a pattern of interpretation applicable not only to Romantic and Post-Romantic poetry but also, Bloom feels, to Freud's own 'prose-rhapsodies', *On Narcissism* and *Beyond the Pleasure Principle*. Certain structures are constitutive: the will figures through verbal acts, the self narcissistically invested against time, belatedness and death – a psychodrama played out as text through 'verbal mechanisms of crisis' which reveal poetic language as the power to project the will across a narcissistically invested field whose dramas silently disrupt the text in the negative moments of the three crossings:

confrontation with the feared loss of creative power, with individual loss, and with death. Poetic enactment is an unconscious system, like the condensements and displacements of the dream work, insofar as it is organized by non-representational effects (the tropic progression) and is also submitted more generally to the disjunctive effects of the narcissistic threats (the crossings) against which poetry defends.

This is a complex and embattled account of poetic expression: it moves strongly against various inadequacies of traditional criticism and it also confronts structuralist limitations. Like Derrida, Bloom has a quarrel with binary rhetoric but his quarrel is only with one articulation of it: Jakobson's 'metaphor/metonymy pseudo dialectic', as he calls it; a structuring of language which for Bloom is too weak to bear the full weight of the constitutive dichotomy which he identifies as being between irony and synecdoche, reduction and representation. Nevertheless, there is trouble in the Bloomian account of creative process; and particularly in his adaptation of Freudian theory to a demonic ego-psychology: 'Lyric celebrates the poetic self . . . what *can* poetry give back, either as successful representation or achieved pathos, and whether to poet or reader, except for a *restitution of narcissism*?'[10]

To go from Bloom's celebration of creative aggression and design back to Lacan's work on *Hamlet* is to feel again the violent *incompatibility* of unconscious processes to any assumed enactment in writing. Lacan makes no adequation of writing and psychic functioning – indeed, the omission of textual energies from his reading of Poe's *Purloined Letter* leads Derrida to describe his seminar as a classic example of applied psychoanalysis. As in the work on *Hamlet*, fictive and linguistic processes are not in any way involved: there is only mourning for the phallus, the relation of objects in desire and the dependence of the subject on the Other. The dramatic events approximate this psychic scene but with no particular assurance: art's power to thrall lies in the reader's unconscious recognition of an inner scene of desire and mourning and a resolution in the symbolic which has no equivalence in the action and events of conscious life. Nothing on the linguistic or semantic level articulates this recognition: there are no moves rhetorically enacted that take part in its release or time its progress. This rejection of writing is the more interesting insofar as when Lacan theorizes painting and its material surface, psychic investment is clearly involved: the gesture of the brush, the strokes that fall 'like rain', enact a descent of desire – unconscious structures are materialized in the relation of painting and the eye invested by the scopic drive,[11] as they are not in writing which neither linguistically nor semantically can become psychically invested – or so it seems. Lacan's account of unconscious functioning is ordered by the relations imaginary, real and symbolic: no other explanatory structures are involved. But 'the incision of deconstruction', as Derrida calls it, cuts into this 'conceptual tripartition': 'dissemination situates the *more or less* that indefinitely resists . . . what Lacan calls . . . the order of the "symbolic". Escapes it and disorganizes it, makes it drift, marks its writing, with all the implied risks, but without letting itself be conceived in the categories of the "imaginary" or the "real"' (P 84). For Derrida, Freud's system of the unconscious is a mythology; the radical importance of his work lies in this: that it touches the originary constitution of objectivity and of the value of the object and that it broaches the classic notion of writing as derivative and transcriptive. 'That which, in Freud's discourse, opens itself to the theme of writing results in psychoanalysis being not simply psychology – nor simply psychoanalysis' (WD 228). In Derrida's re-working, the unconscious has its status in relation to the non-physical and becomes provisionally and for the moment a possible name for radical alterity – for the trace-structure whose effects inhabit all thought and underlie writing: and to move this is to encounter a notion of alterity whose effects implicate critical work as Lacan's triadic scheme does not, and which makes familiar critical positions untenable at their conceptual base, as is not the effect of Bloom's antithetical work.

There are 'destructive discourses' which stand in an important relationship to Derrida's work: Nietzsche's critique of metaphysics, Freud's critique of self-presence, Heidegger's critique of onto-theology. His own repositioning consists in restating these critical texts so that they display effects which are not determined or produced by the system of metaphysics they oppose. (The necessary work of deconstructive translation begins at once – not because a private language is in use, but because deconstruction acknowledges a pre-semantic activity in language which prevents words from being assimilated fully by any context or code.) 'This "new" concept of *effect* borrows its characteristics from both the opposition cause/effect and from the opposition essence/appearance – *effect, reflect – without nevertheless being reduced to them*. It is this fringe of irreducibility that is to be analysed' (P 67).

This irreducible fringe is not the easiest thing to analyse. It's not enough to simply oppose metaphysics – there is an inescapable complicity between a system and its critique: 'According to a law which could be formalized, philosophy always reappropriates for itself the discourse that de-limits it' (MP 177). Deconstruction is not therefore a corrective discourse, a matter of identifying contradictions and incoherencies in philosophical thought and of attributing them to the distortions implicit in certain privileged relations – the idea of presence, of being, identity, etc. It's not oppositional, nor is it a demonstration of texts as a pure showing of contradiction as described by Adorno: 'A successful work according to immanentist criticism is not one which resolves objective contradictions in a spurious harmony, but one which expresses the idea of harmony negatively by embodying the contradictions, pure and uncompromised, in its innermost structure.'[12]

'Extraction, graft, extension: . . . *writing*' (P 71). This is the activity that overruns all contextual boundaries, all restrictions whether of authorial intention or grammatical order itself. 'This is the possibility on which I want to insist: the possibility of disengagement and citational graft which belongs to the structure of every mark, spoken or written, and which constitutes every mark in writing before and outside of every horizon of semio-linguistic communication; in writing, which is to say in the possibility of its functioning being cut off, at a certain point, from its "original" *vouloir-dire* and from its participation in a saturable and containing context.'[13]

The only structure that can give recognition to this divested functioning is that of the remnant, the same inexhaustible resource elsewhere called trace, difference, graft, operating in the same absolute absence of every empirically determined receiver and context. This description unsettles the relation of writing and presence, in classical, phenomenological and psychological writing alike. And yet it is necessary to the functioning of all language, written or spoken, and to the functioning of every mark.

There is a temptation to assume that iteration and iterability can be easily understood: John Searle accused Derrida of confusing iteration with 'the permanence of the text'.[14] But it relates to the trace by refusing the logic of presence and identity. 'It is because this iterability is differential, within each individual element as well as between the elements, because it splits each element while constituting it, because it marks it with an articulatory break, that the remainder, though indispensable, is never that of a full and fulfilling presence.'[15] This relation of break and remnant bears structurally on all writing: 'The break intervenes from the moment there is a mark, at once . . . . It is iterability itself, that which is remarkable in the mark, passing between the *re-* of the repeated and the *re-* of the repeating, traversing and transforming repetition.'[16]

Marked by this condition or effect, writing can hardly be seen as a simple transmitter of meaning: and with that must go also the assumption of there being a homogeneous field of communication – that familiar given space in which writing performs a continuous and consistent reparation of presence. If iterability structures writing in general, then a different logic appears, neatly caught in Derrida's suggested derivation, *iter*, Latin: again, from *itar*, Sanscrit: other, 'a logic that ties repetition to alterity'.[17] There never was/is a homogeneous space of communication: that, too, is a myth, an inherited metaphysical concept, as is the belief that a book is a finished unity, enclosed and sectioned off. 'The text overruns all the limits assigned to it so far (not submerging or drowning them in an undifferentiated homogeneity, but rather making them more complex, dividing and multiplying strokes and lines) – all the limits, everything that was to be set up in opposition to writing (speech, life, the world, the real, history and what not, every field of reference – to body or mind, conscious or unconscious, politics, economics and so forth)' (LO 84).

Derrida quotes a warning of Paul de Man: 'the impossibility of reading should not be taken too lightly'. Language as writing/writing as the activity that over-writes the activity of the trace: the conclusions of aesthetics obscure this possibility: 'If reading means making accessible a meaning that can be transmitted as such, in its own unequivocal, translatable identity, then this title [*Arrêt de mort*] is unreadable. But this unreadability does not arrest reading, does not leave it paralysed in the face of an opaque surface: rather it starts reading and writing and translation moving again' (LO 116).

Deconstructive reading must inhabit the text – insofar as this is possible – by reading into its internal historicity, that is 'into the history of the meaning of the work itself, of its *operation*' (WD 14). No recourse here to psychologism or biography would be relevant; nor can this internal historicity be identified as the product of any determinate unity of construction. 'There is no *space* of the work – if by space we mean *presence* and *synopsis*' (WD 14). In his study of Jean Rousset's *Forme et signification* Derrida criticizes literary formalism for its submission to spatial models to equate the value and force of writing. Against this – but this means of course working an economy that invests and surpasses the system of metaphysical oppositions – Derrida invokes 'the force of the work, ... the force ... of that which engenders in general' (WD 20). This force is the proper object of criticism, identifiable insofar as, in the release of literary production, its structure is most in play. 'It is when that which is written is *deceased* as a sign-signal that it is born as language; for then it says what is, thereby referring only to itself, a sign without signification, a game or pure functioning, since it ceases to be *utilized* as natural, biological or technical information, or as the transition from one existent to another, from a signifier to a signified' (WD 12).

The space for a deconstructive criticism needs a particular clearance: it can't take place as part of the input–output of a communication system wherein meanings are transmitted and aesthetic effects relayed; nor can it operate through the structuralist presentation of the book-in-entirety as a simultaneous network, divested thereby of its force and economy. There is no space of communication, no spatial model of totality which does not include writing itself – 'a certain pure and infinite equivocality which gives signified meaning no respite, no rest, but engages it in its own *economy* so that it always signifies again and differs' (WD 25).

For Derrida, the writer must work '*in* a language and *in* a logic whose proper system, laws, and life, his discourse by definition cannot dominate absolutely' (OG 158). Neither aesthetic commentary nor biographical or clinical documentation has access to this system. Nor can it be defined by structuralist or stylistic analysis. What is most deeply at stake in this 'logic that ties repetition to alterity' is the relation to exteriority: 'the internal historicity' of writing bears on this relation, this outside that we believe we know as the most familiar thing in the world. 'There has never been anything but supplements, substitutive significations which could only come forth in a chain of differential references, the "real" supervening and being added only while taking on meaning from a trace and from an invocation of the supplement, etc.' (OG 159).

Writing enacts iteration: 'one text reads another ... each "text" is a machine with multiple reading heads for other texts' (LO 107). This proliferation is the activity of the break/remnant which lodges, without permanence, in effects that are strictly unreadable: in a play of homonyms, in a neutral beyond dialectical contradictions and all oppositions, in the voicelessness (*aphonie*) of the narrative voice, in parody and in simulacra and in laughter. These effects cannot be assimilated into evaluative criticism which depends on a formal aesthetics, on the reader's trained or natural receptivity and on communal norms worked afresh by individual genius. No system of aesthetics can acknowledge the effects of iteration: critical principles must first be deconstructed, and as Derrida observes – 'the enterprise is hopeless if one muses on the fact that literary criticism has already been determined, knowingly or not, voluntarily or not, as the philosophy of literature' (WD 28).

There are certain quite didactic and exemplary moments in Derrida's writing where deconstruction is worked on a small scale as an operative demonstration. Just as the title *Arrêt de mort* enacts the arrhythmic pulsations of the *récit*, so the word pleasure, 'pleasure', 'Pleasure' which Derrida takes from Nicolas Abraham's essay, *The Shell and the Kernel*, distributes the movement of displacement and dissimulation that marks all language.[18] 'A certain foreign body is here working over our household words.' In the triad, both the homonymic relation between the words and the movement of translation are seen as *designifying*. 'To pass from the word pleasure in ordinary language to "pleasure" in phenomenological discourse, then to Pleasure in psychoanalytic theory, is to proceed to translate in the strangest way . . . since it is a certain identity (or semantic non-alteration) which effectuates this traversal, letting itself be *transposed* or *transported*' (Me 7). It's a matter of recognizing 'a preoriginary and presemantic force' latent in all language but here manifest in the capitalized word whose effect exceeds the orders of sense, of presence and of signification. In Abraham's words, 'Unless one is deaf to its meaning, one is struck, as soon as it is related to the unconscious Kernel, by the vigour with which it literally rips itself away from the dictionary and from language'.[19] Although in Freudian theory, pleasure may be felt as pain – an impossible formulation to common sense, classical logic and phenomenology alike – the homonymic relation of these words is not epistemologically relevant. 'Anasemic translation does not deal in exchanges between significations, signifiers and signifieds, but between the realm of signification and that which, making it possible, must still be translated into the language of that which it makes possible, must still be repeated, reinvested, reinterpreted there' (Me 8).

When put beside iteration, translation is no longer the familiar rendering of one language to another. What is translation? Derrida asks. 'To write . . . *from afar*, in order to get down what *é-loignement, Ent-fernung,* "dis-tance", *mean* in writing and in the voice' (LO 77). The final section of 'Living On' is a play on problems that have an 'irreducible relation to the enigma of translation' which Derrida then presents '*practically*, and in a sense *performatively*, in accordance with a notion of the performative that I feel must be dissociated, by an act of deconstruction, from the notion of presence with which it is generally linked' (LO 90). These problems are sharpened versions of problems of reading: a necessary resistance to the univocal, a recognition of transference, of text superimposed on text, a refusal of the academic ideal of translatability. And behind them lie relations implicit in writing which are neither figural nor literal and do not compose into any familiar epistemological structure.

Abraham's work is inaugural for Derrida by virtue of the problematic it puts in place: not the psychoanalytical 'thing' but the enactments of the Shell-Kernel figure, 'at the origin of every symbolic and figurative act, . . . not merely one tropic or topical mechanism among many' (Me 8–9). There's a point where the problematic is put in play, where image, comparison, analogy cease and a dissymmetry intervenes which no longer permits sense to ally with presentability. Writing takes on this effect. 'Occupied here at the a-semantic origin of meaning, as at the unpresentable source of presence, the anasemic translation must twist its tongue to speak the non-linguistic conditions of language' (Me 10). Writing is marked with absolute non-presence, passes beyond presentability and yet returns to be received as 'familiarity itself'.[20]

It would be possible to reduce the anasemic movement to the abyss structure, *mise en abyme*, but Derrida corrects this. 'I distrust the confidence that it, at bottom, inspires, and I find it too representational to go far enough, not to *avoid* the very thing into which it pretends to plunge us' (Com 120).[21] The encrypting that the anasemic implies has the same spatial, temporal, epistemological disordering that the schematics of differance enact. If psychoanalysis touches this movement in a text, it is through an activity that has no representational or functional status like that relayed by Ernest Jones or Lacan in their readings of *Hamlet*. In his reading of chapter two of *Beyond the Pleasure Principle*, the story of the fort-da, Derrida writes as if into this movement, catching it through Freud's own disturbance of categories – the 'legendary argument' (Com 115) of the wooden reel which is neither history nor myth nor fiction nor scientific example.

The language into which Freud inserts the o/a cannot be fully identified – nor the other sounds that resonate in the chapter, especially the mother's name, Sophie, Freud's daughter, whose death will sound soon enough in the text 'soft and low, in a strange note added after the fact' (Com 122). The text encrypts its claim 'to be nothing less than a genealogy of objectivity in general' (Com 116) within the interest and desire of the speculator himself, Freud, already encrypted in and by a genealogy whereby the abbreviation of the Pleasure Principle, P.P., and the nursery French for grandfather, 'pépé', echo across the pronoun 'il'. 'The P.P. will be surpassed, is already surpassed in advance, by the speculation that he/it incites and by his/its own repetition' (Com 118). Encrypt/superpose the description of the fort/da game with the description of the grandfather writing *Beyond the Pleasure Principle*, but it's not, strictly, a matter of positioning, analogizing, paralleling, abyssing: the movement breaks again as the autobiography of Freud: just as the child, in recalling the object (mother, object or whatever), comes also to recall *himself* in an immediately supplementary operation, in the same way the speculative grandfather recalls *himself*, and produces what is called his text – 'not merely an auto-biography entrusting his life to his own more or less testamentary writing but a more or less living description of his own writing' (Com 119).

Intentionality has no part in the dissymmetry, in its repetition and reappearance; 'what's involved is the *re-* in general . . . ; not some object that goes out and comes back but the very going and returning, . . . the self-presentation of re-presentation' (Com 132). The child's other game, his appearing and disappearing in the mirror, is another enactment, making oneself re-, the re-collecting by sign, voice, writing 'from afar', the play of repetition. Moreover, the re- is also the prefixing of the relict – the bereaved, the survivor, the legatee. Sophie dies soon after, as does Freud's favourite grandson, as did Freud's baby brother when Freud was one-and-a-half, the same age as Ernst at the time of the fort/da game. How do these deaths relate to the writing scene? There's no causality: Derrida only says 'repetition is bequeathed; the legacy is repeated' (Com 146).

Beyond the Pleasure Principle writes the scene, but the notion of truth value, 'adequacy of the external to the emotion', is quite incapable of assessing the performance. It is 'not a space that is open beforehand', merely what Freud tells: that 'every autobiography' – every writing – 'is the going out and the coming back of a *fort:da*' (Com 135–6). In the scene opened by a 'scandalous antisemantics' there is writing, repetition and alterity, the 'auto-bio-thanato-hetero-graphic writing scene' (Com 146). Which is also, I think, Derrida's gift/legacy to literary critics.

Notes

[1] T.S. Eliot, 'Hamlet and his Problems', *The Sacred Wood* (London: Methuen, 1969), p. 101.

[2] Eliot, 'Hamlet and his Problems', p. 103.

[3] Eliot, 'Hamlet and his Problems', p. 102.

[4] Ernest Jones, *Hamlet and Oedipus* (New York: Norton, 1949). Extracts from chapters 3 and 4 are reprinted in 'Hamlet Psychoanalysed', *Shakespeare's Tragedies*, ed. Lawrence Lerner (Harmondsworth: Penguin, 1963).

[5] Jacques Lacan, 'Desire and the Interpretation of Desire in *Hamlet*', in *YFS*, 55–6 (1977), 11–52.

[6] Jacques Lacan, *The Four Fundamental Concepts of Psycho-Analysis*, trans. Alan Sheridan (London: The Hogarth Press, 1977), p. 24.

[7] Lionel Trilling, 'Freud and Literature', *The Liberal Imagination* (Oxford: Oxford University Press, 1981), p. 51.

[8] Harold Bloom, 'Freud's Concept of Defence and the Poetic Will', in Joseph H. Smith (ed.), *Psychiatry and the Humanities* (London and New Haven: Yale University Press, 1980), p. 2.

[9] Bloom, 'Freud's Concept of Defence and the Poetic Will', p. 22.

[10] Harold Bloom, 'The Breaking of Form', in Harold Bloom *et al.*, *Deconstruction and Criticism* (London: Routledge and Kegan Paul, 1979), p. 17.

[11] For Lacan's account of the relations of desire in painting see 'Of the Gaze as Objet Petit a', in Lacan, *The Four Fundamental Concepts of Psycho-Analysis*, pp. 67–199.

[12] Theodor W. Adorno, *Prisms* (London: Neville Spearman, 1967), p. 82, quoted by Rodolphe Gasché in 'Deconstruction as Criticism', *Glyph*, 6 (1979), 212.

[13] Jacques Derrida, 'Signature Event Context', *Glyph*, 1 (1977), 185 (MP 320; LI 12).

[14] See John Searle's 'Reiterating the Differences: A Reply to Derrida', *Glyph*, 1 (1977), 197–208.

[15] Jacques Derrida, 'Limited Inc abc . . .', *Glyph*, 2 (1977), 190 (LI 53).

[16] Derrida, 'Limited Inc abc . . .', 190 (LI 53).

[17] Derrida, 'Signature Event Context', 180 (MP 315; LI 7).

[18] *Diacritics*, 9, 1 (Spring 1979) includes Derrida's 'Me – Psychoanalysis: An Introduction to the Translation of "The Shell and the Kernel" by Nicolas Abraham' [Me] and the translation itself.

[19] Nicolas Abraham, 'The Shell and the Kernel', *Diacritics*, 9, 1 (Spring 1979), 20. Abraham relates this vigour to the action of the psychoanalytic discourse; Derrida recognizes a power in psychoanalytical discourse, as in certain 'literary' texts, 'to operate breaches or infractions at the most advanced points' (P 69). It is interesting to compare Trilling's account of the relations of rhetoric and psychic structures (see note 7) with Abraham's: 'The language of psychoanalysis no longer follows the twists and turns (*tropoi*) of customary speech and writing. Pleasure, Id, Ego, Economic, Dynamic, are not metaphors, metonymies, synecdoches, catachreses; they are, through the action of the discourse, products of de-signification and constitute new figures, absent from rhetorical treatises' ('The Shell and the Kernel', 20).

[20] 'The outside, "spatial" and "objective" exteriority which we believe we know as the most familiar thing in the world, as familiarity itself, would not appear without the grammè, without difference as temporalization, without the non-presence of the other inscribed within the sense of the present, without the relationship with death as the concrete structure of the living present' (OG 70–71).

[21] Ed. note: the text referred to here, 'Coming into One's Own', is an earlier, abridged version of what would subsequently appear in English translation as 'Freud's Legacy' (PC 292–337), Chap. 2 of the essay 'To Speculate – on "Freud"'.

CHAPTER 4

Skepticism and Deconstruction

A.J. Cascardi

There are signs from various directions of a reconciliation between traditional Anglo-American philosophy and contemporary French deconstruction. One may take the concluding section of Richard Rorty's *Philosophy and the Mirror of Nature* (1979), on the American side, and the special issue of *Critique* (1980), on the French, as signal instances of increasing comprehension among the parties involved. In an essay on Stanley Cavell, Jay Cantor drew certain parallels between Cavell's Wittgensteinian critique of skepticism and Jacques Derrida's deconstructive critique of Western philosophy.[1] If Cavell's *The Claim of Reason* (1979) can be compared to the work of Derrida, it is because Cavell's answer to skepticism is that it has no answer, only a certain range of response, or what Saul Kripke, using a phrase of Hume's, has called a 'skeptical solution'.[2] The solution here does not land us on anything like firm ground, but instead is meant to make us aware of the groundlessness of our claims to knowledge and hence of the importance of the ways in which we claim to hold that ground.

But it would be wrong if the rapprochement of French deconstruction and Anglo-American philosophy were to rest on the assumption that deconstruction is a form of skepticism, even of the most radical kind, or displaced to certain areas which have not traditionally been within the scope of skepticism's concern. Jay Cantor says for instance that 'Deconstruction is a classical skeptical argument, recast using linguistic metaphors', that deconstruction 'is a version of skepticism which attacks the claim of consciousness that it has at its disposal a language that is representative of the world or even of itself', or again that deconstruction 'is a thoroughly skeptical enterprise, as was Nietzsche in some of his moods' (pp. 50, 51).

My thesis here is that this alignment of skepticism and deconstruction seriously mistakes the nature and intent of deconstruction, which takes as its target the very ground on which arguments on either side of skepticism rest. But it is because of the notion that deconstruction is a form of skepticism that contemporary analytical philosophy has, by and large, been unable to answer it. To say that skepticism and deconstruction are vastly different amounts in one sense to a statement about a certain division in contemporary philosophy and the historical factors which have brought it about. One has only to look at the texts which contemporary philosophers take as their fixtures to find a divergence that goes back to the time before Socrates. Indeed, one can explain many things about the split between the Anglo-American and the French (or more broadly, Continental) philosophical traditions simply by seeing that the Anglo-American tradition does not feel itself responsible for dealing with the claims raised by the Sophists, Socrates having provided a response to them once and for all, whereas the French tradition wants to call deeply into question the establishment of reason in their defeat. Rather than call deconstruction a form of skepticism, it would be more revealing of its place with regard to analytical philosophy to call it a contemporary version of Sophism. The Anglo-American tradition, by contrast, has been mainly preoccupied by problems of skepticism which rest on an epistemological basis outlined by Descartes and Kant. I mention these considerations at the start to give a sense of the possibility of an alternative account to the one I will offer here. I will be dealing with the arguments and the themes, rather than with the history, which divide skepticism and deconstruction.

I

There are, to be sure, tempting reasons for thinking of deconstruction as a version of epistemological skepticism. In this section I want to press this point as far as I can in order to show how the rapprochement is imperfect. One reason that the alignment of skepticism and deconstruction is made is that skepticism describes our relationship to the provisional objects of our knowledge as one of deep uncertainty, which sounds like what the deconstructionist means when he speaks of textual 'indeterminacy'. But there are significant differences between skeptical doubt and deconstructionist indeterminacy.

Within the scope of traditional philosophy, one can distinguish different species of uncertainty, and thus different facets of the skeptical problem and so, different conceptions of the task of epistemology. The skeptic may see himself as standing before an object and unable to say for certain what that object is. The task of epistemology will then be conceived, along Kantian lines, not so much as providing us with access to things-in-themselves as delimiting the bounds which reason must recognize in attempting to know the thing-in-itself. Rather than offer us transcendental knowledge of the essential object, the Kantian philosopher is more interested in having us avoid transcendental illusions, and so must recognize, as P.F. Strawson's title puts it, the 'bounds of sense'. In another version, the skeptic finds himself confronted with reality as a whole, with an interconnected world of people and things, and pronounces himself unable to say for certain whether this world exists – in which case he imagines himself as standing somehow *outside* of the world and perhaps hallucinating it, or dreaming it. Then the task of the epistemologist becomes one of finding his ties to the world, or of reaffirming his connections with it. In a third version of the skeptical problem, the issue is not the *existence* of objects or the world, but their *identification*. The skeptic denies that there are ways to tell whether things are one way or another. In this case, the task of epistemology becomes one of outlining the criteria on which our capacity for judgment, and hence our knowledge, rests. (In Part Two of *The Claim of Reason*, Cavell provides an unforgettable contrast of the skepticism of existence and the skepticism of identification, which he sees as the main point of contrast between traditional epistemology and ordinary-language philosophy.) Finally, in a version of skepticism which has been of major concern for social scientists, and for some historians and philosophers of science, partly as a result of the work of Paul Feyerabend and Thomas Kuhn, the skeptic claims that he lacks any method for arriving at certifiable knowledge. In this case, the epistemologist may conceive of his project either as one of outlining a decision procedure which is not undermined by its own proof procedure, or along more classically Cartesian lines as one of identifying the ground on which those procedures rest, by securing the method transcendentally in God or immanently in the Cartesian subject.

Unlike the skeptic, the deconstructionist does not have 'provisional objects of knowledge'. Hence his predicament is not uncertainty but radical indeterminacy. He may find himself caught, like Paul de Man, in a seizure of self-conscious doubt about the methods he might use so much as to frame his questions about the communicative mode of a literary text (e.g., 'Any question about the rhetorical mode of a literary text is always a rhetorical question that does not even know whether it is really questioning').[3] And for the deconstructionist, as for the skeptic, there comes a point at which the world drops out. It is converted not into a dream or an hallucination, but into a 'free-play of signifiers', a spider's web of textuality, or a theatrical mime. Unlike the skeptic, the deconstructionist has no idea of what it would take to reduce the proliferation of further indeterminate meanings or to stabilize the free-play of signifiers. Indeed, his point is that this *cannot* be done and that it *ought not* to be done. On the one hand, philosophy has traditionally been guilty of limiting indeterminacy and thus of suppressing much of the real excitement and challenge of dealing with language and the world. And on the other hand, traditional skepticism, in its adversarial but complementary relationship to classical epistemology, has accepted certain ideals of knowledge as setting the parameters of the debate, whereas the deconstructionist wants to call into question those very bounds. This is what Paul de Man sees in Nietzsche's challenge that the principle of non-contradiction is not one of 'necessity' but only a matter of practical inability, that it rests on our inability to affirm and deny one and the same thing. Nietzsche said that it 'is a subjective and empirical law, not the expression of any "necessity" but only of an inability. If, according to Aristotle, the law of contradiction is the most certain of all principles, if it is the ultimate and most basic, upon which every demonstrative proof rests, if the principle of every axiom lies in it; then one should consider all the more seriously what presuppositions already lie at the bottom of it.'[4]

Certainly Nietzsche's mood here is something other than skeptical. In a recent discussion of Derrida, Charles Altieri refers to him as a skeptic as well, but some of what he says suggests that this 'skepticism' does not have the traditional purpose of the articulation of doubts, but aims instead to provide a formulation of uncertainty in a way that will not be undercut by that same formulation. Altieri credits Derrida with certain original developments of skepticism 'by which the skeptic can actually state, if not argue the grounds of, and possible values in, a skeptical perspective.'[5]

Thus Derrida's 'formulation' amounts to no formulation at all. He is seeking to free himself from the skeptical circle in order to question the axis on which it turns. He will for instance criticize certain concepts to which he would not commit himself, and which he would hardly pronounce, by placing them *sous rature*. Or he will undercut the assertive force of utterances by placing their seriousness in doubt, instead couching his 'claims' in textual performances. These tactics may infuriate some readers, as if Derrida has by some trick or simple self-indulgence allowed himself the privilege of discourse on subjects of which he is at the same time depriving them. Yet a performance like *Glas* is undeniably exhilarating. Among many practising deconstructionists, the need to avoid the oppressive self-consciousness towards which discussions of indeterminacy naturally tend, and to escape eventual incrimination or conviction by their own methods, the 'performative' posture has been an important, some would say abused, resource. But of course the deconstructionist would not accept the description of 'performative' as a charge against him. His point is precisely that all communication is performance, that language is play in both senses of the word.[6]

Looking back, with Nietzsche, to Aristotle's *Metaphysics* as a target, he finds that if the 'play' of language is not to be overlooked, he must deny the fundamental tenet of logic, the principle of non-contradiction. By that principle, everything either is something or it is not; 'either P or ~P'. By denying this logical sentence, the deconstructionist is able to fashion for himself what amounts to a utopian (non)place for his inspection and questioning of every determinate position in any 'topographical' (i.e., propositional) logic – which is to say, any position pro or contra skepticism. Hence Derrida's selective interest in the Kierkegaardian 'either/or', to which he alludes at the beginning of his essay on Foucault: 'The instant of decision is madness' (WD 31).

I will not insist on it here, because it would take me too far afield of the contrast between skepticism and deconstruction that I want to pursue, but there are further grounds which support the view of deconstruction as a form of utopian discourse. The favoured metaphors of textuality, of play, of the abyss, of the graph, and of the trace, all suggest what strikes me as a utopian topography, and in fact some of the most provocative work on utopias has been done by French post-structuralist thinkers.[7] On his own account of himself, or course, the charge of utopianism would be incomprehensible to the deconstructionist. Derrida has in fact given a reading of Descartes that sees the Cartesian Cogito as a form of utopianism, in this case a temporal one (i.e., a denial of history, the escape of an 'original' moment). The Cogito, he says, is 'the return to an original point which no longer belongs to either a *determined* reason or a *determined* unreason, no longer belongs to them as opposition or alternative' (WD 56).

A further explanation of what Derrida has to say about madness and the Cartesian Cogito will have to wait until I can discuss the problem of the reasonableness of doubt in the following section. For now it is enough to see that in contrast, the skeptic and the epistemologist – at least on their account of themselves – remain wholly within the constraints of the principle of non-contradiction, and recognize that every 'place' from which they might argue, every position which they might hold, is *some* place or position and that it is not any other. Consequently, each must be ready for conviction in his position. Even if he is solitary (like Descartes, seated beside the fire, or like Montaigne, in his circular reading room), the skeptic's position is an identifiable place, a determinate locus. The deconstructionist, by contrast, will not sit still.

The deconstructive rejection of the principle of non-contradiction and the 'performative' nature of deconstructive practice may suggest that deconstruction is a skeptical methodology of literary analysis. Certainly some of the consequences of deconstruction, by which it seems impossible to be secure in the received meaning of a text, or by which the difference between literature and criticism has been blurred, may seem like methodological skepticism, but deconstruction alone is not responsible for this state of critical affairs. If deconstruction were a skeptical method of literary analysis (and I am suggesting that it is not), one would have to see it as saying not just that there is no basis for choosing among various readings of a text, but that the methods of literary criticism themselves render impossible any judgment of the relative adequacy of competing interpretations. As Steven Fuller put it, 'If this were mathematics . . . rather than literary criticism, the deconstructionist would be claiming, in effect, that his discipline's proof procedure undermines the possibility of its ever serving as a decision procedure.'[8]

For deconstruction, what invalidates a proof procedure from ever serving as a decision procedure is the fact that the instrument of analysis, namely human language, is itself the source of the uncertainty that is discovered in the object of analysis. But human language could hardly be called a discipline's 'method' (although it might be its medium), and for the deconstructionist language is as much the *object* as it is his method. Language is at the heart of what prompts the deconstructionist in his entire project. Thus I think it is true, but too little, to say with Jay Cantor that deconstruction differs from skepticism in that it uses 'linguistic metaphors'. That substantially underestimates the place of language in the deconstructionist's methods and in his conclusions, although it is certainly right to credit him with having discovered a breach between signifiers and signifieds.

The deconstructionist is supremely aware of the ambiguities of ordinary discourse which, he claims (as for instance in Derrida's discussion of J.L. Austin),[9] the 'ordinary-language' philosopher must deny. He rejects the idea that literary language is a special type of language, to which ambiguities and polysemia are 'proper'.[10] He demonstrates, as Paul de Man has done, that the rhetorical and semiological axes of a text consistently undercut and destabilize one another. And perhaps most important, in the work of Derrida, the deconstructionist denies the claim he finds implicit in classical arguments for and against skepticism that we may ever be in possession of a language capable of expressing the contents of consciousness directly, im-mediately. Thus when a Derridean calls into question the basis on which the Cartesian Cogito rests, he means not only to question the principle of identity and the law of non-contradiction, but to charge that the Cogito cannot be made known without the intervention of language – or, stated in terms of Derrida's discussion of Husserl, that the contents of consciousness are always tacitly assumed as taking some form, as being impressed in some language.[11]

If the deconstructionist's insistence on the play of language is of the consequence he says it is (and we can do nothing here but take him at his word), then what I pointed to earlier as moments at which the world drops out and madness sets in are not as similar as they might at first appear for the skeptic and the deconstructionist. For the skeptic, the world is a dream, a vision, an hallucination; for the deconstructionist, there is no world beyond the text. The skeptic remains always in possession of his own consciousness; in this sense, all traditional forms of skepticism are also forms of philosophical idealism; madness for him takes the form of solipsism, the spectre against which Wittgenstein guarded throughout both periods of his career. The skeptic's greatest worry is that what he thinks he sees as the external world may *also* be a product of his consciousness. This is the point at which Descartes, for instance, considers himself 'in the habit of sleeping, and in my dreams representing to myself the same things or sometime even less probable things, than do those who are insane in their waking moments'.[12] And this is the reason that Descartes can, without contradiction, go on to begin his programme of doubt by *assuming* 'that we are asleep and that all these particulars, e.g., that we open our eyes, shake our head, extend our hands, and so on, are but false delusions' (p. 146). By contrast, the deconstructionist who loses the world in a web of language is saying that it would do no good to try to get 'behind' the Cartesian (or Husserlian) Cogito, because there is no such place to which to aspire. All there is is language. And in so saying, what the deconstructionist loses, rather than the external world, is consciousness, or his own connection to his consciousness, his presence to himself, and this is a loss he does not lament, because it sustains his textual performances. For the deconstructionist, madness is detachment from self-consciousness, but as I shall discuss in the following section, he envisions no reattachment to consciousness to be gained through the work of reason. He stands literally beside himself, in ecstasy, or hilarity; hence Derrida's interest, in 'The Double Session', in the figure of Pierrot, who 'mimes all the way to the "supreme spasm", the rising of ecstatic hilarity' (D 201).

II

So far, I have been outlining certain features of deconstruction and skepticism in order to understand why the traditional philosopher – the epistemologist – finds dialogue with the deconstructionist so uncommonly difficult and why the deconstructionist, for his part, finds the traditional philosopher so unaware of the slipperiness of his own discourse; why, in other words, they have been talking past one another. This contrast shapes up along lines which look something like the following: the skeptic knows what it would take on the part of epistemology to relieve him of his world-shattering doubts, and he seeks to prove that what he demands – a secure method, viable criteria, the reaffirmation of his ties to the world, and so forth – cannot be forthcoming. As Stanley Cavell showed in earlier work on skepticism, the epistemologist who wishes to prevail over the skeptic will have to show that the skeptic cannot possibly mean what he says when he makes his demands; he will, so to speak, have to stupify the skeptic to himself.[13] But the deconstructionist, wrongly thought of as a skeptic, has no idea what an epistemology counter to his uncertainties and indeterminacies would look like. This is because he is out to question the very axis of which skepticism and epistemology are the opposite poles. Because his questioning shows up as a denial of the principle of non-contradiction, one is likely to think that deconstruction is a form of irrationalism. That is a tempting idea for the deconstructionist's opponent, because it would relieve him of the burden of a response; or rather, the charge of irrationalism would itself be his response. The deconstructionist's opponent may, moreover, find support for this view in what the deconstructionist himself has to say about the nature of traditional, skeptical doubt, viz., that doubt itself must be reasonable if it is to have any place in the skeptic's programme. In the following pages, I want to look more closely at the place of 'reasonable doubt' in skepticism and deconstruction. I hope to show that the charge of 'irrationalism' aimed at the deconstructionist is in fact ill-aimed, hence that it cannot be used to free his opponent from the burden of response. The basis from which this charge is levelled, moreover, seriously misrepresents what the deconstructionist has to say about the place of reason in epistemology.

For Descartes, the requirement of 'reasonable doubt' poses the following problem. Descartes must achieve the reasonableness which he demands of himself in the face of his own avowal that his skeptical worries seem unreasonable. In the First Meditation he asks '. . . how could I deny that these hands and this body are mine, were it not that I compare myself with certain persons, devoid of sense, whose cerebella are so troubled and clouded by the violent vapours of black bile, that they constantly assure us that they think they are kings when they are really quite poor, or that they are clothed in purple when they are really without covering, or who imagine that they have an earthenware head or are nothing but pumpkins or are made of glass' (p. 145). Descartes is worried that since he has *sometimes* found himself in error in the past, he may *never* be able to rest secure in his opinions: 'It is now some time since I detected how many were the false beliefs that I had from my earliest youth admitted as true, and how doubtful was everything I had since constructed on this basis' (p. 144). And since his senses have in the past deceived him, they might never be trusted: 'it is sometimes proved to me that these senses are deceptive, and it is wiser not to trust entirely any thing by which we have once been deceived' (p. 145). The problem, if the requirement of the reasonableness of doubt is to be met, is to explain how one could make this progression, so seemingly precipitous, from the *local* worry that *sometimes* my claims to knowledge fail, to the *general* worry that they *never* can succeed.

An explanation of this progression occupies Cavell for a large part of his discussion of traditional epistemology in *The Claim of Reason*. The traditional philosopher feels that the doubts he raises are reasonable insofar as they arise in connection with ordinary objects in ordinary contexts (e.g. Descartes inspecting a piece of wax). For this reason, they are the very considerations which the philosopher who, like Austin, proceeds from ordinary-language, should be in a position to capture. Do the methods of ordinary-language philosophy succeed here? Austin's investigations of the bases of claims to knowledge characteristically focus on specific rather than general instances. He looks at cases where the identification of an object, not its existence, is in doubt. Thus the work of the ordinary-language philosopher makes even more apparent the problem of the traditional epistemologist who wants to proceed from his local worries ('sometimes I am deceived') to his general conclusion ('I never can be certain'). The ordinary-language philosopher like Austin seems more to want to ward off skepticism before it has a chance to take root than to voice skeptical doubts.

Consider one of Austin's typical cases from the essay 'Other Minds'.[14] A claim of knowledge is introduced, such as 'There's a bittern at the bottom of the garden' (p. 79); then the bases for the claim are requested by asking 'How do you know?' In one set of answers the question is taken to be asking about my position with respect to the claim (hence the replies 'I was brought up in the fens'; 'The keeper reported it'). In a second set of answers the question is taken to be asking about the object, about the ways in which I can identify it in the way that I have (hence the replies 'By its booming'; 'From the booming noise'). But in some cases where a claim has been entered, the bases for it are not felt to be exhausted by either of these two classes of response. The question 'How do you know?' is taken not to mean either 'How do *you* come to know?' (asking about my position or training) or 'How can you *tell*?' (asking about the distinctive features of the object), but something more like the skeptical question 'How can you *ever* know *anything*?' Someone might object not to my competence for this particular task of knowledge, and not to the fact that the features I have identified are not definitive marks, but that the goldfinch might be 'stuffed, painted, dummy, artificial, trick, freak, toy, assumed, feigned', and so on (p. 87). I cannot simply reject these objections out of hand as long as they are expressions of 'reasonable doubt', which is to say as long as they make some sense in some context.

As Austin's discussion of these kinds of objections makes clear, however, what will happen is that in providing them with a context I will have to reduce the force by which they are meant to question the possibility of knowledge *überhaupt*: I know what it means for this bird to be stuffed or toy or dreamed, and I have procedures which in each case will tell me how to distinguish it from a 'real' bird (Austin: 'These doubts are all to be allayed by means of recognized procedures . . . appropriate to the particular case'). But in so doing I will be answering local questions about my ability to tell or to know a particular thing in a particular case. Hence the *skeptical* question ('But is it a *real* one?') is felt as requiring a special basis: 'there must be some "reason for suggesting" that it isn't real, in the sense of some specific way . . . in which it is suggested that this experience or item may be phoney' (Austin, p. 87), and it seems that there is no general basis to be found: no 'special basis' is general enough. Hence the metaphysician's question seems out of order: 'The wile of the metaphysician consists in asking "Is it a real table?" (a kind of object which has no obvious way of being phoney) and not specifying or limiting what may be wrong with it, so that I feel at a loss "how to prove" it *is* a real one.'

Given the threats of the skeptic, who means to challenge the possibility of knowledge *überhaupt*, it is not enough for the epistemologist to enter specific claims to knowledge; he cannot conceive of making a general claim about certainty from the fact that he knows this *particular* thing, as the skeptic conceives of making a general objection about knowledge from the fact that he may be *mistaken* about this particular thing.[15] What he needs is a context, a reasonable basis, for entering some general claim of knowledge such as 'I know': not 'I know this (particular thing)', but 'I am a knowing being, one who has certain capacities, knowledge (certainty) among them'. But the question is, to whom could one imagine oneself saying such a thing? This was Wittgenstein's most important contribution to our understanding of the epistemologist's predicament, his having shown us how in making such a general claim, in succumbing to the temptation to knowledge, the epistemologist can only be speaking 'outside language games'. 'There is nothing we cannot know', Cavell said in *The Claim of Reason* (p. 239): 'That does not mean we can know everything; there is no everything, no totality of facts or things, to be known. To say that we do not (cannot) know things-in-themselves is as much a Transcendental Illusion as to say we do.'

The originality of this critique of skepticism is that it shows that the requirement of 'reasonable doubt' is not as great a problem for the skeptic as the requirement of a 'reasonable claim' is for the epistemologist seeking to claim certitude for his knowledge of the world. The problem with skepticism lies with its conception of epistemology. It is tempting for this reason to draw a parallel between the *Philosophical Investigations* or *The Claim of Reason* and the work of Derrida. But a look at Derrida's discussion of this same problem will reveal as many significant differences as similarities.

On Derrida's reading of Michel Foucault's *Folie et déraison*, Foucault says that Descartes makes a categorical distinction between madness, or 'unreason', and sensory error: he treats cases in which empirical knowledge fails as unassimilable to cases of dreams, feigning, and imagination. The former are local failures of knowledge, such as are produced where part of an object under consideration is hidden from our view, or where it is too distant to be seen ('things which are hardly perceptible, or very far away', Meditation I). To mark the parallel with *The Claim of Reason* up to this point, these are cases where it would make sense to ask whether we saw 'all' of an object (e.g., the earth viewed from space, but not the earth viewed from earth; or the moon viewed from the earth, but not from the moon). Descartes then supposedly exiles the remaining cases (dreams and imagination) 'by decree'.

This would have one of two related effects: either it would trivialize the epistemologist's project, because he could then only make local, particular, or empirical claims to knowledge; or it would deprive the skeptic of the basis that he needs in order to aim his attack against knowledge *überhaupt*. If I read him correctly, Derrida interprets Foucault as saying that the requirement that doubt be reasonable has this second effect, that of silencing skepticism; hence the difficulty Derrida sees in an enterprise such as Foucault's, which proposes to allow madness to 'speak for itself'.

The parallel with Austinian-styled epistemology breaks down, however, when we look to Derrida's own response to Descartes. Derrida does not accept the 'exile of madness' in the Foucauldian reading of Descartes, saying in effect that cases of dreams and madness present serious worries because they are *similar* to local, individually threatening cases of sensory error. He sees no breach between the instance of a particular doubt of a particular thing (sensory error) and skeptical doubt (madness): 'It must be understood that the hypothesis of dreams is the radicalization or, if you will, the hyperbolical exaggeration of the hypothesis according to which the senses could *sometimes* deceive me' (WD 48). If the Cartesian project is not to be trivialized, then none of these considerations – dreams or sensory error – can simply be dismissed. Thus if the skeptical philosopher is finally to come to affirm the Cogito, he must do so in full acknowledgement of the possibility that he may be mad or dreaming the world. Madness thus becomes 'reason's possibility'. And certainty 'need not be sheltered from an imprisoned madness. It is valid *even if I am mad* – a supreme self-confidence that seems to require neither the exclusion nor the circumventing of madness. Descartes never interns madness, neither at the stage of natural doubt nor at the stage of metaphysical doubt' (WD 55).

Thus unlike the Wittgensteinian dissolution of skepticism, which shows that there is no (reasonable) context in which to project our general claims of knowledge and no general claim of knowledge able to provide the relevance of a context, the Derridean deconstruction of skepticism shows that the Cartesian affirmation of the Cogito includes radical doubt (madness) as its 'other' or 'exterior', as the possibility on which it rests. The point of contrast with the Wittgensteinian response to skepticism is that reason there remains the stable anchor, the pivot around which doubt and knowledge turn: when a general claim of knowledge is rejected as suspicious or out of order, it is because of a prior requirement of reason, i.e., that no *reasonable* (meaningful, sensible) context can be found for it.

Perhaps the key to these differences lies in Derrida's idea of madness as the condition of *possibility* of the Cogito. Read in a certain light, in a certain mood, the idea that knowledge has conditions has a Kantian ring. Derrida gives what I take to be his most explicit formulation of the requirement that doubt be reasonable when he says that 'Even if I do not *in fact* grasp the totality, if I neither understand nor embrace it, I still formulate the project of doing so, and this project is meaningful in such a way that it can be defined only in relation to a precomprehension of the infinite and undetermined totality' (WD 56). I call this a statement of the requirement of the *reasonableness* of doubt not only because what is reasonable must be meaningful, must make sense, but because reasonable discourse, logical discourse, is discourse about the whole.[16] But Derrida says that the Cogito 'exceeds the totality'. As the point on which Descartes stakes all knowledge, the Cogito is imagined to be outside of reason, 'invulnerable to all determined opposition between reason and unreason'; this accounts for the 'utopianism' that Derrida sees in the Cartesian Cogito, 'the point starting from which the history of the determined forms of this opposition [between reason and unreason] . . . can appear as such and be stated'. The Cogito is in excess of the totality in the sense that it is outside of it, or anterior to it, so that thanks to it, 'even if the totality of what I think is imbued with falsehood or madness, even if . . . nonmeaning has invaded the totality of the world, up to and including the very contents of my thought, I still think, I am *while I think*' (WD 56).

The theme of reason in excess of reason, beside itself, outside the totality, is of major importance in Derrida's discussion of Hegel and the Preface of the *Phenomenology of Spirit* in *Dissemination*. Here I want simply to point out that Derrida's analysis of Descartes comes out sounding surprisingly like Kant's Preface to the *Critique of Pure Reason*: 'Human reason has this peculiar fate that in one species of its knowledge it is burdened by questions which, as prescribed by the very nature of reason itself, it is not able to answer.'[17] Except that Derrida would revise Kant on the point of it being reason in excess of what reason can conceive, not only know, which determines reason's fate. I pick up the Kantian, rather than the Hegelian theme, because Kant's words are one of the epigraphs to *The Claim of Reason* and because Cavell has given one of the clearest summaries of Kant's anti-skeptical achievement, saying that 'the limitations of knowledge are not failures of it' (p. 241). Some of what there is of Kant in Wittgenstein is visible in *The Claim of Reason*. The reasonableness of doubt for instance is measured by the possibility of what we can or cannot say within the 'bounds of sense' of ordinary language-games. But when Cavell, reading Wittgenstein, revises Kant and asks us to give up our hope of knowing the thing-in-itself, it is not because of any excess of reason beyond the totality of that 'thing'; rather it is by our having exceeded reason, our having spoken outside the bounds of sense, that we have wrongly been led to the illusion of there being a totality, an 'everything' to be said or known. The idea of a comprehending Reason is not so much deconstructed as dissolved. There is no temptation for philosophy to allow madness to speak 'for itself', as in the Foucauldian project. Instead, our temptations to knowledge are silenced. Philosophy itself is eventually put to rest.

These comments suggest a final similarity between skepticism, as Wittgenstein sought to respond to it, and deconstruction, as exemplified in the writings of Derrida. It is that both, as images of what philosophy has become, mean to question the very nature of philosophical discourse and what this is, or might be. But then what should we expect of these writers, the one who saw it as his task to bring words back from their philosophical to their everyday use, the other who has shown us the literal extravagance of reasoned speech? It may be a consequence of this shared purpose not to remake philosophy but to stop philosophy from trying to remake itself again, that both Derrida and Wittgenstein seem to run so close to nihilism. In deconstructionist practice, where the world is a web of language and where language is an unstable trace, we are always in danger of talking things to death. The deconstructionist who stands beside himself in ecstasy or hysteria and realizes that rational discourse is itself reason (speech) in excess of reason (the *logos*, the whole), may be unable to bring his own discourse to an end. Hence when a neo-pragmatist thinker like Richard Rorty embraces deconstruction from within the language of analytic philosophy, as a form of 'conversation' (one hears echoes of Heidegger and Gadamer), and as a conversation 'without end', one can see how he might rest comfortably with that as an idea of the history of philosophy, as an image of what happens as paradigms change; but the analytic bias removes the threat of nihilism, which is deconstruction's cutting edge.[18] Since Wittgenstein approaches philosophy from somewhat the opposite place, he launches other threats and runs contrasting risks. In his writing the danger is not speech, but silence, not saying everything, or just anything, but saying nothing, a condition in which philosophical wisdom is indistinguishable from boredom (i.e., having nothing to say).

It may be that nihilism is the price to pay for asking the questions that Wittgenstein and Derrida have raised. But then if they show us what we have not yet had it at heart to say, that may not be any price to pay. When Wittgenstein said that what he wanted to do was to replace philosophy, as when Derrida parodies and mimics its high seriousness, both mean to question nothing less than the conditions for philosophy, the conditions under which we might have anything meaningful to say. If the contrast of skepticism and deconstruction has anything to show, it is perhaps that 'philosophy' has already reached the end that Nietzsche and Heidegger and Wittgenstein foresaw for it, and that its post-history has been developing along rather disparate lines. If that is indeed the case, then it means that Wittgenstein and Derrida silence as much as they echo one another's words.

Notes

[1] Jay Cantor, 'On Stanley Cavell', *Raritan*, 1 (1981), 49; and Stanley Cavell, *The Claim of Reason* (Oxford: Oxford University Press, 1979).

[2] Saul Kripke, *Wittgenstein on Rules and Private Language* (Cambridge, MA: Harvard University Press, 1982).

[3] Paul de Man, *Allegories of Reading* (New Haven: Yale University Press, 1979), p. 19.

[4] Friedrich Nietzsche, *The Will to Power*, trans. Walter Kaufmann and R.J. Hollingdale (New York: Random House, 1967), section 516.

[5] Charles Altieri, *Act and Quality: A Theory of Literary Meaning and Humanistic Understanding* (Amherst: University of Massachusetts Press, 1981), p. 29.

[6] See, for example, Derrida's reply to John Searle, LI 105–6.

[7] See, for example, Louis Marin, *Utopiques: Jeux d'espace* (Paris: Minuit, 1973).

[8] Steven Fuller, 'A French Science (With English Subtitles)', *Philosophy and Literature*, 7 (1983), 3–14.

[9] See Derrida's 'Signature Event Context', in MP 307–30.

[10] See, for example, Barbara Johnson, 'Poetry and Performative Language: Mallarmé and Austin', in *The Critical Difference* (Baltimore: Johns Hopkins University Press, 1980), pp. 52–66.

[11] See Derrida's discussion of Husserl in 'Form and Meaning: A Note on the Phenomenology of Language', in MP 155–73. These concerns have been taken up in recent work by Jean-François Lyotard, with some reference to Wittgenstein, on the problem of presentation. See 'Presentations', trans. Kathleen McLaughlin, in Alan Montefiore (ed.), *Philosophy in France Today* (Cambridge: Cambridge University Press, 1983), pp. 116–35.

[12] Descartes, Meditation I. I follow the translation of Elizabeth S. Haldane and G.R.T. Ross, in *The Philosophical Works of Descartes*, vol. 1 (1911; rpt Cambridge: Cambridge University Press, 1975), pp. 145–6.

[13] See Stanley Cavell, 'Knowing and Acknowledging', in *Must We Mean What We Say?* (1969; rpt. Cambridge: Cambridge University Press, 1976), pp. 238–67.

[14] In *Proceedings of the Aristotelian Society*, Supp. Vol. 20 (1946); references are to J.L. Austin, *Philosophical Papers*, 2nd edn (Oxford: Oxford University Press, 1970).

[15] There is one important exception to this: that in which a particular case is advanced as a 'best case' of knowledge. A 'best case' might be thought of as having the following formulation: 'If I know *anything*, I know *this*' (see Cavell, *The Claim of Reason*, p. 429).

[16] See Stanley Rosen, *Nihilism* (New Haven: Yale University Press, 1969).

[17] I follow the Norman Kemp Smith translation (1929; rpt New York: St Martin's Press, 1965), p. 7.

[18] See Richard Rorty, *Philosophy and the Mirror of Nature* (Princeton: Princeton University Press, 1979), especially Part Three; and 'The World Well Lost', in *Consequences of Pragmatism* (*Essays: 1971–1980*) (Minneapolis: University of Minnesota Press, 1982), pp. 3–18. The matter of the absorption of philosophy into criticism is taken up in his 'Philosophy as a Kind of Writing: An Essay on Derrida's also in that collection. Regarding the expression of deconstructionist concepts in the language of analytic philosophy, see Fuller, note 8, above.

CHAPTER 5

Un dialogue de sourds?
Some Implications of the Austin–Searle–Derrida Debate

Ian Maclean

It would clearly be unwise to claim that philosophy had been the same discipline for all its practitioners in every age and in every place. When Guillaume Du Val published in 1620 what was to be the standard edition of Aristotle for two centuries, he prefaced the first volume with a definition of philosophy, which at one point he describes as 'that true salvation and panacea of souls, that most certain governor of human life, that leader, light, torch, peace, inventor of laws, mother of cities, indicator of virtue, expeller of vice, mistress of customs and of discipline'; such a description would hardly be adopted now for inclusion in a university prospectus or a publisher's catalogue. Philosophy is a discipline which is taught and examined in different institutional contexts, although with the same name; two of these contexts are geographically designated as 'Anglo-American' and 'continental'. Philosophers like Richard Rorty and Arthur Danto see these traditions in historical terms – Kant (or Frege) and Hegel (or Husserl) are seen respectively as founding fathers.[1] A genealogical view like this one is tolerant of differences of approach, and does not necessarily imply comparative evaluation; other philosophers do not proceed in this Irenic mode. The 'Anglo-American' John Searle, assessing the most recent productions of 'continental' philosophy, sees them as wrongheaded, lacking in rigour, loose in thought and expression; the 'continental' philosopher Jacques Derrida sees all philosophy as prey to certain 'présupposés métaphysiques'. Are there two traditions? Is there one common tradition? Is there one sound tradition, and one impostor? These questions have emerged in sharp focus from the polemical exchanges between Searle and Derrida. It is highly questionable whether there exists a neutral position from which to adjudicate this debate; if there were one, it would presumably be the place of true philosophy. My modest aims in this paper are to ask the questions: does a dialogue take place between Searle and Derrida? Do they validate their enquiries in the same way, or in different ways? Do they share presuppositions, or are the premises of their arguments different? Is it possible to characterize their methods? If a dialogue does not take place, why does it fail?

Both Searle and Derrida treat language as a place of philosophical investigation. Searle allies himself to the tradition of analytical philosophy which pursues the thesis that the philosophy of thought is to be accomplished by the philosophy of language, in the sense that it is through the philosophy of language that we can elucidate how our thoughts relate to the world.[2] Searle distinguishes the philosophy of language ('the attempt to give philosophically illuminating descriptions of certain general features of language such as reference, truth, meaning and necessity') from linguistics ('the attempt to describe the actual structures of natural languages (phonological, syntactical, semantic)') and from linguistic philosophy ('the attempt to solve particular philosophical problems by attending to the ordinary use of particular words or other elements in a given language').[3] Derrida, on the other hand, draws no maps of disciplinary boundaries, and confines himself to describing his enterprise as the reading of philosophical texts in a certain way. In an essay on Paul Valéry, he writes:

> Une tâche est alors prescrite: étudier le texte philosophique dans sa structure formelle, dans son organisation rhétorique, dans la spécificité et la diversité de ses types textuels, dans ses modèles d'exposition et de production – au-delà de ce qu'on appelait autrefois les genres –, dans l'espace aussi de ses mises en scène et dans une syntaxe qui ne soit pas seulement l'articulation de ses signifiés, de ses références à l'être ou à la vérité, mais l'agencement de ses procédés et tout ce qui s'y investit. Bref, considérer aussi la philosophie comme 'un genre littéraire particulier'. . . .[4]

I do not believe that Derrida is reduced to the status of interpreter of texts by this passage: rather, he declares his task to be the examination – in an almost impossible mode – of the necessary conditions of language which they contain, and which by his own admission are beyond the reach of language. This project is incompatible with that of Searle: so it is hardly surprising that Derrida's 'reading' of J.L. Austin – Searle's forerunner in speech act theory – should provoke from Searle a spirited defence of his conception of the philosophy of language. In order to attempt to describe their differing approaches, it is expedient to begin with a short account of Austin's *How To Do Things With Words*, before considering the writings of Derrida and Searle themselves.

How To Do Things With Words is a transcript of Austin's lecture notes which were used by him at Harvard in 1955; I shall refer also to a lecture he delivered in France in 1958 entitled 'performatif/constatif'.[5] The content of these lectures is very well known, and I shall offer only a brief résumé of them. Austin begins by distinguishing 'constatives' from 'performatives': 'constatives' are statements in the form of sentences which philosophers believed (then) to be verifiable; 'performatives' are not subject to the opposition true/false, since issuing the utterance is performing an action, which can be 'happily' or 'unhappily' performed, but cannot be 'true' or 'false'. For several lectures, Austin investigates this doctrine of infelicities, before abandoning it as unsatisfactory; in his French lectures he is more direct, and proceeds to make the claim that constatives, like performatives, are subject to his rules of 'happy' or 'unhappy' performance, and that there can be no linguistic criterion for distinguishing constatives from performatives: all utterances are speech acts (p. 139; P/C 279). In his Harvard lectures, he does not state this until the end: instead he creates mid-way a new division – locutionary/illocutionary/perlocutionary – which he relates to another triad: rheme/phone/pheme. There is a certain slipperiness about some of these distinctions (force, meaning and sense, for example, appear at different points with apparently different senses), but Austin is careful to make limited claims for them, and to stress their provisional nature.

Two features of Austin's schemes are worthy of note here. The first is convention(ality). As Jonathan Culler points out, Austin claims that 'what makes an utterance a command or a promise is not the speaker's state of mind at the moment of utterance but conventional rules involving features of the context'.[6] These conventional rules mean necessarily, as the semiologist Umberto Eco points out, that an utterance must be able to be used to tell a lie if it can be used to tell the truth: so that if a lie is to be distinguished from the truth (or if sincerity is to be distinguished from insincerity), then an extralinguistic criterion needs to be found: and Austin seems to be forced at certain points in his argument to appeal to intention as such a criterion.[7]

The second feature worthy of note is Austin's recourse to context in his search for firm ground. At the end of the Harvard lectures, he declares that 'the total speech act in the total speech-situation is the only actual phenomenon which, in the last resort, we are engaged in elucidating' (p. 148): in his French lecture, the context is said to be 'les faits: la situation de celui qui a parlé: le but dans lequel il parlait: son auditoire: questions de précision' (P/C 281).[8] This context sounds like the definition of it given in linguistics: it seems to have important psychological implications; but most strikingly, it impinges on the law. Austin makes many references to performatives and the law: he refers to operatives and 'verdictives'; he claims that 'lawyers have always known about infelicities . . . only the still widespread obsession that the utterances of the law, and utterances used in, say, "acts of the law", must somehow be statements true or false, has prevented many lawyers from getting this whole matter straighter than we are likely to': elsewhere he declares that it is 'better to apply than to make law'; most telling is his reference to the 'consensus ad idem': 'when two parties are involved "consensus ad idem" is necessary'.[9] By invoking the law and the legal conception of context, the *mens rea* as well as the *actus reus* is invoked, and intention, mental states, real human beings, decisions, even true and false all return to the arena.

Austin claims at the end of his lecture that he has been attacking the 'true/false fetish' and the 'value/fact fetish' (p. 151). To do this, he engages in a number of presuppositions, and a number of procedures of argument which deserve some attention. There is a general problem of anteriority in his work, which has been adumbrated already: is philosophy dependent on grammar and psychology? At various points in his argument, Austin seems to rely on prior grammatical categories (e.g. singular, present, indicative, active): indeed this reliance on grammar draws a comment from a member of the audience of Austin's French lecture, who pointed out that the grammar of French, being different, made a difference also to the status of performatives in that language (P/C 295-6, 301). The questioner (Chaim Perelman) went on to say that this being so, Austin would need a metalinguistic or extralinguistic criterion for the performative: but Austin denied that this would need to be a 'sentiment intérieur' ['inner feeling'] which might have a psychological or an ontological status. His French audience were not convinced: for them a 'logique des énoncés performatifs' ['logic of performative utterances'] would entail a (prior) 'logique des pensées performatives' ['logic of performative thoughts']: as René Poirier pointed out, we need to know the meaning of 'j'ordonne' ['I command': an example of a performative] before we can categorize it. But he conceded also that the relationship of thinking to speaking was not simple, and was made more complex by the philosophical enterprise itself (P/C 297-8).

Austin's enquiry reads informally and untechnically: he indulges also in a certain intellectual playfulness, which makes two aspects of *How To Do Things With Words* somewhat surprising. The first is his dismissal of 'non-serious' as opposed to 'serious' aspects of performatives. While he concedes that a performative is mimicable, as is any phatic or phonetic act, he feels it necessary *ab initio* to banish the possibility of a non-serious performative from his enquiry: 'Surely [performative words] must be spoken "seriously" and so as to be taken "seriously"?' (p. 9, cf. p. 122) As well as this, he both begins and ends with reference to truth – whereas he claims that his writing is directed against the 'true/false fetish'. The first lecture opens with the words: 'What I shall have to say here is neither difficult nor contentious: the only merit I should like to claim for it is that of being *true*, at least in parts' (p. 1: my emphasis); and he returns at times to the criterion of truth (e.g. p. 45) eventually claiming that 'true and false' is 'a general dimension of being a right or proper thing to say as opposed to a wrong thing, in these circumstances, to this audience, for these purposes, and with these intentions' (p. 145). These references to truth are not only surprising because of his attack on the true/false fetish (one might claim that he would still like true/false to retain a limited efficacy): they are also surprising because Austin refuses to be reflexive about his own enterprise. Is not lecturing a speech act? Why does he not relativize his own discourse? It would be wrong to deduce that Austin believed that there was such a thing as the neutral transmission of ideas especially in view of his deliberate jokiness and informality; but it remains odd that he did not speculate at all on the problems of metalanguage.[10]

I do not wish to spend much time on John R. Searle's *Speech Acts* (1969): a book which developed out of Searle's Oxford D.Phil. thesis on sense and reference. Searle's undertaking is in the philosophy of language, which he defines as being concerned with the following sorts of questions: how do words relate to the world? how does meaning relate to phonetics? how does communication occur? what is the difference between saying something and meaning it and saying something and not meaning it? how do words stand for things? what is the difference between meaningful and meaningless? what is it for something to be true? or false? Searle follows Austin in claiming that to *say* something is also to *do* something, and that a whole class of utterances explicitly, and perhaps all utterances implicitly, depend for their (proper) performance upon conventions other than purely linguistic ones. Unlike Austin, Searle rejects marginal cases, and concentrates on what he (intuitively?) sees as 'central instances'; his method is first to explain his notions (e.g. his version of an illocutionary act), then to formulate rules; then, and only then, to deal with marginal cases and exceptions. His central tenet is that 'speaking a language is engaging in a highly complex form of rule-governed behaviour . . . talking is performing acts according to rules'.[11] Like Austin, Searle excludes 'non-serious' utterances; unlike Austin, he foregrounds his connections with well-known philosophical issues — sense and reference, fallacies in the philosophy of language, brute *versus* institutional facts, nominalism and universals, ontological commitment — and he engages in 'technical' exercises in logic which are inaccessible to laymen. His is not a modest or unaggressive book.

Two years after the publication of Searle's *Speech Acts*, Jacques Derrida addressed a conference on communication in Canada: his paper was entitled 'Signature événement contexte', and it dealt in part with Austin's *How To Do Things With Words*. It was published in 1972 in *Marges de la philosophie*, and translated into English for the first issue of *Glyph* in 1977. The same number of *Glyph* produced Searle's critique of Derrida ('Reiterating the differences: a reply to Derrida'); the following number included Derrida's critique of Searle's critique of Derrida ('Limited Inc').[12] Derrida's paper is not just devoted to speech acts: it constitutes also an attack on the homogeneity of the 'field of communication', and on the implicit principles it contains, namely: that men write to communicate; that men communicate their ideas and thoughts; that 'ideas' and 'thoughts' precede communication; that men were (historically) communicating orally before writing came into existence. The aspect of the field of communication which Derrida has particularly in mind is the pure logical grammar proposed by Husserl in his *Logical Investigations* (1900–01): this would be the universal conditions of possibility for a morphology of significations in their cognitive relation to a possible object — not a pure grammar in general, considered from a linguistic or psychological point of view. Husserl's pure logical grammar is the most reduced form of communication possible (epoché has taken out the contingent sender and receiver and reduced the 'message' to its conditions of possibility). It is as 'pure' a version of thought on communication as Derrida believes possible. What it has in common with Austin is its privileging of *speech* and *presence*, and its reference to notions of code and context (even though these are only considered as virtual).

Derrida does not suggest that Husserl and Austin are bad or incompetent philosophers: rather that their projects are doomed from the beginning for similar reasons which concern the intrinsic conditions of speech, presence, code, and context. This is to some degree acknowledged by Austin (see P/C 278), and Derrida is clear in his approval of this part of Austin's text. Derrida questions however Austin's enterprise of considering the speech act as an event whole and complete to itself, accessible to consciousness. I have already said that Austin was constrained to reintroduce the intending subject of speech even though he wished not to: Derrida examines these passages in his work, and especially those among them where Austin excludes 'non-serious' uses of language: for example language used by actors, language teachers and the like. These cases are described by Austin as 'impure', 'diseased' or 'parasitic'.[13] For Derrida, a signature is a clear case of the absence of an intending subject in an event whose conditions of possibility demand that it is repeatable, hence imitable:[14] for Austin, it is a performative event, linked to a moment in time and to an intention.

I have quoted Austin's words on the need to consider the 'whole context of utterance'. Derrida accuses Austin of failing to see that his insistence on presence, totality, consciousness, intention allows the value/fact fetish which Austin wishes to banish to slip back into his writing: the value being attached to presence, intention, consciousness and totality. For Derrida there is no central, unified, isolatable, present-to-itself speech event organized by an intention: no 'vouloir-dire absolument plein et maître de lui-même' ['absolutely full meaning that is master of itself'], no 'conscience libre et présente à la totalité de l'opération' ['free consciousness present for the totality of the operation'], no 'contexte exhaustivement définissable' ['exhaustively definable context', MP 323]: and what I am 'saying now' is of course as much impugned by Derrida's claims as was Austin's own discourse. Context is never 'saturated';[15] it is indeterminate, because speech can operate without it, and its constituents are never fully present to themselves. No meaning can be determined out of context (Austin would agree with this); no context is 'closed' or 'complete': therefore no meaning can be definitive. There is, according to Derrida, an indefinite or infinite loss of meaning which he describes by the word 'dissemination': communication is therefore not a unified field since its 'horizon' is broken by the non-wholly-present elements of its constituents – speaking subject, message, receiver. Derrida implicitly recognizes that consensus and law can limit this dissemination but not *philosophically*, only *politically*: he speaks at one point of a 'conscience comme autorité de dernière instance' ['consciousness as the authority of the last analysis'] which appears to have the legal force of 'mens rea' (*Marges*, pp. 368, 376 [MP 310, 316]). Even the code of the message (in speech, this might be 'grammar') is not total or present, because the code can only be considered a finite set of rules if the context in which it is used is also finite, and this condition is not met (*Marges*, p. 375 [MP 315–16]). 'Repetition', 'quotation' is therefore only relatively possible.

It is this sort of analysis which leads Derrida to postulate his notion of 'general writing' ('l'écriture'). When he says (paradoxically) that speech is a form of writing, he is reversing this hierarchy to show that one of the (repressed) conditions of possibility of speech (absence of intending subject present to himself or herself) is something associated with writing which leads it to be considered as less than speech. If speech contains non-presence, non-intention as part of its condition of being (or rather not-altogether-being) then it is indeed a form of writing. All writing can function in the absence of its speaking and intending author and its intended receiver: so, argues Derrida, can speech. The oral sign, like the written sign, contains the structural possibility of being 'weaned from referent and signified' (*Marges*, p. 378 [MP 318: trans. modified]). There is no such thing as pure presence in either place or time. A signature is a sign of iterability (repeatability) which confirms this: 'son avoir-été présent' is written in 'un maintenant passé, qui restera un maintenant futur, donc un maintenant en général . . . la forme [générale] de la maintenance' (*Marges*, p. 391).[16] It is important to stress that Derrida does *not* conclude from this that speech acts are impossible, *nor* that presence is an effect of speech, *nor* that performatives do not exist; but rather that the 'general space of the possibility' of presence, speech and performance presupposes absence, writing and dissemination.

Nor does Derrida, in arguing thus, exempt himself from the charge of idealism (from which, in one way or another, he would claim there is no escape: see 'Limited Inc', 82 [LI 93–4]): he turns his own discourse against itself as a *mise en abyme*, and finishes it with a printed version of his own signature which exemplifies and ironizes at the same time his own argument. This argument was conducted as an exercise in textual analysis (of Austin and Husserl) – an analysis taken out of context (that is, out of the teleological and metaphysical horizon of the writing): this causes Derrida again to reflect on his own enterprise ('[l']opération dont nous devons nous demander comment et pourquoi elle est toujours possible' ['an operation about which we must ask how and why it is always possible'], *Marges*, p. 380 [MP 319]). The analysis employed a form of logic which was used first to identify what Austin and Husserl repressed (absence, quotation, incompleteness of context, imperfection of code, lack of full consciousness): then to promote a series of transformations of the kind 'if possible, then *necessarily* possible; if *necessarily* possible, then conditional *ab initio*; if conditional *ab initio*, then integral; if integral then disseminational'. (See *Marges*, p. 385 [MP 323–4] for an example). In this logical process, the forms of grammar indicating passivity, activity, possibility, abstraction are taken as sense-bearing in some neutral way (they are bracketed out): he talks, for example, of 'the suppressed predicates of writing' (absence, non-intention, non-presence) 'dont la force de générali*té*, de générali*sation* et de géné*rativité* se trouve libérée, greffée sur un "nouveau" concept d'écriture' ['whose force of generali*ty*, generali*zation*, and gene*rativity* finds itself liberated, grafted onto a "new" concept of writing'] (*Marges*, p. 393 [MP 329]: my emphases). He also uses, without commentary or explanation, words from the storehouse of phenomenology.

Not all Anglo-American philosophers have reacted to this as though it were obscure pretentious rubbish: but John Searle was scathing about it. In his reply in the first issue of *Glyph* he accuses Derrida of incompetence as a philosopher, perversion of the truth, lack of clarity, internal inconsistency, and failure to understand such distinctions as use/mention and type/token. Derrida does not represent another philosophical tradition (the 'continental' one); he is simply not worthy of the name of philosopher. Searle's pugnacious style gives rise to sentences such as 'Derrida has a distressing penchant for saying things which are obviously false'; and 'I find so many confusions in this argument of Derrida I hardly know where to get started on it'. He represents Derrida as a latter-day scholastic who does not quite fully understand the rules of syllogistic reasoning, and accuses him of misunderstanding the term 'parasitic' in Austin by attributing to it moral connotations (where Austin merely uses it to mean 'pertaining to something defined in terms of something else') and failing to grasp the meaning of 'ordinary language'. Derrida does not, according to Searle, distinguish between historical and logical dependence in relation to writing *versus* speech; he confuses iterability of a term or sentence (that is, its type) with the permanence of a given text (that is, a token). Searle claims furthermore that Derrida thinks that intentions are prior to speech, and psychologically separate; that Derrida muddles up the use of a sentence with its mention (as an example); and that he misrepresents Austin. Searle accuses Derrida of failing to see that to begin a philosophical investigation with standard cases (as opposed to *cas-limites*) does not imply that standard cases have chronological or metaphysical priority; and Derrida is indicted therefore of failing to see the logical priority of 'a set of questions about serious discourse'.

One might say that here is the exact point (if there were such a thing) of incomprehension between Searle and Derrida: Searle cannot take seriously Derrida's claim that the *ab initio* conditions of investigation into speech repress absence, non-seriousness, non-presence, imperfection. Searle therefore provides two examples of writing messages to oneself which are supposed to show that writing can operate self-reflexively as can speech. He misrepresents Derrida when he quotes him as saying that there is an essential absence of intention in any utterance *without adding* that intention of a certain kind is also present (in a certain way) in an utterance. Searle also provides an example of a sentence in written form ('on 20th September 1793 I set out on a journey from London to Oxford') designed to show that 'a meaningful sentence is just a standing possibility of the corresponding (intentional) speech act', and that, 'understanding the sentence apart from its utterance is knowing what linguistic act its utterance would be the performance of'. Searle, in all his article, does not accept that there can be statements about the general conditions of speech (of the kind Derrida wishes to make) which can be separated from hypotheses used to test 'real speech': Searle insists that one can only test notions about language and formulate its rules on the assumptions that its rules are recursive; that language is real; and that it exists prior to the investigation.

Derrida's reply to Searle in the second issue of *Glyph* is no less vituperative: but this is only to be expected. It is not easy for a philosopher to put up with accusations of incompetence and lack of rigour. Because Searle accused him of 'misunderstanding', Derrida is forced into the role of hermeneut (it is a role which might in any case have suited him best): he is reduced paradoxically to demonstrating that he read Austin in an attentive and accurate way, and in a way which distinguished the 'whole' from the 'parts', and the 'unimportant' from the 'important' in Austin's text (see 'Limited Inc' 15–16, 64–5, 69–70 [LI 43–4, 91–2, 96–7]). He also sets out to show that Searle has misread him, and a reader of

'Limited Inc' might be forgiven for detecting in Derrida's text a tone of anger, in spite of his claims that he is made 'gai' by Searle's accusations. At one point Derrida even declares that 'Searle *falsifie* gravement les choses. Je me mets par contagion à écrire comme lui. C'est bien la première fois que j'accuse quelqu'un de tromper ou de se tromper' ('Limited Inc' 50),[17] and in so doing consciously betrays his own claim about the ultimate unfalsifiability of interpretation (in the face of boundless meaning in an 'unsaturable' context). I did not myself find 'Limited Inc' a particularly comfortable text to read.

But Derrida is able to make a good case for his gross misrepresentation by Searle on a number of points. Searle does not concede that Derrida allows a degree of intention, presence and a limited 'totality'. Searle also fails to distinguish 'necessary' and 'possible'. His accusations of confusion over iterability, repetition, identity and difference can be countered in Derrida's terms, and do not, according to Derrida, arise from a 'faiblesse conceptuelle' ['conceptual weakness'] or a 'lâcheté théorique' ['theoretical laxity']. Searle's characterization of Derrida as a pre-Saussurean substantialist – a scholastic straw-man believing in mentalism – is vigorously rejected by Derrida. And Searle's implicit attack on Derrida's presentation of his argument – his 'non-serious' style – seems to sting Derrida into a flurry of elucidations, as the opposition serious/non-serious lies close to his project in writing, together with the other (impugned) oppositions normal/abnormal; originality/quotation; full/empty; strict/non-strict; literal/metaphorical. It was precisely in Austin's rejection or repression of the 'non-serious' performative that Derrida identified his repression of the conditions of speech which threatened his (Austin's) whole enterprise: namely absence, non-totality, the presence (or trace) of the conventional or contextual in a 'pure act of consciousness' and so on. Derrida picks up Searle's exemplary sentence 'On 20th September 1793 I set out on a journey from Oxford to London' to rehearse his case again:

> ... au moment même où quiconque voudrait dire, écrire 'On the twentieth ... etc.', cela même qui assurera, au-delà de ce moment, le fonctionnement de la marque (psychique, orale, graphique, peu importe), à savoir la possibilité d'être répété une *autre* fois, cela même entame, divise, exproprie la plénitude ou la présence à soi 'idéales' de l'intention, du vouloir-dire et *a fortiori* de l'adéquation entre meaning and saying. L'itérabilité altère, elle parasite et contamine ce qu'elle identifie et permet de répéter; elle fait qu'on veut dire (déjà, toujours, aussi) autre chose que ce qu'on veut dire, on dit autre chose que ce qu'on dit *et* voudrait dire, comprend autre chose que ... etc. ('Limited Inc' 33)[18]

It is worthy of note here that 'peu importe' disguises a major 'bracketing out': what is 'la marque'? Furthermore the attack on the semantic integrity of the sentence is not engaged in at a legal or political level, but at a theoretical level, relating to the conditions of being of language itself. This argument is not, in fact, new: it was used in the Middle Ages by jurists to justify the trade of legal interpreter.[19] Derrida's exposure here of the problems of *vouloir-dire* [*Bedeutung*] may well serve a similar function: but he goes further than medieval jurists by applying his strictures to himself. 'Limited Inc' is a reflexive piece which foregrounds its own dubious claims to 'full' statement or 'neutral metalanguage' in a highly self-conscious way.

Unlike Searle, Derrida is a philosopher (if that word is appropriate) who dislikes verbal engagements: 'J'ai horreur de la discussion, des arguties, et des ratiocinations' ['I detest discussions, quibbling and hair-splitting'] ('Limited Inc' 56 [LI 84: trans. modified]). He claims that impromptu speech is not a good medium for the expression of his philosophical beliefs.[20] 'Limited Inc' is in this respect characteristic of his 'method': the close textual approach, the exploitation of the uncontrolled and connotative forces in language (puns, metaphors, rhyme), and (like Austin) the investigation of *cas-limites*. Where Searle in *Speech Acts* takes 'central' or 'standard' performatives before examining the marginal or aberrant, Derrida attaches himself specifically to these: 'Je m'étonne . . . que Searle ait écarté les "cas limites". Ce sont pourtant, pour toute saisie des conditions essentielles, les index les plus sûrs, les plus décisifs' ('Limited Inc' 42).[21] Hence Searle takes the distinction between 'use' and 'mention' to be obvious; Derrida pushes hard at the distinction until he has found an undecidable frontier case and begins his analysis from there. Derrida claims that there is no enquiry which does not at some point call itself into question: Searle accepts this as an *eventual* effect of all enquiries, but claims that language and object language can be kept apart for 'standard cases' and 'central points at issue'. The rules of type and token, use and mention seem to him to be sufficient as rules of thumb to invalidate Derrida's marginal exercises.

Searle has in fact replied to Derrida in his review in the *New York Review of Books* of Culler's *On Deconstruction*.[22] As well as repeating earlier criticisms, he specifically attacks Derrida for being a latter-day metaphysician – something which Derrida attacked Heidegger for accusing Nietzsche of and being himself.[23] The great mistake which (Searle alleges) Derrida makes is to look for metaphysically certain foundations of knowledge, language, meaning, being, etc. Language is not *founded* on sense data because sense data are infused with linguistic and social practices: such an attempt to *found* a science of language is necessarily misguided. 'The real mistake of the classical metaphysicians', asseverates Searle, 'was not the belief that there were metaphysical foundations, but rather the belief that such foundations are necessary' (p. 77). No-one, I suspect, will be more surprised than Derrida to find himself accused of such metaphysics: and it is a measure of the distance which separates Searle and Derrida that the former could accuse the latter of a naïve allegiance to the very aspect of philosophy – classical metaphysics – which Derrida believes himself to be denouncing.

To do full justice to the differing premisses of Searle and Derrida, their differing procedures of argument, and their differing conceptions of the distinction true/false, it would be necessary to extend this discussion beyond the typographical limits set by *Paragraph*. Here I should merely like to examine briefly three points of issue concerning principles: the distinction type/token: the distinction use/mention; and the concept of the infinity of language. It is worth making the general point that

Un dialogue de sourds? 59

although both Searle and Derrida are in some sense 'philosophers of language', the implications of this description are very different for them: for Searle, the philosophy of language does not call into question the prior (separate) existence of thought, language, and world and it accepts implicit oppositions such as self/other, before/after, cause/effect (or, if not this last, then at least 'intention/effect' and 'purpose/uptake') and the intrinsic conditions of ordinary speech – passive *versus* active, indicative *versus* non-indicative, singular *versus* plural etc. Derrida, on the other hand, allows his discourse to be infused with Husserlian and Heideggerian terms in which self/other, before/after, cause/effect are oppositions treated phenomenologically – that is, as non-psychic, transcendental categories accessible to the subjective consciousness. Searle makes no allowance for this (he does not 'recognize' the context of Derrida's discourse), and brutally denies that phenomenology can be in any sense a critique of the philosophy of language as he conceives it.

Searle adduces two rules which he sees as beyond question: the type/token rule (from C.S. Peirce) and the use/mention rule (whose guarantor seems to be common sense, that well-known Cartesian authority). The first of these rules allows him, he believes, to refute the claim made by Derrida (according to Searle) that difference (absence) is present in language as a condition of its being: the passage Searle refers to here comes from *Positions* (1972), whose text he quotes in translation:

> The play of differences supposes, in effect, syntheses and referrals which forbid at any moment, or in any sense, that a single element be *present* in and of itself, referring only to itself. Whether in the order of spoken or written discourse, no element can function as a sign without referring to another element which itself is not simply present. This interweaving results in each 'element' – phoneme or grapheme – being constituted on the basis of the trace within it of the other elements of the chain or system. This interweaving, this textile, is the *text* produced only in the transformation of another text. Nothing, neither among the elements nor within the system, is anywhere ever simply present or absent. There are only, everywhere, differences and traces of traces. (P 26)[24]

It is pertinent, before looking at Searle's refutation of this passage, to point to some of the problems which his reading of Derrida in translation raises:

(i) 'the play of differences' ('le jeu des différences') refers to a metaphor not so much of play as leisure-time rule-governed activity as of play as in a machine (that is, mechanical inefficiency). Searle does not understand the metaphor in this way.

(ii) 'a simple element' ('un élément simple') refers to the concept used in structuralism of 'minimal unit', and perhaps also to the irreducible thing-in-itself [*Ding an sich*] as developed by phenomenology. This is not a statement about *the real* but about the *a priori* conditions of language, as is made clear in 'no element can function *as a sign* without referring to another element...' ('aucun élément ne peut fonctionner comme signe sans renvoyer à un autre élément'). Searle appears insensitive here to the difference between sign-based semantics and proposition-based semantics.

(iii) The 'referrals' ('renvois') refer to Derrida's analysis of the (impossible) 'origin' of any text or speech act, not to any notion of reference found in analytical philosophy. We may again note Searle's confident assumption that continental philosophy can be understood in terms of analytical philosophy, or not at all, and that if it cannot be understood, it is meaningless.

(iv) The final remark about 'simple presence or absence' does not deny impure or imperfect presence: it merely denies that language is a closed system in which words can have a *punctual* existence (that is, can be plotted phonetically or semantically, paradigmatically or syntagmatically, etc. to a given intersection or confluence of codes). It is a further complication on the structure/event paradox known best in terms of the classical example of Zeno's arrow. Searle appears to believe that such paradoxes have either been solved by the elimination of systematic error through the identification of category mistakes; or that they can be avoided by the rigorous use of formal logic.

It is in the light of these remarks that we can turn to Searle's refutation of Derrida. Searle denies Derrida's claim about the trace of absence or difference in the sign, and offers the following corrective account:

> I understand the sentence 'the cat is on the mat' the way I do because I know how it would relate to an indefinite – indeed infinite – set of other sentences 'the dog is on the mat', 'the cat is on the couch' etc. But I understand the differences between the two sentences 'the cat is on the mat', 'the dog is on the mat' in precisely the way I do because the word 'cat' is present in the first while absent in the second, and the word 'dog' is present in the second, while absent from the first. The system of differences does nothing whatever to undermine the distinction between presence and absence: on the contrary, the system of differences is precisely a system of presences and absences. (p. 76)

Here is a claim that the recursive rules of language allow us to understand sentences which seem to be guaranteed by the (empirical? or mental?) difference in our *understanding* of 'cat' and 'dog'. In a later riposte, Searle tries to tighten this up:

> If we consider the two sentences as abstract sentence *types*, apart from any particular *context* of utterance, then the words don't refer to anything. If we consider the sentences as occurring in actual *token* utterances, in *particular real-life contexts* then the expression 'the dog' would normally be used to refer to a dog, and the expression 'the cat' would normally be used to refer to a cat. The topic of self-reference is one that logicians and philosophers have been discussing now for over three-quarters of a century; but no-one to my knowledge has ever supposed that examples of that sort, whether as tokens or as types, had 'exclusive self-reference'. (*NYRB*, 31, 1, 48: my emphases)

Un dialogue de sourds? 61

One or two points need some elucidation here:

(i) the distinction token-type answers the *ab initio* conditions of enquiry of Searle, and reflects his acceptance of a number of principles in the form of objects or oppositions: the rules of language, the world, thought, reference, intention are all subjects of enquiry, but their existence is not called into doubt.[25]

(ii) Derrida, following the modes of enquiry of phenomenologists and structural linguists, is operating in the context of *a priori* systems in which consciousness and corpus, minimal units, structure etc. are principles, but *not* Searle's realist oppositions and premises. In phenomenology and structuralist linguistics, the real world is a *construct* of the consciousness of the individual perceiver or the language system: and to write, as Derrida does, a critique of the limitations of these lines of enquiry is to engage oneself *within* those discourses. Searle, from different principles, seems to be unwilling or unable to perceive the coherence of this approach.

(iii) It is possible to argue also, as Paul Ricoeur has done, that Derrida's point is being made about terms or words whereas Searle's point is being made about propositions (subject and predicate), which alone can be true or false, and alone can have meaning and reference.[26]

(iv) In saying that 'logicians and philosophers have now been discussing [self-reference] for over three-quarters of a century', Searle shows himself to be concerned only with self-reference as understood in Fregean terms and to exclude all else other than analytical philosophy from the realm of philosophy.

A similar non-meeting of minds can be discerned over the opposition use/mention of a word, which Searle treats as a distinction equivalent to normal use/abnormal use. Without rehearsing Searle's argument (which includes a refutation of Tarski), I should perhaps briefly state that it concerns proper *versus* common nouns, nomination, convention and reference in a characteristically pugnacious way.[27] Derrida's reply is conducted at length in 'Limited Inc' (pp. 53–7 [LI 81–5]): the following short quotation is again an indication of their difference in principles:

> Si les conventions ne sont en fait jamais adéquates, si l'opposition du 'normal' et de l''anormal' manque toujours de rigueur et de pureté, si le langage peut toujours 'normalement' devenir 'anormalement' son propre objet, cela ne tient-il pas encore à l'itérabilité structurelle de la marque? ('Limited Inc' 54)[28]

Here Searle's points, which relate to a model of normality, convention and reference accepted by Anglo-American philosophers of language, are carried across the divide into the phenomenological–structuralist world of Derrida's philosophy, where the opposition normal/abnormal (like that of use/mention) is not allowed a guarantee outside language, and hence has no firm anchorage within it.

The final point at issue which I should like to mention is the debate about the infinity of language. Infinity is associated with language in a number of ways: first, language can be said to be infinite because any sentence can be prolonged *ad infinitum* (this is the sense mainly encountered in transformational grammar): sometimes this species of linguistic infinity is referred to as 'transfinity' or 'transinfinity'.[29] Secondly, language can be said to be infinite because, although it is made up of a finite lexicon and phonetic structure, it operates through recursive rules which can generate sense-bearing sentences *ad infinitum*.[30] According to a third theory, language can be said to be infinite because it is inextricably linked in its sense-making dimension to a context which can never be fully accounted for or re-created: it is therefore infinite because its necessary context is indeterminate.[31] In these three theories, the infinity of language is located differently: in aggregation; in the application of the language system; in the necessary extralinguistic component of language. In the case of the first two theories, language has to be considered as a *finite* entity in order for it to be given an infinite dimension. The finiteness resides in the possibility of seeing either the grammar or the system ('langue') of language as mathematically computable: in Saussure's and Ricoeur's terms, the idea of an infinite lexicon is absurd in principle, and for language to be analysable, it must have a finite number of elements.[32] Searle robustly grasps this potential aporia (the infinity of language being dependent on its finiteness): 'it is a condition of the adequacy of a precise theory of an indeterminate phenomenon that it should precisely characterize the phenomenon as indeterminate: and a distinction is no less a distinction for allowing for a family of related, marginal, diverging cases.'[33] Here a *practical* heuristic decision grounds the examination of language by banishing its infinity until a set of rules have been generated to regulate and control it – these rules having the statistical force of rules of probability but not of truth-conditions. Implicit in this quotation from Searle (who, as I have said, accepts the 'recursive' form of linguistic infinity) is a critique of Derrida for his 'metaphysical' demand for certainty, purity and determinacy (Searle omits to mention that this demand is more obviously associated with phenomenology and not with Derrida at all).

In his article in *Glyph*, Searle attacks Derrida for locating the infinity of meaning in context and declares stoutly: 'speakers and hearers are the masters of the set of rules we call the rules of language, and these rules are recursive . . . they allow for the repeated application of the same rule'.[34] This recourse to rules does not entirely solve the problem, because their status is not fixed: are they neurological imprints on the brain? do they arise from the inherent logic of natural languages? how do they affect the discussion of rules (i.e. the metalanguage, for example formal logic, designed to talk about them)? Are these rules metaphysical in the Aristotelian sense (that is, descriptions of the general conditions of possibility of language, set in a knowable mode) or are they heuristic in character? Searle's defence of his notion of rules is made in *Speech Acts* and is important to his argument in that book: rather than become embroiled in that, I should like for the purposes of this paper to compare the use of the concept 'recursive rules' to the explanation of indeterminacy in Derrida's account of language. The generation of French philosophers who precede Derrida had looked to the notion of a 'mixed system' (an amalgam of approximate mental categories with apophantic statements in pure logical form) as the source of indeterminacy;[35] Derrida refers instead to the need for context in the determination of the meaning, and the fact that as no context can saturate the meaning of an utterance (i.e. as no utterance is only comprehensible in a given context (whose 'completeness' Derrida would in any case contest)), there is the possibility of an infinity of meanings in any utterance (just as there is a possibility for the utterance to be placed in an infinity of new contexts).[36] For Searle, meaning is a delimited content – delimited, within the parameters of the indeterminacy of language, by conformity to rules and its 'real' 'linguistic' 'context'; for Derrida, meaning is an open set of discursive possibilities in which the notion of a 'real linguistic context' is disqualified (*Marges*, p. 376 [MP 316]). Both Searle and Derrida accept the imprecise nature of meaning in language: Searle, practically and forcefully, sets out to work in an area where the imprecision affects the philosophy least; Derrida, with no little hint of Unamuno's 'tragic sense', demonstrates the impossibility of meaning at the level of code, context, intending utterer and implied receiver. What is more, Derrida, in stressing the impossibility of full meaning to the intending subject, goes beyond those theorists of interpretation (such as Hirsch and Ricoeur) who locate a meaning (finite, determined and certain) in the author and a significance (infinite, historical and contextual) in the text.

It would clearly be impertinent to attempt to draw grandiose conclusions from this brief and incomplete examination of the Searle–Derrida debate. Some mutual incomprehension clearly arises from the different philosophical vocabularies adopted by the two protagonists; some arises, at least on Searle's part, from an unwillingness to accept the coherence of a philosophical discourse which is not reducible to, or reproducible in terms of, analytical philosophy; an element of personal style which is exacerbating to the adversary cannot be ruled out. A more serious dissension may be detected at the level of legitimation: Searle and Derrida do not, it seems, accept the same procedures of validation or verification, and are divided on the issue of presupposition (that is, what it is licit to assume or 'bracket out' of an enquiry) and on that of the nature and place of truth in philosophical investigations. In reply to J.L. Austin's lecture at Royaumont in 1958, René Poirier characterized truth as, first, 'that which it is necessary to believe', and, secondly, 'that which we agree are given positions' (P/C 300). In the first characterization, the word 'necessary' evokes the role of logic in truth, and Augustus de Morgan's now venerable notion of 'universe of discourse'; no common ground can be found here in the debate between Searle and Derrida. The second description of truth recalls Austin's 'consensus ad idem'. At several points in the Derridean texts, reference is made to the role of 'consensus implicite' ['implicit consensus'] and to the 'horizon d'une intelligibilité et d'une vérité du sens de telle sorte qu'un accord puisse finalement en droit s'établir' ['the horizon of an intelligibility and truth of meaning, such that in principle a general agreement may finally be established'] (*Marges*, pp. 368–9, 375 [MP 310, 315]). These important concessions to the (eventual) political and legal determination of any discourse find no echo in Searle's text, unless it is in his stout presupposition of the relationships between word and world, word and thought, self and other and sense and reference. Analytical philosophy, phenomenology; propositional logic, semiology; verification, unverifiability; such choices in the end assume a theological character, which is perhaps why these verses from Racine's *Athalie* came irresistibly to my mind when looking for an epitaph for this debate:

> Athalie: J'ai mon Dieu que je sers: vous servirez le vôtre;
> ce sont deux puissants dieux.
> Joas: Il faut craindre le mien;
> Lui seul est Dieu, madame, et le vôtre n'est rien.
> (ii.7)[37]

Notes

[1] See Richard Rorty, 'Philosophy as a Kind of Writing: An Essay on Derrida', *New Literary History*, 10 (1978), 141–60; idem, *Philosophy and the Mirror of Nature* (Princeton: Princeton University Press, 1979), pp. 364ff.; Danto's review of Alan Bass's translation of Derrida's *Marges de la philosophie*, *TLS* (30.9.1983), 1035–6; also Michael Rosen, *Hegel's Dialectic and its Criticism*, ch. 1 (Cambridge: Cambridge University Press, 1982).

[2] The classical expression of this thesis is found in Michael Dummett's *Truth and Other Enigmas* (London: Duckworth, 1978), p. 458: 'Only with Frege was the proper object of philosophy finally established: namely, first, that the goal of philosophy is the analysis of the structure of *thought*; secondly, that the study of *thought* is to be sharply distinguished from the study of the psychological process of *thinking*; and finally, that the only proper method for analysing thought consists in the analysis of language . . . the acceptance of these three tenets is common to the entire analytical school.' L. Jonathan Cohen's *The Dialogue of Reason: An Enquiry into the Purposes and Presuppositions of Analytical Philosophy* (Oxford: Clarendon, 1986) challenges this characterization of 'the entire analytical school'.

[3] J.R. Searle, *Speech Acts: An Essay in the Philosophy of Language* (Cambridge: Cambridge University Press, 1969), p. 4.

[4] *Marges de la philosophie* (Paris: Minuit, 1972), pp. 348–9: 'A task is then prescribed: to study the philosophical text in its formal structure, in its rhetorical organization, in the specificity and diversity of its textual types, in its models of exposition and production – beyond what previously were called genres – and also in the space of its mises en scène, in a syntax which would be not only the articulation of its signifieds, its references to Being or to truth, but also the handling of its proceedings, and of everything invested in them. In a word, the task is to consider philosophy also as a "particular literary genre"' (MP 293).

[5] Page references are to J.O. Urmson's and M. Sbisà's edition of *How To Do Things With Words* (Oxford: Oxford University Press, 1962). 'Performatif/constatif' is reprinted in J. Béra (ed.), *La Philosophie analytique* (Paris: Minuit, 1962), pp. 271–304 (references to this lecture and the ensuing discussion of it are preceded by the letters P/C).

[6] J. Culler, *On Deconstruction* (London: Routledge, 1983), p. 111 (but see also pp. 110–34).

[7] Culler, *On Deconstruction*, pp. 114–15.

[8] 'the facts: the situation of the speaker: his/her purpose in speaking: his/her audience: matters of detail' [Ed. trans.].

[9] Austin, *How To Do Things With Words*, pp. 7, 13, 19, 32, 36, 42, 122: see also P/C 271–2, 280.

[10] For indications of the rich field of research in philosophy, linguistics and literary theory which emanates from Austin's posthumous text, see D. Holdcroft, *Words and Deeds: Problems in the Theory of Speech Acts* (Oxford: Clarendon, 1978); John R. Searle and Daniel Vanderveken, *Foundations of Illocutionary Logic* (Cambridge: Cambridge University Press, 1984); P. Cole and J. Morgan, *Syntax and Semantics 3: Speech Acts* (New York: Academic Press, 1976); Stephen C. Levinson, *Pragmatics* (Cambridge: Cambridge University Press, 1983); Mary L. Pratt, *Toward a Speech Act Theory of Literary Discourse* (Bloomington: Indiana University Press, 1977); Shoshana Felman, *The Literary Speech Act: Don Juan with J.L. Austin or Seduction in Two Languages* (Ithaca: Cornell University Press, 1983).

[11] Searle, *Speech Acts*, p. 22.

[12] The full bibliography of the exchange is as follows: J. Derrida, 'Signature événement contexte', in *Marges*, pp. 367–93; translated in *Glyph*, 1 (1977), 172–97 [MP 307–30; LI 1–23]; J.R. Searle, 'Reiterating the Differences: A Reply to Derrida', *Glyph*, 1, 198–208 [summarized by Gerald Graff in LI 25–7]; J. Derrida, 'Limited Inc', supplement to *Glyph*, 2 (1977); translated in *Glyph*, 2, 162–254 [LI 29–110].

[13] Austin, *How To Do Things With Words*, pp. 21–2, 139–40; P/C 288. Later speech act theorists (e.g. Mary L. Pratt, who follows Grice) seem to accept the need to include imitative with real speech acts: 'fictive or imitation speech acts are readily found in almost any realm of discourse, and our ability to produce and interpret them must be viewed as part of our normal linguistic and cognitive competence, not as some special by-product of it': Pratt, *Toward a Speech Act Theory of Literary Discourse*, p. 200.

[14] See Culler, *On Deconstruction*, pp. 125–6.

[15] This term, which is used quite frequently by Derrida (e.g. *Marges*, pp. 369, 381 [MP 310, 320]), is Fregean in origin (see Searle, *Speech Acts*, pp. 99–100).

[16] 'its having-been present [is written in] a past now, which will remain a future now, and therefore in a now in general, in the [general] form of nowness (*maintenance*)' (MP 328).

[17] Searle 'gravely *falsifies* matters. I note here that I seem to have become infected by [his] style: this is the first time, I believe, that I have ever accused anyone of deception, or of being deceived' (LI 86).

[18] 'at the very moment when anyone might mean to say or to write, "On the twentieth . . . etc.", the very factor that will permit the mark (no matter whether it be psychic, oral or graphic) to function beyond this moment – namely the possibility of its being repeated *another* time – breaches, divides, expropriates the "ideal" plenitude or self-presence of intention, of meaning (to say) and, a fortiori, of all adequation between meaning and saying. Iterability alters, contaminating parasitically what it identifies and enables to repeat "itself"; it leaves us no choice but to mean (to say) something other than what we say *and* would have wanted to say, to understand something other than . . . etc.' (LI 61–2: trans. modified).

[19] See Ian Maclean, 'The Place of Interpretation: Montaigne and Humanist Jurists on Words, Intentions and Meaning', in Terence Cave and Grahame Castor (eds), *Neo-Latin and the Vernacular in Renaissance France* (Oxford: Clarendon, 1984), pp. 261–4.

[20] See *Positions* (Paris: Minuit, 1972), p. 91: 'la parole improvisée de l'entretien ne peut se substituer au travail textuel' ['the improvised speech of an interview cannot substitute for the textual work', P 67] (said in an interview with Jean-Louis Houdebine and Guy Scarpetta).

[21] 'I note with astonishment that Searle chooses to ignore "marginal, fringe" cases. For these always constitute the most certain and most decisive indices wherever essential conditions are to be grasped' (LI 70).

[22] See *NYRB*, 30, 16 (1983), 74–9; and also Searle's reply to correspondence, 31, 1 (1984), 47–8.

[23] See *L'Ecriture et la différence* (Paris: Seuil, 1967), p. 413 (WD 281–2).

[24] In *Positions*, pp. 37–8, the French text reads: 'Le jeu des différences suppose en effet des synthèses et des renvois qui interdisent qu'à aucun moment, en aucun sens, un élément simple soit *présent* en lui-même et ne renvoie qu'à lui-même. Que ce soit dans l'ordre du discours parlé ou du discours écrit, aucun élément ne peut fonctionner comme signe sans renvoyer à un autre élément qui lui-même n'est pas simplement présent. Cet enchaînement fait que chaque "élément" – phonème ou graphème – se constitue

à partir de la trace en lui des autres éléments de la chaîne ou du système. Cet enchaînement, ce tissu, est le *texte* qui ne se produit que dans la transformation d'un autre texte. Rien, ni dans les éléments, ni dans le système, n'est nulle part ni jamais simplement présent ou absent. Il n'y a, de part en part, que des différences et des traces de traces.'

[25] The distinction token/type has found a rather different use in hermeneutical theory: E.D. Hirsch makes it match his own word pair meaning/significance in the *Validity in Interpretation* (New Haven: Yale University Press, 1967), pp. 78–9, and Paul Ricoeur assimilates token/type to reference/sense in the *Interpretation Theory* (Fort Worth: Texas Christian University Press, 1976), p. 20.

[26] Ricoeur, *Interpetation Theory*, ch. 1.

[27] See Searle, *Speech Acts*, pp. 73–6. His points are, however, not uncontentious within the field of analytical philosophy: see, for an example of an approach nearer to Derrida's, P.F. Strawson, 'On referring', *Mind*, 59 (1950), 320–44.

[28] 'If conventions are, in fact, never entirely adequate; if the opposition of "normal" and "abnormal" will always be lacking in rigour and purity; if language can always "normally" become its own "abnormal" object, does this not derive from the structural iterability of the mark?' (LI 82).

[29] This view is rehearsed and contested by D. Terence Langendoen and Paul M. Postal in *The Vastness of Natural Languages* (Oxford: Blackwell, 1984).

[30] This view is rehearsed and contested by P. Hacker and G.P. Baker in *Language, Sense and Nonsense* (Oxford: Blackwell, 1984).

[31] This view is implicit in Austin's *How To Do Things With Words* and in most studies in pragmatics (e.g. Levinson, *Pragmatics*).

[32] See Ricoeur, *Interpretation Theory*, p. 5; also Hirsch, *Validity in Interpretation*, p. 30.

[33] *NYRB*, 30, 16, 78.

[34] *Glyph*, 1, 199, 208.

[35] See P/C, 299–303 for brief accounts of this view.

[36] See *Marges*, pp. 377–8 (MP 317–18), and 'Limited Inc' 37, 50–51 (LI 65, 78–9).

[37] 'Athalie: I have my God whom I serve: you shall serve yours; both of them are powerful gods./ Joas: Mine is to be feared; He alone is God, Madame, and yours is nothing'. [Ed. trans.]

CHAPTER 6

Autobiography and the Case of the Signature: Reading Derrida's *Glas*

Jane Marie Todd

Jacques Derrida's *Glas* seems to defy the familiar categories of genre. Each page is divided into two columns: on the left, a meticulous discussion of Hegel's philosophical works, from his early writings to the *Phenomenology of Spirit* and the *Aesthetics*; on the right, a fragmented, lyrical celebration of Jean Genet's literary writings. Straddling the distance between philosophy and literature, *Glas* combines widely diverse writing styles, modes, levels of discourse and even type-faces. Each of the two columns splits again to allow for marginalia, supplementary comments, lengthy quotations, and dictionary definitions. Paragraphs break off in mid-sentence to make way for undigested material, excerpts from Hegel's correspondence or translations of Poe's poetry, only to resume several pages later. Despite or because of its 'defiance' of categorization, this curious and challenging text offers a direct contribution to literary theory: in both form and subject matter, it details a new way of viewing genre definitions.

In his discussion of Genet's autobiographical writings, Derrida suggests that the status of the signature is a 'préliminaire indispensable à l'explication de la formalité (par exemple, "littéraire") avec tous les juges musclés qui l'interrogent depuis des instances apparemment extrinsèques (question du sujet – biographique, historique, économique, politique, etc. – classé). Quant à la textualité générale, le seing représente peut-être le cas, le lieu de recoupement (topique et tropique) de l'intrinsèque et de l'extrinsèque' (pp. 9–10, right column).[1]

To realize the role that the signature plays in the discourse of literary criticism, and in autobiography criticism in particular, one need only look at Philippe Lejeune's *Le Pacte autobiographique*, one of a half-dozen books that Lejeune has written on autobiography. In his generic definition, he argues that the author of an autobiography must be *identical* to both the narrator and the main character of the work in order for it to conform to the genre. He adds that 'il n'y a ni transition ni latitude. Une identité est, ou n'est pas. Il n'y a pas de degré possible et tout doute entraîne une conclusion négative' (p. 15).[2] Lejeune grounds autobiography in the honesty and sincerity of the author's intentions to truthfully convey his own life and personality. But if his notion of 'identity' is necessarily founded on the immediacy of a subject present to itself, this is quickly supplemented by an exterior sign that would guarantee this intention. He thus makes an appeal to the institutional value of the proper name: the name that appears on the cover of the book must be identical to that of the narrator and the main character *in* the book. That proper name, Lejeune claims, is the 'seule marque dans le texte d'un indubitable hors-texte, renvoyant à une personne réelle, qui demande ainsi qu'on lui attribue, en dernier ressort, la responsabilité de l'énonciation de tout le texte écrit' (Lejeune, p. 23).[3] The empirical existence of the author who bears the same name as the narrator and main character thus becomes the sole means of authenticating the 'pact'.

Lejeune makes it clear that by 'personne reélle', he means one 'dont l'existence est attestée par l'état civil et vérifiable' (p. 23).[4] It is thus to a legal contract assumed by the author and guaranteed not only by the signature but by the state that Lejeune must eventually have recourse. Everything comes to depend on the proper name, the signature, and eventually on the legal status of the subject as author.

Although Lejeune has greatly underestimated the problematic status of the signature, especially in relation to a literary discourse, he has identified the essential issue involved in autobiography. For whatever the strategy of establishing a genre definition, whether by locating it in the reader, in shared conventions, in formal characteristics, or in the historical transformations of a general structure, the issues inevitably involve the supposed identity between the author and his main character, and the opposition between referential (or, more recently, performative) and figural modes. These suppositions, in turn, are eventually grounded on certain assumptions about the relation between signature and text.

Elizabeth Bruss's *Autobiographical Acts*,[5] to take a recent example, appears more subtle than Lejeune's work; it is, in fact, simply more oblique. She notes at one point that 'the title page or mode of publication alone may be enough to suggest its illocutionary force' (p. 10), a phrasing less strong than Lejeune's insistence that the signature on the title page always determines the genre. But in the next paragraph she adds that 'in fact, we must have something on the order of rules which accounts for our ability to recognize that there is something wrong, paradoxical in a title like *Everybody's Autobiography*'. These rules, in turn, invoke the author's 'individual responsibility' for the authorship of the text, his shared identity with the 'individual to whom reference is made via the subject matter of the text', the 'existence of this individual, independent of the text itself . . . susceptible to appropriate verification procedures', and so on (p. 11). All of these criteria, as Lejeune very rightly points out, rest on the signature-function, the articulation between text and culture or institution.

Considering autobiography as fictional, as Northrop Frye and others have done, does not solve the legal and ethical problems of the author's responsibility, but only displaces them. The signature is effaced in favour of the text, except where it is a question of the legal functions of the canon (the assumed integrity of an author's corpus, the critical literature attached to that corpus, and the aesthetic and historical information that provides the background for 'formal' interpretations), when the signature is simply reinvoked. The situation is not essentially different if, with Barbara Herrnstein Smith, one locates the distinction between autobiography and fiction in the reader. Here, it is simply the reader's responsibility to validate the signature, to recognize the author's responsibility by means of a countersignature, or to remove the text from its historical context by amputating the author's signature, and hence read the text as 'fictive'.[6] As long as autobiography criticism fails to address the problematic of the signature, the fundamental issue, the 'indispensable preliminary' to understanding what autobiography is about, will not have been addressed.[7]

Derrida's strategy is to show how Genet's autobiographical writings comment on and eventually undermine the very assumptions about the role of the signature which inform all definitions of autobiography. Derrida takes on the additional task of commenting on the way his own signature, the name that signs *Glas*, operates, just as he claims Genet has done. The result is not only a theoretical critique of the question of the signature, but a reevaluation or displacement of the genre of autobiography, and a revised genre definition that includes *Glas* as one of its examples.

The first step is to question the assumption that the signature is a mark in the text that points to an extratextual source of the text. For if it lies within, the signature 'ne signe plus, elle opère comme un effet à l'intérieur de l'objet, joue comme une pièce dans ce qu'elle prétend s'approprier ou reconduire à l'origine. La filiation se perd. Le seing se défalque' (p. 10, right column).[8] In this case, it is not a signature at all, but simply a name, a word, itself a bit of text. It cannot guarantee an ultimate signified, cannot function as the expression of an author's intentions or as the source of the text. If, on the other hand, the signature is simply outside the text, 'elle émancipe aussi bien le produit qui se passe d'elle, du nom du père ou de la mère dont il n'a pas besoin pour fonctionner. La filiation se dénonce encore, elle est toujours trahie par ce qui la remarque' (p. 10, right column).[9] If the signature is simply outside the text, then the text does not depend on it and is already complete without it.

Drawing on a persistent metaphor that he analysed in 'La Pharmacie de Platon', Derrida describes the relation of author to text as one of filiation. Throughout *Glas* he uses and distorts Plato's metaphor: whereas for Plato the parent in question is always the father, Derrida suggests here that the author is alternatively the father and the mother of the text. Furthermore, since the signature takes the place of the absent author, it becomes its surrogate parent, watching over it in the real parent's place. The duties of paternity fall to the signature itself.

These distortions of Plato's model allow Derrida to assimilate his discussion of the family, and of Genet's family in particular, to the question of the signature. As it happens, 'Genet', the author's *nom de plume*, is also the name of the mother: illegitimate and abandoned by his parents at birth, all he knows of his genealogy is the name 'Gabrielle Genet' that appears on his birth certificate. In the mother who abandons her bastard child, leaving only her name, Derrida finds a figure for the author/text/signature relationship.

Having established the two possible functions of the signature, Derrida adds that whether the signature lies within or outside the text, 'la perte sécrétée du reste' ['the secreted loss of the remain(s)'] is recuperated by the signature. The text is somehow reappropriated by the name that signs it. In fact, 'tout le texte . . . se rassemblerait dans tel "cerceuil vertical" . . . comme l'érection d'un seing' (p. 10, right column).[10] The 'cerceuil vertical', an allusion to Genet's *Miracle de la Rose*, is a prison: the signature would imprison the text, enclose it in a tomb. There is, then, a certain conflict between the text and the signature: the text seems to be able to function on its own; it seems to kill off the father or mother that produces it so as to engage in the free play of signification. Nevertheless, the signature tries to imprison the text, to make it a tomb or a dwelling for the signature. Derrida compares this conflict to a reciprocal work of mourning: 'La signature reste demeure et tombe. Le texte travaille à en faire son deuil. Et réciproquement' (p. 11, right column).[11] Signature and text work against each other, each trying to bury the other.

In the next paragraph, Derrida offers a definition of literary discourse. Although at first it seems to have little to do with the question of the signature, the discussion that follows makes the connection clear: 'Le grand enjeu du discours – je dis bien discours – littéraire: la transformation patiente, rusée, quasi animale ou végétale, monumentale, dérisoire aussi mais se tournant plutôt en dérision, de son nom propre, *rebus*, en choses, en nom de choses' (p. 11, right column).[12] The passage presents itself as a general formulation of the nature of literature, or rather, of literary *discourse*. If literature is conceived as a set of norms, practices, and conventions, literary discourse converts these norms into figures in the text in order to demonstrate how language operates. For this reason, literary discourse is essentially subversive: it undermines language, in particular, metalanguage, by constantly turning against itself.

The phrase 'quasi animale ou végétale' also refers to the two meanings of Genet's proper name: a *genet* is a kind of horse native to Spain, whereas a *genêt* is a type of flower called 'broom'. Much of the right column of *Glas* is concerned with how Genet incorporates his name into his texts by representing it as flowers or horses. The passage thus suggests that one of the conventions that literary discourse puts into play is precisely the signature: the transformation in question is also of the *author's* proper name into a thing. In fact, this passage immediately follows the first use of Genet's name in *Glas* and announces the discussion of the act of naming (of others and himself) in Genet's texts. This nomination is precisely the kind that Derrida describes in relation to literary discourse: it consists of transforming proper names into names of things or using common nouns to refer to individuals.

It is no accident that most of Derrida's examples are drawn from Genet's autobiographical writings, since the fundamental issue in defining the genre involves the relation of the 'I' in the text to the name that signs it. The founding law of autobiography is folded into the work.

The phrase 'quasi animale ou végétale', in addition to alluding to Genet's proper name, also echoes the first of two passages from Hegel that Derrida quotes in the first pages of the left column of *Glas*. In fact, he writes that these 'figures en train de s'effacer' (p. 7, left column)[13] are the only parts of Hegel's corpus that he will 'donner à lire' ['give to be read'], and although he does not discuss the passage explicitly until the very end of the book, it takes up the issues that will surface in the discussion of Genet's signature.

The passage in question occurs in Hegel's discussion of religion in the *Phenomenology of Spirit*. Natural religion is the first phase of the development towards absolute religion, and the religion of plants and animals is the second moment in the syllogism of natural religion. Derrida focuses on the religion of *flowers*, which is not even a moment, only part of the religion of plants and animals. The religion of flowers is innocent, whereas the religion of animals is guilty (*coupable*). In fact, the religion of flowers 'procède à sa propre mise en culpabilité, à sa propre animalisation' (p. 8, left column).[14] This is because the flower, not yet a self, a subject, a destructive being-for-itself, nonetheless is the representation (*Vorstellung*) of such a self: '"L'innocence de la *religion des fleurs*, qui est seulement représentation de soi-même sans le soi-même (*die nur selbstlose Vorstellung des Selbsts*) passe dans le sérieux de la vie agonistique, dans la culpabilité de la *religion des animaux*; la quiétude de l'impuissance de l'individualité contemplative passe dans l'être-pour-soi destructeur"' (Hegel, quoted in *Glas*, p. 8, left column).[15]

The passage from the religion of flowers to the religion of animals corresponds to the passage from *genêt* to *genet*, plant to animal. That is in fact the order that Derrida follows in discussing Genet's signatures in the first pages of *Glas*. The Hegelian passage that he leaves out at this point, and only takes up at the very end of *Glas*, is the moment that immediately precedes the religion of plants and animals (the first moment of the syllogism); it in fact corresponds to the transformation of Genet into *genêt*, of the signature as origin or source of the text to the name as figure within the text. For the first moment of natural religion is the religion of the sun, and the characteristic feature of this religion is that it does not involve representation or figuration: 'Cette première figure de la religion naturelle figure l'absence de figure, un soleil purement visible' (p. 264, left column).[16] The movement from the religion of the sun to the religion of plants and animals is the passage from the realm of pure phenomenality to the realm of figuration. The development of religion in the *Phenomenology* proceeds as a development of the figure – as representation, work of art, language, and so forth. Moreover, the stage that follows the last phase of religion (i.e. absolute religion) is absolute knowing and it, too, is characterized by the absence of figure. 'La figure se dérobe à l'origine et à la fin de la religion, avant et après la religion: dont le devenir décrit littéralement une consumation de la figure, entre deux soleils' (p. 264, left column).[17] This stage of absolute knowing, then, which is also the last section of Hegel's text, brings an end to figuration or representation. If the development of religion is assimilated to the operation of reading (of reading the *Phenomenology*, for example), we find that Hegel's ideal text is made up of figures or symbols that are consumed as they are apprehended; it is the model of a text that always returns to its source, to its author or to the signature that guarantees the author's intentions.

The figures in the texts would finally be consumed by the light of the sun, leaving no residue to be read.

Tracing the passage from the religion of the sun to the religion of flowers, Derrida offers an alternative to this apocalyptic mode of reading: 'Alors au lieu de tout brûler, on commence à aimer les fleurs. La religion des fleurs suit la religion du soleil' (p. 268, left column).[18] This, then, is the model of reading that Genet's texts institute: they transform the signature as source, sun, non-figure, into the proper name as flower, that is, the proper name as common noun.

Genet's signature becomes a flower in two senses. First, the word *genêt* refers to a type of flower, and the proliferation of flowers in his texts can be taken as so many signatures. Secondly, the transformation of proper name into common noun is itself a rhetorical figure, that is, a *flower* of rhetoric, namely an antonomasia, a type of synecdoche that consists in taking a proper name for a common noun, or the reverse (p. 204 [G 181], right column). As a result, *genêt* is not only a figure for Genet's signature but a figure for figuration in general. The flower *genêt* describes at once Genet's signature and the operation that allows that signature to be transformed into a thing. Furthermore, since the flower is 'l'objet poétique par excellence' ['the poetic object par excellence'] (Sartre, quoted in *Glas*, p. 21 [G 14], right column), it can also stand as a figure for poetry or poetic language.

Derrida writes: 'En apparence, cédant à la Passion de l'Ecriture, Genet s'est fait une fleur. Et il a mis en terre, en très grande pompe, mais aussi comme une fleur, en sonnant le glas, son nom propre, les noms de droit commun, le langage, la vérité, le sens, la littérature, la rhétorique et, si possible, le reste' (p. 20, right column).[19] Derrida claims, first, that Genet's use of antonomasia is a subversive activity: by figuring his signature as a thing in the text, Genet undermines the function of the signature which guarantees truth and meaning. And, since the flower of rhetoric, the antonomasia, is itself a flower (a *genêt*), it turns the expression 'flowers of rhetoric' into a pun and so parodies rhetoric and poetry. No doubt Derrida is also alluding to other aspects of Genet's texts, for example, his use of mythological *topoi* and of sophisticated literary devices to render the life of the criminal-homosexual. That is why, in Derrida's formulation of what is at stake in literary discourse, the phrase 'la transformation . . . quasi animale ou végétale . . . de son nom propre' can refer just as well to Genet's proper name as to the proper name of literature. The use of antonomasia is only one example of Genet's practice of commenting on and undermining literature by parodying it.

Yet Derrida qualifies his appraisal of Genet's use of the signature, suggesting that the subversive aspect is only an appearance. If we take Derrida's discussion of Hegel as a commentary on Genet's practice of antonomasia, we discover the reason for this qualification.

The plant remains 'innocent' for Hegel because it is brought out of itself by an external force rather than by an internal, subjective act: 'La plante est arrachée à elle-même, vers l'extérieur, par la lumière', that is, by the sun. The plant's flower, however, 'libère un progrès dans le mouvement de réappropriation et de subjectivation' (p. 274, left column).[20] The flower is not only acted upon, altered, made exterior *by* light, it also produces its own light as colour. Although the flower's colour is only a figure (a *Vorstellung*) of self-representation and not true subjectivity, it is the first step towards subjectivity in the form of self-representation or self-figuration. This self-figuration, as we have seen, involves guilt and reappropriation, in particular, the reappropriation of the sun. This raises the question: if Genet's use of antonomasia is a self-figuration of this kind, is it also a reappropriation? Does the transformation of the signature as sun into a flower involve the reappropriation of the sun *into* the text? Are Genet's flowers also little suns?

This is in fact one of the major issues that Derrida addresses in his discussion. Genet's self-figuration is only one case of his use of antonomasia. In general, his literary texts glorify thievery, cowardice, betrayal, prostitution, poverty, homosexuality, all negative values of what he calls 'votre monde'. Derrida explains that Genet often defines this 'opération "magnifiante"' ['"magnifying" operation'] as an act of naming (p. 11 [G 5], right column). This leads him to examine the function of naming in Genet's writing. As it happens, this naming is also an antonomasia, since he often converts common nouns into proper names, calling his characters, for example, 'Mimosa, Querelle, Divine, Yeux-Verts, Culafroy, Notre-Dame-des-Fleurs, Divers, etc.' (p. 13 [G 7], right column):

> Quand Genet donne à ses personnages des noms propres, des espèces de singularités qui sont des noms communs majusculés, que fait-il? . . . Arrache-t-il violemment une identité sociale, un droit de propriété absolue? Est-ce là l'opération politique la plus effective, la pratique révolutionnaire la plus signifiante? Ou bien, mais voici la rengaine des contraires qui se recoupent sans cesse, les baptise-t-il avec la pompe et le sacré – la gloire est son mot – qu'il confère toujours à la nomination? (pp. 14, 15, right column)[21]

It is not a question of deciding between these two possibilities. Genet's use of antonomasia, like his glorification and aestheticization of the underworld in general, is both an expropriation and a reappropriation, a decapitation and a 'recapitation', a dissemination and a recapitalization (p. 19 [G 12], right column). 'Quand Genet donne des noms, il baptise et dénonce à la fois' (p. 12, right column).[22] The use of antonomasia simply foregrounds what is true of naming in general: no name is absolutely proper to the person it designates; it operates within a system, classifies the individual, grants him a place within language and within the state. Further, the proper name can always be used to refer to someone else, can be repeated, expropriated and reappropriated. In this sense, antonomasia uncovers the lie of the proper name which, like private property, is presumed to belong properly to someone. Antonomasia is, then, a kind of theft, but one that reveals the thievery involved in the original act of naming.

On the other hand, antonomasia is quite literally an appropriation, the making proper of a common noun. By adorning the word with a capital letter, one attempts to take it out of circulation, out of the system of language, and make it one's own.

From this point of view, antonomasia is a kind of theft, but like the orphan Genet who steals, not because he scorns private property but because he wishes to possess something that is truly his,[23] this use of the rhetorical figure simply reaffirms the institutional status of the proper name. The use of antonomasia, then, like the 'opération "magnifiante"' in general, is a double gesture that both calls into question the institution (of literature or of the proper name) and reaffirms it.

Having concluded the discussion of Genet's use of antonomasia in naming *others*, Derrida adds that 'la division se complique à peine quand le dénominateur . . . s'institue ou s'érige lui-même dans sa propre signature. Habitat colossal: le chef-d'oeuvre' (p. 17, right column).[24] In other words, Genet's transformation of his signature into a thing, a plant or animal, functions in the same (double) way as his naming of others. In the process, antonomasia emerges as the trope of literary authorship.

The major example of this trope is drawn from *Le Journal du voleur*. Genet writes:

> Je suis né à Paris le 19 décembre 1910. Pupille de l'Assistance Publique, il me fut impossible de connaître autre chose de mon état civil. Quand j'eus vingt et un ans, j'obtins un acte de naissance. Ma mère s'appelait Gabrielle Genet. Mon père reste inconnu . . . . Quand je rencontre dans la lande . . . des fleurs de genêt, j'éprouve à leur égard une sympathie profonde . . . . Je suis seul au monde, et je ne suis pas sûr de n'être pas le roi – peut-être la fée de ses fleurs . . . . Elles savent que je suis leur représentant vivant . . . . Elles sont mon emblème naturel . . .
>
> Par [cette fleur] dont je porte le nom le monde végétal m'est familier. Je peux sans pitié considérer toutes les fleurs, elles sont de la famille.[25]

The passage begins with an account of Genet's civil and legal status and thus establishes his place in a genealogy and in an institution (the state). Yet Genet refuses that genealogy: taking on his mother's name and adorning it with a circumflex accent, he denies his heritage and establishes his own natural genealogy. The antonomasia serves to extract the proper name from its civil status and places it in the natural world; as a result, Genet becomes, if not the mother of flowers, at least their king or fairy. He scatters his name over a field of flowers and makes those flowers his family.

Derrida characterizes the operation whereby Genet takes on his mother's name in the following terms: 'Je . . . me surnomme fleur (le baptême est une seconde naissance), je nais une fois de plus, je m'accouche comme une fleur. La race étant condamnée, l'accent circonflexe se sacre en ouvrant la bouche et tirant la langue . . . s'élève et se place lui-même en tête couronnée' (p. 203, right column).[26] Thus Genet becomes a mother, the mother of his own life, in taking on the name of his mother. 'L'accent circonflexe' is Derrida's nickname for the 'narrator' (as opposed to the author) of *Le Journal du voleur*; the passage, then, also points to Genet's activity as a writer, his act of making himself into a rhetorical or poetical 'flower' in his texts. Derrida thus displaces the commonplace notion of autobiography as the telling of a life (of one's birth and genealogy) to a different plane: Genet engages the specifically legal aspect of identity, only to refuse it in favour of a poetic or rhetorical one.

In one of the passages leading up to the 'hymne au nom propre' ['hymn to the proper name'] (p. 193 [G 171], right column) cited above, Genet, having described the baseness and poverty of his life of crime, explains: 'Mon talent se développait de donner un sens sublime à une apparence si pauvre. (Je ne parle pas encore de talent littéraire.)' This talent consists in creating a religion of abjection, a new, mythical world out of the criminal underworld he is thrown into. This talent for transforming his life anticipates his literary talent, since Genet's texts involve precisely a transformation of this sort. In the next paragraph, Genet compares his activities to that of a mother of a monstrous child. He writes:

> Je me voulus semblable à cette femme qui, à l'abri des gens, chez elle conserva sa fille, une sorte de monstre hideux, difforme, grognant et marchant à quatre pattes, stupide et blanc. En accouchant, son désespoir fut tel sans doute qu'il devint l'essence même de sa vie. Elle décida d'aimer ce monstre, d'aimer la laideur sortie de son ventre où elle s'était élaborée, et de l'ériger dévotieusement .... Avec des soins dévots, des mains douces malgré le cal des besognes quotidiennes, avec l'archarnement volontaire des désespérés elle s'opposa au monde, au monde elle opposa le monstre qui prit les proportions du monde et sa puissance.

In a footnote, Genet adds that

> ... par les journaux j'appris qu'après quarante ans de dévouement cette mère arrosa d'essence – ou de pétrole – sa fille endormie, puis toute la maison et mit le feu. Le monstre (la fille) succomba. Des flammes on retira la vieille (75 ans) et elle fut sauvée, c'est-à-dire qu'elle comparut en Cour d'assises.[27]

Derrida once more takes this scene as a description of Genet's relation to his text. In taking on his mother's name, the name that he uses to sign his texts, Genet becomes the mother of his text, and by dispersing his name throughout it (through antonomasia), keeps it to himself, devotes himself to it, and finally, kills it off, keeps it away from 'the world', from the reader:

> Rêvant visiblement de devenir, à résonner, son propre (glas), d'assister à *son propre* enterrement après avoir accouché de lui-même ou opéré sa propre décollation, il aurait veillé à bloquer tout ce qu'il écrit dans les formes d'une tombe. D'une tombe qui se résume à son nom, dont la masse pierreuse ne déborde même plus les lettres, jaunes comme l'or ou comme la trahison, comme le genêt. (pp. 51–2, right column)[28]

In this view, Genet's practice of antonomasia would stem from the desire for the proper, the wish to erect his signature into a tomb or dwelling or to shape his entire corpus into the tomb of his proper name. As his own mother, he would give birth to himself as a flower (a name or figure in a text) only to keep the text for himself:

> Genet . . . aurait, le sachant ou non . . . silencieusement, laborieusement, minutieusement, obsessionnellement, compulsivement, avec les gestes d'un voleur dans la nuit, disposé ses signatures à la place de tous les objets manquants. Le matin, vous attendant à reconnaître les choses familières, vous retrouvez son nom partout, en grosses lettres, en petites lettres, en entier ou en morceaux, déformé ou recomposé. Il n'est plus là mais vous habitez son mausolée ou ses chiottes. (p. 51, right column)[29]

Rather than a representation of a 'life', the familiar thing one expects to find in an autobiography, Genet's writings have no other content than 'literariness' itself, that is, the investigation of their own literary conventions, including the regulatory convention of the signature. Just as Genet scatters his name over a field of flowers by transforming it into a *genêt*, he disseminates his signature throughout the text, through the operation of antonomasia. He does nothing but sign with the flower of his proper name; his corpus is a sepulchre for the signature.

The question remains, however: does Genet *succeed* in signing his text? Can any text, even one littered with signatures, be ultimately governed, regulated by a signature? Summarizing his argument that the flowers in Genet's texts are anagrams or figures for the proper name, Derrida writes:

> Genet anagrammatise son propre, sème plus que tout autre et glane son nom sur quoi qu'il tombe. Glaner égale lire . . . [Mais] si cette (double) opération . . . était possible, absolument praticable ou centrale, si s'effectuait l'irrépressible désir qui l'agit (de mort ou de vie, cela revient ici au même), il n'y aurait ni texte ni reste. Encore moins celui-ci. Le résumé serait absolu, il s'emporterait, s'enlèverait lui-même d'un coup d'aile. (pp. 55, 56, right column)[30]

Genet's efforts to gather his dispersed signature back to himself, to reclaim his text, cannot but fail. The text falls; it escapes the prison of the signature; Derrida reads it and writes another text. Derrida gleans and glosses Genet's text, reads it; in so doing, he steals it away from its author.

A text, like a name (common or proper), can always be appropriated. One can always use another's text to describe oneself, or name oneself in feigning to name another. If Genet does not succeed entirely in signing his text, it is partly because Derrida also signs it, in an autobiographics that appropriates the other into the self. This points to a second trope of autobiography, the chiasmus, a figure of the reader and not the author, or rather, the figure that blurs the distinction between writer and reader.

Following the preliminary discussion of the signature, Derrida returns to Genet's autobiographical essay, 'Ce qui est resté d'un Rembrandt déchiré en petits carrés bien réguliers et foutu aux chiottes' which serves as a model of sorts for *Glas*. Describing the double-columned form of the short essay, he writes: 'X, chiasme presque parfait, plus que parfait, de deux textes mis en regard l'un de l'autre: une galerie et une graphie qui l'une l'autre se gardent et se perdent de vue. Mais les tableaux sont écrits et ce(lui) qui (s')écrit se voit regardé par le peintre' (p. 53, right column).³¹ The chiasmus in question is, in the first place, the effect produced by placing two texts on the same page so that they exchange gazes, gloss each other.

As Derrida realizes, however, the form of Genet's texts stages the experiences that Genet relates in each column. On the left, the narrator tells us how, seated in a train compartment, he happened to look up and catch the gaze of a stranger sitting across from him. He had the overwhelming sensation of looking, not into the eyes of another, but into his own eyes. He relates the 'expérience désagréable' ['unpleasant experience'] in these terms:

> Ce que j'éprouvais je ne pus le traduire que sous cette forme: je m'écoulais de mon corps, et par les yeux, dans celui du voyageur *en même temps que le voyageur s'écoulait dans le mien* .... Qu'est-ce donc qui s'était écoulé de mon corps – je m'ec ... – et qu'est-ce qui de ce voyageur s'écoulait de son corps?³²

Thus, the autobiographical essay relates an exchange of identities, the reversal of position between self and other. Derrida associates Genet's 'je m'ec' with, among other things, 'je m'écrivais', suggesting that the activity of writing (oneself) involves such an exchange of identity. In the circulation between the two columns, the very foundation of autobiography, the identity of the self, begins to crumble. The first person narrator, in telling his story, finds his identity blurred in the telling.

In the right column, the narrator is looking at a portrait by Rembrandt that not only returns his gaze, but also exchanges its gaze with the painting that hangs on the opposite wall of the gallery. This situation, in turn, provides a specular image of the reader before Genet's facing columns. 'Vous croyez regarder et c'est le texte du tableau (Rembrandt) qui vous surveille et vous indique, vous dénonce' (p. 53, right column).³³ The reader too is drawn into the exchange of identities.

This exchange is quite common in *Glas*: the gloss that describes Genet's writing turns back upon itself and comments on Derrida's textual practice. There are, for example, numerous instances of antonomasia in *Glas*, the transformation of Derrida's signature into a common noun: most appear in the *judas* of the Genet column, those pockets that occasionally interrupt the main text. They involve a chiastic movement between Genet and Derrida who, for instance, takes up the specific details of Genet's life and shapes them into his theory about the signature, then stages this theory in the play of his proper name.

One of the first of these moments appears as a *judas* that runs alongside Derrida's discussion of naming in Genet. He first quotes a passage from *Le Journal du voleur* in which the narrator, discussing the name of another, turns to consider his own name: 'Armand était en voyage. Encore que j'entendisse parfois qu'on l'appelât de noms différents, nous garderons celui-ci. Moi-même n'en suis-je pas, avec celui de Jean Gallien que je porte aujourd'hui, à mon quinze ou seizième nom?' (quoted in *Glas*, p. 12, right column).³⁴ In his gloss, Derrida suggests that he will remotivate the apparent arbitrariness of the proper name 'Gallien' and of the initials 'J.G.'. He adds that in Genet's *Pompes funèbres*, the initials are not 'J.G.' but 'J.D.'. Thus, in a move that parallels Genet's shift from Armand's name to his own, Derrida introduces *his* initials into the discussion and, in so doing, remotivates an apparently arbitrary signifier that figures prominently in Genet's novel.

In the following paragraph, still ostensibly discussing Genet, Derrida raises a number of issues about the signature, the text, and their relation to death and genealogy. As he proceeds, he insinuates his name and his text into the analysis. 'Quant au sigle, dans *Pompes funèbres*, c'est J.D. Jean D. . . . Le D majuscule à qui il échoit de représenter le nom de famille ne revient pas forcément au père. Il intéresse en tous cas la mère et c'est elle qui bénéficie de son titre, "la mère était anoblie par cet écusson portant le D majuscule brodé d'argent"' (p. 12, right column).[35] *Pompes funèbres* is a study in mourning: the book is dedicated to one of Genet's lovers, Jean Decarnin, and the entire novel is organized around his funeral and the period of mourning that follows. The coat of arms with the capital D appears on the hearse that bears the corpse to the place of burial. It thus names and envelops a corpse, but also brings prestige to the mother who presides at the burial. But the initials of the dead man are also Derrida's initials, and he exploits this ambiguity in order to further develop his theory of signatures in figuring his own name.

Derrida continues: 'Quant à celui qui organise les *Pompes funèbres* – c'est-à-dire littéraires – de J.D., dira-t-on que c'est l'auteur, le narrateur, le narrataire, le lecteur, mais de quoi? Il est à la fois le double du mort . . . qui reste vivant après lui, son fils, mais aussi son père et sa mère' (p. 12, right column).[36] On the one hand, this passage is simply a further discussion of *Pompes funèbres*: Genet does characterize himself as both Jean D.'s son and his mother and father. In fact, the novel enacts the sort of chiastic movement, the exchange of identities that we noted earlier. Aided no doubt by the shared first name of the lovers, but due primarily to the operation of mourning itself, Jean Genet becomes Jean Decarnin: 'Aujourd'hui je me fais horreur de contenir, l'ayant dévoré, le plus cher, le seul amant qui m'aimât. Je suis son tombeau'; 'Mais Jean vivra par moi, je lui prêterai mon corps. Par moi, il agira, pensera.' In the next lines, Genet even compares this lending of his body to a dead man to an actor's performance of a role on stage: 'J'assume un rôle très grave . . . . Avec la même émotion le comédien aborde le personnage qu'il rendra visible.'[37] This links mourning as incorporation and reactivation to the performance, the quoting, of a work of art.

But the doubt that Derrida attaches to the source of the text's meaning or 'organization' tends to bring the question around to this use of quotation in Derrida's autobiographics. That is, he characterizes his *own* activity in *Glas* as the reactivating, the taking on the role of a dead man. Genet's notion of mourning as the performance of the dead man's role is extended to the activity of reading. As in *Pompes funèbres*, where Genet exploits the similarity of names, Derrida allows the ambiguity of the initials 'J.D.' to effect a blurring of identities. In fact, since a 'glas' is obviously associated with a funeral rite, the phrase 'les *Pompes funèbres* . . . de J.D.' can be taken as a reference to Derrida's work as well as to Genet's. Derrida, as well as Genet, is 'le double du mort': in rewriting Genet's texts, he imitates them, doubles them, claims them as an ancestor; at the same time, he also (re)produces them, stitching together a tissue of quotations or an anthology of Genet's writings. He is, then, Genet's son as well as his father and mother.

In the last section of the *judas*, Derrida speaks of Genet's fear that someone will steal his death from him and that to guard against such an expropriation 'il a d'avance occupé tous les lieux où ça meurt. Bien joué? Qui fait mieux, qui dit mieux, le mort' (p. 12, right column).[38] This issue is also related to the signature and the text: Genet tries to occupy his tomb (tome) by scattering his signature throughout the text. But Derrida is enacting as well as reporting the expropriation of Genet's death: by taking the initials and the quotations from *Pompes funèbres* and applying them to himself and to his theory of the signature, Derrida is stealing away Genet's death and text in order to stage his own. And it is through the act of reading that this expropriation occurs.

Since the name 'Derrida' does not have any semantic value in French, Derrida's use of antonomasia involves a number of mutations of his name: the two most common are 'Derrière' and 'Déjà'. As for Genet, the figure of antonomasia stands not only for Derrida's signature, but also for the operation of figuration, of antonomasia itself. And, as for Genet, the signature stands in a certain relation to death and to ancestry. Thus, he writes in a *judas*:

> Derrière: chaque fois que le mot vient en premier, s'il s'écrit donc après un point, avec une majuscule, quelque chose en moi se mettait à y reconnaître le nom de mon père, en lettres dorées sur sa tombe, avant même qu'il y fût.
>
> *A fortiori* quand je lis *Derrière le rideau*. (p. 80, right column)[39]

At the beginning, the term 'Derrière' seems to involve a simple, largely unmotivated referentiality: its similarity to 'Derrida' leads him to recognize not his own name, but that of his father. But the word quickly takes on its semantic value as well. It points to something *behind* – specifically, to the corpse that lies behind the tombstone. The word 'derrière' is not itself behind; it is the name engraved on the outside of the tombstone. It stands in the place of the father, and it points to the father presumed to lie behind it. Oddly, his reading of 'Derrière' as the father's name on a tombstone occurs even before the father's death; the tombstone points to something behind itself, but the grave is empty. This undermines the simple referentiality of the proper name. Not only does the word refer to nothing behind it, it appears to bring about the illusion of reference. It is as if the word itself, or the meaning of the word, invoked the image of a tomb and of the father within.

Derrida describes the functioning of the signature or of the proper name on the cover of a book in precisely the same terms. The name of the book's 'father' appears on the cover of the book, but its very appearance *outside* the text announces the death of the father and makes of the book a tomb for its author. Hence, the personal confession in the mode of an autobiographical anecdote is used to exemplify the theory of signatures that he is developing.

In the next paragraph, the link between 'Derrière' as the proper name of Derrida's father, and 'Derrière' as figure for the signature in general, is made explicit: 'Derrière n'est-ce pas toujours déjà derrière un rideau, un voile, un tissage. Un texte toisonnant . . .' (p. 80, right column).[40]

Whereas in the first instance the word 'derrière' was visible on the outside on the tombstone and only indicated something else presumed to lie behind it, it now appears that the signature 'Derrière' is itself behind a text, and a text 'toisonnant'. The term, a combination of *toison*, 'fleece' or 'pubic hair', and *foisonnant*, 'abundant', alludes to the notion of text as textile and, in this context, to Freud's belief that women invented weaving out of the desire to weave their pubic hair into a penis or, at least, to cover their lack with the braided pubic hair (p. 79 [G 67], right column). Thus, if the text is a *toison*, what it conceals is precisely a lack: if the signature lies behind the text, the signature is simply an empty space, like the mother's missing phallus.

The text and the signature have exchanged places: in the first formulation, the signature was on the outside, the text was a tomb, and the grave was empty. In the second example, the text is the covering or veil, the signature is within, but void, disappearing behind the weave of the text. Thus, in these few lines, Derrida stages the two functions of the signature that he posits at the beginning of *Glas*, the reciprocal work of mourning between text and signature in relation to his own (and his father's) name.

Immediately following the allusion to the 'texte toisonnant', Derrida quotes Genet: 'Un autre de mes amants orne de rubans sa toison intime. Un autre a tressé pour la tête de noeud de son ami, miniscule, une couronne de pâquerettes. Avec ferveur un culte phallique se célèbre en chambre, derrière le rideau des braguettes boutonnées' (p. 80, right column).[41] Like the term 'toisonnant', which both alludes to castration and, in its similarity to 'foisonnant', compensates for castration by multiplying the penis in peril, this passage describes a type of fetishism that, rather than substituting an object for an absent phallus (as in Freud's theory), adorns an existing member. If the signature is seen as a phallus that can be cut off from the body of the text, then this fetishism involves a multiplication of the signature, a staging of the signature in the text.

Like a number of other scenes in *Glas*, the above passage moves by association from the 'derrière le rideau' that points to a corpse, the father's dead body, to a 'derrière le rideau' that refers to the phallus behind the buttoned fly. This association of the corpse with the erect phallus (the shared trait of rigidity and the verbal bridge *bander* supply the link) is developed in relation to Derrida when he turns to speak of the signature as his own death:

> déjà. La mort a déjà eu lieu, avant tout. Comment déchiffrer cette étrange antériorité d'un *déjà* qui vous met toujours un cadavre sur les bras? . . . Il veut que vous ne puissiez jamais vous défaire du corps très raide que sa littérature, sa pompe funèbre, aura bandé pour vous. Comment séduire, comment se faire aimer sans vous dire *je suis mort*? . . . Qui fait mieux? Qui dit mieux? . . . le *déjà*

que je suis sonne son propre glas, signe lui-même son arrêt de mort, vous regarde d'avance, vous voit avancer sans rien comprendre à ce que vous aurez aimé, suivant, en colonne, la marche funèbre d'une érection dont tout le monde entendra désormais disposer. (p. 92, left column)[42]

The expression 'Qui fait mieux?' echoes Derrida's comments about Genet's efforts to guard against the theft of his death. Derrida is expressing the same desire. By pronouncing himself dead on arrival, he manages to seduce the reader with a monument erected to his death; he delivers his text, his cadaver, to the reader who cannot be rid of it. The text remains proper to him; the reader can do nothing but bear the text or pay tribute to it in a eulogy or funeral march.

We are already approaching the figure of the mother who bears a child only to keep it to herself, then finally, to kill it, to take it back into herself. Derrida develops this train of thought in another use of antonomasia:

Je suis *déjà* (mort) signifie que je suis *derrière*. Absolument derrière, le Derrière qui n'aura jamais été vu de face, le Déjà que rien n'aura précédé, qui s'est donc conçu et enfanté de lui-même, mais comme cadavre ou corps glorieux. (p. 97, right column)[43]

Earlier associated with the name of the father, 'Derrière' now clearly represents the mother, the signature as mother who gives birth to a child already dead, a child who will never belong to anyone besides herself, who will never venture out of the home. We begin to see why the signature of preference is that of the mother: in taking on his mother's name, Derrida can give birth to himself, kill himself, bury himself, and thus remain absolutely proper to himself.

Nevertheless, Derrida recognizes the impossibility of this desire. Alluding once more to the details of Genet's genealogy, he writes:

On sait que la paternité s'attribue toujours au terme d'un procès, dans la forme d'un jugement. Donc d'une généralité. Mais la mère? Surtout celle qui se passe de père? Ne peut-on espérer une généalogie pure, purement singulière . . .? Le propre n'est-il pas finalement de la mère? (p. 170, right column)[44]

That, in any case, is the hope or desire. But in the next paragraph, alluding to Genet's encounter with a thief or beggarwoman whom he imagines to be his mother, Derrida concedes: 'Pas plus que le glas qu'elle met en branle. La mère est une voleuse et une mendiante. Elle s'approprie tout mais parce qu'elle n'a rien en propre' (p. 170, right column).[45]

The mother is a thief: the signature as mother steals its status from the state and from language. To appropriate and reappropriate the signature is to admit that nothing is proper, not even one's own death. Thus, explaining that through his use of antonomasia he has given birth to himself as a corpse, Derrida adds: 'Le Derrière et le Déjà me protègent, me rendent illisible . . . . Toutes les fleurs de rhétorique dans lesquelles je disperse ma signature, dans lesquelles je m'apostrophe et m'apotrope, lisez-les aussi comme des formes de refoulement. Il s'agit de repousser la pire menace' (p. 97, right column).[46]

What is repressed in the recourse to antonomasia, in the effort to sign and resign the text, is the possibility of being read. Derrida has said that Genet's text is only readable because, at some point, he has failed to keep it subsumed under his signature. Derrida admits the same thing in reference to his own text: 'vous ne pouvez vous intéresser à ce que je fais ici que dans la mesure où vous auriez raison de croire que – *quelque part* – je ne sais pas ce que je fais . . . . Ni ce qui s'agit ici' (p. 76, right column).[47] Despite all the protective efforts to keep the text to himself, despite the multiple signatures that attempt to reappropriate it, there remains a text to be read, and the reader's interest in it lies precisely in those moments in *Glas* that reveal a *je m'ec*: a 'je m'écarte' ['I'm removed'], or a 'je m'écrase'['I'm crushed'] (p. 76 [G 64], right column). The antonomasia, which attempts to reappropriate the text, will once more be expropriated through the chiasmus between the author of *Glas* and the reader.

Elizabeth Bruss writes that 'if anything happens to alter or obscure' the boundaries between fiction and nonfiction or 'empirical' and 'rhetorical' first person narration, 'the nature and scope of autobiography will be changed', a change that could involve the 'obsolescence of autobiography or at least its radical reformulation' (p. 8). Derrida's reading of Genet as well as his own textual practice in *Glas*, suggest that this obscuring of boundaries is involved in autobiographical discourse itself. What Bruss views as a historical eventuality is in fact a structural feature of figural language. Autobiography may be nothing more than the sounding of its own knell. Through the figures of antonomasia and chiasmus, the outside is brought inside, the signature placed in the text, the reader's identity blurred with the author's, and genre definitions transgressed in the process. It is not by accident that autobiography is often considered 'marginal' to literature, since it is the genre that incorporates literature's margin, the signature that links it to its outside, into itself. The resulting text can no longer simply 'belong' to the genre it takes as its object. Taking the issues of self, identity, and self-representation as their subject matter, autobiographers produce a counter-discourse (but not a metadiscourse) that questions and also reaffirms the legal claims of genre definitions. And the critical and legal discourses that assign a text to an author and to a genre do so at the expense of reading the text, which transforms the very terms of the definition into flowers and things.

Notes

[1] Jacques Derrida, *Glas* (Paris: Galilée, 1974): 'an indispensable preliminary to discussing (for example "literary") formality with all the muscled judges who interrogate it on apparently extrinsic authority (a question of the classified – biographical, historical, economic, political, and so on – subject). As for general textuality, perhaps the signum [*seing*] represents the case, the place of (topical and tropical) intersection of the intrinsic and the extrinsic' (G 3–4, right column; trans. modified). [Ed. note:

the term 'le seing' used by Derrida is an archaic form, meaning 'signature'; it is also an exact homophone of 'le sein', meaning 'breast'.]

² Philippe Lejeune, *Le Pacte autobiographique* (Paris: Seuil, 1974): 'there is no question of transition or latitude. An identity either is or is not. There can be no matter of degree and any doubt would lead to a negative conclusion' [Ed. trans.].

³ 'the only marker in the text of an indubitable outside-text, referring to a real person who thereby demands ultimately to be deemed responsible for the enunciation of the entire written text' [Ed. trans.].

⁴ 'to whose existence a verifiable civil status attests' [Ed. trans.].

⁵ Elizabeth Bruss, *Autobiographical Acts* (Baltimore: Johns Hopkins University Press, 1976).

⁶ Barbara Herrnstein Smith, *On the Margins of Discourse* (Chicago and London: University of Chicago Press, 1978), p. 48 and passim.

⁷ See also Paul de Man's discussion of these questions in 'Autobiography as De-facement', *MLN*, 94 (1979), 919–30, an article that has influenced me on a number of points.

⁸ 'no longer signs, operates as an effect within the object, acts as a piece in what it claims to appropriate or to lead back to its origin. The filiation is lost. The signum [*seing*] retrenches itself' (G 4, right column; trans. modified).

⁹ '[it] emancipates as well the product that dispenses with the signature, with the name of the father or of the mother the product no longer needs to function. The filiation again gives itself up, is always betrayed by what remarks it' (G 4, right column).

¹⁰ 'the whole text . . . would gather itself in such a "vertical coffin" . . . as the erection of a signum [*seing*]' (G 4, right column; trans. modified).

¹¹ 'The signature remain(s) resides and falls (to the tomb), the signature remain(s) house and tomb. The text labours to give the signature up as lost [*en faire son deuil*]. And reciprocally' (G 5, right column).

¹² 'The great stake of literary discourse – I do say discourse: the patient, crafty, quasi animal or vegetable, untiring, monumental, derisory too, but on the whole holding itself up to derision, transformation of his proper name, *rebus*, into things, into the name of things' (G 5, right column).

¹³ 'figures in the act of effacing themselves' (G 1, left column).

¹⁴ 'proceeds to its own placement in culpability, its very own animalization' (G 2, left column).

¹⁵ '"The innocence of the *flower religion*, which is merely the self-less representation of self, passes into the seriousness of warring life, into the guilt of *animal religions*; the quiet and impotence of contemplative individuality pass into destructive being-for-self"' (G 2, left column).

¹⁶ 'This first figure of natural religion figures the absence of figure, a purely visible . . . sun' (G 238, left column).

¹⁷ 'The figure withdraws at the origin and end of religion, before and after religion: whose becoming literally describes a consuming destruction of the figure, between two suns' (G 237, left column).

¹⁸ 'Then in place of burning all, one begins to love flowers. The religion of flowers follows the religion of the sun' (G 240, left column).

¹⁹ 'Apparently, yielding to the Passion of Writing, Genet has made himself into a flower. While tolling the *glas* (knell), he has put into the ground, with very great pomp, but also as a flower, his proper name, the names and nouns of common law, language, truth, sense, literature, rhetoric, and, if possible, the remain(s)' (G 12–13, right column).

²⁰ 'The plant is uprooted from itself, toward the outside, by the light . . . the flower sets free an advance in the movement of reappropriation and subjectivization' (G 246, left column).

²¹ 'When Genet gives his characters proper names, kinds of singularities that are capitalized common nouns, what is he doing? . . . Does he violently uproot a social identity, a right to absolute proprietorship? Is that the most effective political operation, the most significant revolutionary practice? Or else, but this is the refrain of ceaselessly intersecting opposites, does he baptize them with the pomp and the sacredness – glory is his word – that he always confers on nomination?' (G 7, 8–9, right column; trans. modified).

²² 'When Genet gives names, he both baptizes and denounces' (G 6, right column).

²³ See Jean-Paul Sartre, *Saint Genet*, Vol. I of Genet's *Oeuvres complètes* (Paris: Gallimard, 1952–68), pp. 16–17.

[24] 'The division becomes only a little more complex when the denominator . . . institutes or erects himself in his own proper signature. Colossal habitat: the masterpiece' (G 11, right column).

[25] Jean Genet, *Le Journal du voleur* (Paris: Gallimard, 1949), pp. 46, 47: 'I was born in Paris on 19 December 1910. As a child in care, I was unable to find out anything else about my civil status. When I turned twenty-one I got hold of my birth certificate. My mother's name was Gabrielle Genet. My father is still unknown . . . . When I'm on the moors and come across . . . broom flowers [*fleurs de genêt*], I feel a deep sympathy with them . . . I'm alone in the world, and for all I know I may be the king – perhaps the fairy of its flowers . . . . They know I am their living representative . . . . They are my natural emblem . . . . By virtue of [this flower] whose name I bear, the vegetable world is familiar to me. I am able to contemplate all flowers without pity, they are part of the family'. [Ed. trans.]

[26] 'I . . . nickname myself [*me surnomme*] flower (baptism is a second birth), I am born once more, I deliver myself [*je m'accouche*] as a flower. The race being condemned, the circumflex consecrates itself in opening the mouth and drawing the tongue . . . raises and places itself on the crowned head' (G 181, right column; trans. modified).

[27] Genet, *Journal*, pp. 29, 30: 'I had a growing talent for giving a sublime sense to such a paltry appearance. (I'm not yet talking about literary talent)'; 'I took myself to be like the woman who kept at home, hidden from the world, her daughter, a sort of hideous, deformed monster, grunting, walking on all fours, stupid and pale. When she gave birth, her despair was doubtless such that it became the very essence of her life. She decided to love this monster, to love the ugliness sprung from her womb where it had fashioned itself, and to erect it in devotion . . . . With pious care and hands which were gentle although callused by daily tasks, with the relentless tenacity of the desperate, she set herself against the world, and set against it too the monster that assumed the proportions of the world as well as its power'; 'I read in the newspapers that after forty years of devotion this mother poured petrol – or paraffin – over her sleeping daughter, then over the whole house, and set light to it. The monster (the daughter) died. The 75-year-old woman was dragged from the flames and saved, and then brought to trial'. [Ed. trans.]

[28] 'Visibly dreaming about becoming, by resounding, his own proper knell [*glas*], about attending *his own* interment after giving birth to himself or performing his own decapitation, he would have taken care to block up all that he writes in the forms of a tomb. Of a tomb that comes down to his name, whose stony mass no longer even extends beyond the letters, yellow as gold or betrayal, like broom [*genêt*]' (G 42, right column; trans. modified).

[29] 'Genet . . . would have, knowing it or not . . . silently, laboriously, minutely, obsessionally, compulsively, and with the moves of a thief in the night, set his signatures in (the) place of all the missing objects. In the morning, expecting to recognize familiar things, you find his name all over the place, in big letters, small letters, as a whole or in morsels, deformed or recomposed. He is no longer there, but you live in his mausoleum or his latrines' (G 41–2, right column).

[30] 'Genet anagrammatizes his own proper(ty), sows more than any other, and gleans his name over whatever it falls [*tombe*]. Gleaning equals reading . . . . [But] if this (double) . . . operation were possible, absolutely practicable or central, if the irrepressible desire that activates it were effected (for death or for life, here it comes down to the same thing), there would be neither text nor remain(s). Even less so this text here. The summary would be absolute, it would sweep (itself) off, take (itself) off with the flap of a wing [*un coup d'aile*]' (G 46, right column; trans. modified).

[31] 'X, an almost perfect chiasmus, more than perfect, of two texts, each one set facing [*en regard*] the other: a gallery and a graphy that guard one another and lose sight of each other. But the pictures are written, and whatever/whoever writes itself/oneself sees itself/oneself regarded by the painter' (G 43–4, right column; trans. modified).

[32] 'Ce qui est resté . . .', in Vol. IV of Genet's *Oeuvres complètes*, pp. 22, 23: 'What I was experiencing I could only translate in the following form: I was seeping out of my body – through my eyes – into that of the other passenger *at the very same time as the passenger was seeping into mine* . . . . What was it then that had seeped from my body – *je m'ec* . . . – and what was it of this passenger that was seeping from his body?' [Ed. trans.]

33 'You think you are the one looking and it is the text of the picture (Rembrandt) that watches over you and points you out, denounces you' (G 44, right column; trans. modified).

34 'Armand was away on a trip. Although I heard that he was sometimes called by other names, we shall keep this one. Am I myself not up to my fifteenth or sixteenth name, including Jean Gallien, my current one?' (G 6, right column).

35 'As for the siglum in *Funeral Rites* it is J.D. Jean D. . . . The capital D, to which falls representing the family name, does not perforce revert to the father. In any case, it concerns the mother, and she is the one to benefit from its title, "the mother was ennobled by this escutcheon on which the capital D was embroidered in silver"' (G 6, right column).

36 'As for the one who organizes the *Funeral* – i.e., literary – *Rites* of J.D., is one to say it is the author, the narrator, the narratee, the reader, but of what? He is at once the double of the dead . . . the one who remains alive after him, his son, but also his father and his mother' (G 6, right column).

37 *Pompes funèbres*, in Vol. III of Genet's *Oeuvres complètes*, p. 14 and p. 57: 'Today I am disgusted at myself for containing, having devoured him, the dearest, the only lover who really loved me. I am his tomb'; 'But Jean will live on through me, I will lend him my body. Through me, he will act and think'; 'I'm taking on a very serious role . . . With the same emotion, the actor approaches the character that he will make visible.' [Ed. trans.]

38 'he has, in advance, occupied all the places where that (*ça*) dies. Well played? Who does it better, who says it better, the dead' (G 6, right column; trans. modified).

39 '*Derrière*: every time the word comes first, if written therefore after a period and with a capital letter, something inside me used to start to recognize there my father's name, in gold letters on his tomb, even before he was there. *A fortiori* when I read *Derrière le rideau* [*Behind the Curtain*]' (G 68, right column).

40 '*Derrière*, behind, isn't it always already behind [*déjà derrière*] a curtain, a veil, a weaving. A fleecing text' (G 68, right column).

41 'One of my other lovers adorns his intimate fleece with ribbons. Another once wove a tiny crown of daisies for the tip of his friend's prick. A phallic cult is fervently celebrated in private, behind the curtain [*derrière le rideau*] of buttoned flies' (G 68, right column).

42 '*déjà*, already. Death has already taken place, before everything. How is one to decipher this strange anteriority of an *already* that is always shouldering you with a cadaver? . . . He wishes you never to be able to get rid of the very stiff body his literature, his funeral rite, will have banded erect for you. How does one seduce, how does one win love without telling you *I am dead*? . . . Who does it better? Who says it better? . . . the *already* [*déjà*] that I am (following) [*je suis*] sounds its own proper *glas*, signs itself its own death sentence [*arrêt de mort*], regards you in advance, sees you advance without any comprehension of what you will have loved, following, in a column, the funeral march of an erection everyone will intend to have available from now on' (G 79, right column).

43 'I am *already* [*déjà*: also, D.J.] (dead) signifies that I am *behind* [*derrière*]. Absolutely behind, the *Derrière* that will never have been seen from the front, the *Déjà* that nothing will have preceded, which therefore conceived and gave birth to itself, but as a cadaver or glorious body' (G 84, right column).

44 'Paternity, as you know, is always attributed at the end of a trial and in the form of a judgment. Hence of a generality. But the mother? Above all the mother who dispenses with the father? May one not hope for a pure genealogy from her, purely singular . . . ? Isn't the proper finally from the mother?' (G 150, right column).

45 'No more than the *glas* that she sets ringing [*met en branle*]. The mother is a thief and a beggar. She appropriates everything, but because she has nothing that is properly hers' (G 150, right column).

46 'The Behind and the Already, the *Derrière* and the *Déjà*, protect me, make me illegible . . . Also read, as forms of repression, all the rhetorical flowers in which I disperse my signature, in which I apostrophize or apotropize myself. It is a matter of repulsing the worst threat' (G 84, right column).

47 'you can take interest in what I am doing here only insofar as you would be right [*auriez raison*] to believe that – *somewhere* – I do not know what I am doing . . . Nor what activates itself here' (G 64, right column).

CHAPTER 7

Metaphorics and Metaphysics: Derrida's Analysis of Aristotle

Irene E. Harvey

Contents

INTRODUCTION
A. Concepts of Metaphor
   (a) Transference
   (b) Resemblance
   (c) Strange Names
   (d) Intentional Tropes
B. The Metaphor of Metaphor: Constituting Philosophical Discourse
   (a) Proper Tropes
   (b) The Economy of Metaphor
   (c) Forgetting
C. Metaphysics as a Metaphor of Theory: Heliotropes
   (a) The Literal Metaphor
   (b) The Concept of Sensibility
   (c) The Heliotropic Structure of Metaphor
   (d) The Metaphor of Philosophy
D. The Death of Metaphor and the Resurrection of Metaphysics

Introduction

> ... philosophy is deprived of what it provides itself. Its instruments belonging to its field, it is incapable of dominating its general *tropology* and *metaphorics*. It could perceive its metaphorics only around a blind spot or central deafness. The concept of metaphor would describe this contour, but it is not even certain that the concept thereby circumscribes an organizing centre; and this *formal law* holds for every philosopheme. (my emphasis)[1]

It will be the task of this paper to articulate precisely what Derrida means by 'this formal law' and the 'blind spot'. We suggest that the relation between metaphor, as a philosophic concept, and metaphorics, as a process and a movement within philosophic textuality, will form the focus for this articulation and in turn serve to ground Derrida's own theoretical notion of metaphor as it exceeds the possibility of a philosophic concept. In order to elucidate this shift from metaphysics to metaphorics we propose an analysis of Derrida's 'deconstruction' of the 'concept of metaphor', specifically as it is articulated by Aristotle. In this process it will become apparent that the strategy of 'deconstruction' operates on at least two levels of the text simultaneously. On the one hand, it is concerned with the thematized and theoretically articulated notion: 'what the writer commands of the patterns of language that he uses'. On the other hand, it is concerned with precisely *how* this notion, idea or concept is articulated and thus with 'what the writer does *not* command of the patterns of language that he uses'.[2] For Aristotle, in particular, with reference to the problems of metaphor as it relates to philosophy and specifically to philosophic discourse, Derrida finds that the former's theoretical claims concerning the role, status, function and structure of metaphor are belied (betrayed) by the role, status, function and structure of metaphor that he in fact uses or perhaps, uses him, within his own discourse. This shadow of a praxis within a praxis is, as we shall show, the nature of the 'blind spot' that Derrida seeks to articulate and further to bring to light within the notion of a 'formal law'. As contradictory as this project may appear, we suggest that the *telos* of an articulated formal law does not return us to a pre-Derridean metaphysics but points towards a philosophy of textuality which we have certainly not yet begun to thematize. The directions of contemporary hermeneutics, archaeology, and certainly deconstruction do, however, coincide on this issue, we suggest, and our conclusions in this paper will attempt to 'go beyond' this formal law and the blindness of the blind spot which Derrida here situates within the notion of metaphysics.

A. Concepts of Metaphor

> Metaphor is the application of a strange term either *transferred* from the genus and applied to the species or from the species and applied to the genus, or from one species to another or else by analogy. (my emphasis)[3]
>
> Sometimes there is *no word* for some of the terms of the analogy but the metaphor can be used all the same.
>
> Besides this another way of employing metaphor is to call a thing by the *strange name* and then to deny it some attribute of that name. (my emphases)[4]
>
> It is a great thing to make *proper use* of each of the elements mentioned, and of double words and rare words too, but by far the *greatest thing* is the *use of metaphor*. That alone *cannot be learnt*; it is the token of genius. For the *right use* of metaphor means an *eye for resemblances*. (my emphases)[5]

There is little doubt that this multiple determination of the notion of metaphor by Aristotle does not necessarily coalesce into one coherent concept of the same. Indeed they can be shown to be contradictory in more than one respect; i.e. the transfer of a name of one thing to that of another and yet there being the possibility that at least one of the terms of the analogy need not have a name; the structure of *resemblance* that allows for metaphorical transfer yet also the possibility of *inadequation* of the 'strange name' minus one or some of its attributes to its new home. These problems will not however be our main focus here. Instead, Derrida's analysis/deconstruction begins with what is presupposed in each of these concepts and therefore with that which *allows* Aristotle to articulate these notions as such. Thus we turn towards the unthematized infrastructure within the above claims.

(a) Transference

Apart from its apparent clinical connection, the notion of transference here will be used to designate the 'transfer process' which is required, according to Aristotle, for the production of 'metaphor'. As he says, the 'transfer' can take place in a number of ways and can transcend the categorial specificity of particular levels of abstraction; for instance, the transfer from genus to species, or species to genus. In addition, Derrida claims, the transfer can be and often is from one disciplinary specific discourse, i.e. biology, to another, i.e. philosophy. And in turn we find a metaphorics, or a system of metaphors, employed for example in the following way. The borrowing of one term, i.e. 'symptom', leads in turn in the articulation of a problem to the employment of 'similar' metaphors; i.e. disease, treatment, diagnosis, etc. This is not a necessary relation but a description of a phenomenon which can be found in the textuality of any 'particular' field of inquiry. The regional discursive transfer is of course an extension of Aristotle's claim but not inconsistent with it. In turn, if one were to aim to articulate this process philosophically one could classify the 'types' of metaphors according to their *proper*, original home discourse; i.e. roots, stems, flowers, stamens as proper terms in the field of biology. But when these same terms are employed in philosophic discourse, for example, they become instantly metaphoric. Thus it is, as Aristotle described, the *transfer* that constitutes metaphor, not the substance or essence of the term. Prior to an elucidation of the 'excess' of metaphorics which such concepts are 'powerless to describe' we shall pursue Aristotle's attempt to circumscribe the problem and Derrida's gloss on the same.

(b) Resemblance

'To have an eye for resemblance', Aristotle says, is the gift of genius that promotes the 'right use of metaphor'. Indeed, it is 'resemblance' that makes 'analogy' the 'metaphor par excellence'. In order that one can 'see such resemblances' and in turn constitute such correct metaphors one must necessarily reduce the metaphoric process to a *means* to an end. More specifically, the metaphor, once constituted, *serves* as a sign for – represents – that previously seen resemblance. In short, resemblance is the *archè* and *telos* of the process of metaphorization. What this entails, Derrida claims, is none other than the process of idealization that characterizes philosophy as such. Consequently he argues:

> . . . metaphor is charged with *expressing an idea*, with placing outside or representing the content of a thought that naturally would be called 'idea'. (*Marges* 266; MP 223)

The role of the sign in the history of philosophy has been none other than to express the truth, carry it, represent it and in particular to efface itself as the bearer or 'facteur'.[6] Thus we have here, in Aristotle's notion although not explicated as such, the metaphor which is not simply metaphorical, or a metaphor, as we shall see.

The notion of *resemblance* orienting the production of metaphor and subsequently destroying it can also be seen as the moment of the Hegelian *Aufhebung*, Derrida claims. This process entails an overcoming yet sustaining of an origin which thereby 'gives way' to a process of usurpation. In short, a kind of 'transfer' in which that from which and that towards which the movement is made are both sustained in the leap. According to Hegel, following Aristotle, the production of oppositions which characterize metaphysics (i.e. nature/mind, nature/history, nature/freedom) is necessarily related to a process of *metaphorization* which (a) serves to overcome the original sensible level; (b) is in turn itself overcome as one reaches the level of truth, ideality, or intelligibility. Derrida describes this complex process, which subsequently articulates the conditions of possibility of metaphorics, in the following way:

> And in order to think and resolve them, this framework sets to work the oppositions nature/spirit, nature/history, or nature/freedom, which are linked by genealogy to the opposition of *physis* to its others, and by the same token to the oppositions sensual/spiritual, sensible/intelligible, sensory/sense (*sinnlich/Sinn*). Nowhere is this system as explicit as it is in Hegel. It describes the space of the *possibility of metaphysics*, and the *concept of metaphor* thus defined belongs to it. (*Marges* 269; MP 226: my emphasis)

The point is that the shift which inaugurates philosophy, from the sensible to the intelligible, is the precise analogue of the shifting process that produces metaphor and in turn effaces it. This latter process we shall address later in the section entitled 'The Death of Metaphor', but for now we wish to articulate this profound originary sphere which is prior to both philosophy and metaphor as such and yet constitutes the possibility of both. For Aristotle, as we have seen, this *shift* in ground which constitutes the 'ground', the proper, and the notion of origin itself *in* philosophy is constrained by the, albeit paradoxical, notion of resemblance, or mimesis or representation, which in turn presupposes some claim of identity. Thus metaphor is 'charged with expressing an idea', as Derrida claims, and hence becomes indistinguishable from the 'sign' of metaphysics, or more precisely, the concept of the sign according to metaphysics. This latter entails an 'external' relation to that which it signifies and thus a certain expediency. As we mentioned earlier, it is a means to an end, which once served can be discarded since it is assumed to *not be constitutive* of that same product which is also an origin.

Along with this process we have a moment of *nonsense* which characterizes metaphor, according to Aristotle and others more recently who have emphasized this as distinct from Aristotle (i.e. Ricoeur).[7] The shift which allows for metaphor is also a displacement that threatens the meaning or the semantic production 'sought for' in that same displacement. Aristotle himself articulates this movement but only as 'on the way' to a meaningful representation. As he says, 'a jumble of words is simply jargon'.[8] The guiding thread for the displacement is of course 'not to be learned' but one has the capacity for creating 'proper metaphors' (which make sense) or not, by nature; or more precisely, via the quality of genius that one either has or does not have. Reversing the priority he establishes, one could argue that the 'meaningfulness' of the metaphor is the criterion for the title of genius or not for its author, but we shall address this issue in more detail shortly. For the moment let us return to Derrida's analysis of this 'risk' which metaphor at once constitutes and overcomes, if done properly.

> It risks disrupting the semantic plenitude to which it should belong. Marking the moment of the turn or of the detour [*du tour ou du détour*] during which meaning might seem to venture forth alone, loosened from the very thing it aims towards, from the truth which attunes it to its referent, metaphor also opens the wandering of the semantic. The meaning of a name, instead of designating the thing which the name ought normally to designate, takes itself elsewhere. (*Marges* 287; MP 241: trans. modified)

The issue is of course the locus of the 'elsewhere' and the conditions of the possibility of this becoming meaningful; or as Aristotle puts it, the metaphor being *fitting* or not, *appropriate* or not. The guardrail is, in addition, as Derrida says of Aristotle:

> If metaphor, the chance and risk of *mimesis*, can always miss the true, it is because it must take a determined absence into account. (*Marges* 288; MP 241: trans. modified)

The nature of this 'determined' or circumscribed absence entails the structure of a syllogism, Derrida claims. In turn, the hidden structure of metaphor, as Aristotle explicates it, can be described (albeit paradoxically) as syllogistic. The transformation process – from non-meaning to meaning – in the deciphering of a 'metaphor' (indeed, more precisely in its *recognition* as a metaphor since metaphor by definition already entails the *success* of this process) entails a tripartite process, albeit implicitly formulated if formulated at all, in the act of its comprehension. Let us consider an example of metaphor and its analytic decipherment into the classic parts of a syllogism. For instance, 'The man is a fox'. First, we should note, according to Aristotle, this is a proper type of metaphor since it represents the transfer of the name of one species to another: fox to man. The syllogistic implicit structure which produces the meaning of the metaphor would be one of the following possibilities:

(i) The man is a cunning animal.
(ii) All cunning animals are foxes.
(iii) The man is a fox.

Despite the fact that the minor premise (ii) is not valid, the structure above would depict a valid syllogism. Another possible syllogistic extrapolation of the metaphor above would be this:

(i) The man is a cunning animal.
(ii) Foxes are cunning animals.
(iii) The man is a fox.

This is of course an 'invalid' syllogism unless one adds to the conclusion that 'the man *could be* a fox', which of course would reduce the metaphor to a mere proposition of possibility. The potency of metaphor is in the juxtaposition; the forcing together of categories that 'normally' are not found together. In short, it is the *nonsense* (as Ricoeur and Hausman have described)[9] that one meets initially in the 'would-be' metaphor that promotes the shift from the literal non-sensical level to the metaphoric and in turn, meaningful level. It is what allows for this shift, which is not simply nonsense, nor simply the *telos* of meaning (be that desire, need or habit) which Derrida has pointed out as the syllogistic structure.

Returning to the problem of the 'absence of meaning' and the circumscription of this, we find that for Derrida the unthematized notion of teleological non-meaning inhabits Aristotle's distinctions between 'mere sounds', made by animals, and 'letters' (phonemes) articulated by human beings. Although the 'actual sound' can be identical, the difference is that a letter is on the way to a word, which is on the way to meaning and in turn the truth. The animal cry has no such implicit or necessary *telos*. The presupposition of a semantic teleology within 'human nature' is placed in question by Derrida on more than one occasion[10] and in particular, for our purposes here, with respect to the structure of metaphor. Since metaphor portrays a hidden syllogism in its proper, that is meaningful, manifestation (if the syllogism cannot be found, it cannot be made meaningful) there is, Derrida argues, also a profound parallel here to the manifestation of truth claims for Aristotle. In fact, metaphor as the medium for the transfer from non-sense to meaning is the precise analogue of the movement from nonsense to truth for philosophy. The key to the parallel here is the condition of the possibility of both and that is resemblance, Derrida claims.

> Metaphor thus, as an effect of *mimesis* and *homoiosis*, the manifestation of analogy, will be a means of knowledge, a means that is subordinate, but certain. (*Marges* 283; MP 238)

The residue of metaphor is thus the recognition of the *same* in the apparently different. Is the philosophic concept based on anything else? Aristotle claims that mimesis however is based on pleasure, and this is the pleasure of knowing.

> For the same reason, pleasure, the second 'cause' of *mimesis* and metaphor, is the pleasure of knowing, of learning by resemblance, of recognizing the same. (*Marges* 284; MP 238)

Of course the difference between resemblance and identity is precisely resemblance here. The difference within resemblance is *reduced* in the recognition of the same. In this way metaphor itself is the mid-point between language not yet born, and the fulfillment of language – its meaning – as truth. As Derrida explains, for Aristotle:

> In non-meaning, language is not yet born. In the truth, it should fulfill itself, accomplish itself, actualize itself to the point of erasing itself, without any possible play, before the thing (thought) which is properly manifested in the truth. (*Marges* 288; MP 241: trans. modified)

Thus the role of language, or the sign (as we mentioned earlier) for Aristotle is analogous in the revelation of truth to that of metaphor in the establishment of meaning. The very means of production in the fulfilment of its aim is thereby effaced, sacrificed in the 'as if' of a pure presentation of either meaning or truth, regardless. The point is that the structure of metaphor and the structure of the revelation of truth are homologous. And this is no accident, as we shall see.

Let us now turn to the notion of the nameable in, or within, Aristotle's claims which Derrida articulates once again as a paradox inhabiting the former's discourse.

(c) Strange Names

There are two important references to names as they relate to the concepts of metaphor for Aristotle and these are: (i) the 'transfer of names' from different 'categories' of the articulation of Being: from the 'proper' to the 'improper' realm; and (ii) using a 'strange name' for something and denying the newly named item some or one of the attributes 'normally' attributed or represented by that 'same' name (or as Heidegger called it using a term 'under erasure'[11]).

In order to make such claims Aristotle must presuppose a theory of the *nameable* and in turn, the *unnameable* and it is this that concerns Derrida. Aristotle's theory of names, that is the concept of 'name', entails a 'proper' relation of the name to its referent, or the named. What this entails, for Aristotle, is that there be, in proper cases, a one-to-one correspondence between name and thing named. That is, in short, that polysemy is a bastardized form of naming and the aim of properly naming is to reduce the polysemic, ambiguous and hence treacherous (as we shall see shortly) aspects of univocity, singularity, and simplicity. With unity achieved so will the injunction of the *proper* and hence the concept of name.[12] This system of reduction entails the demarcation of the limits of the nameable, Derrida claims. This becomes relevant for the concept of metaphor since it in turn circumscribes the conditions of the possibility of the metaphoric transfer of names, with its subsequent additions or subtractions of attributes or markers. As Derrida says:

> Therefore it seems that the field of *onoma* – and consequently that of metaphor, as the transport of names – is less that of the name in the strict sense . . . than that of the nameable. Every word which resists this nominalization would remain foreign to metaphor. (*Marges* 278; MP 233: trans. modified)

The most obvious example of that which has no 'name', or is not a name would be any term which has no meaning in itself. For instance, syntactical elements in a discourse; shifters such as 'but', 'or', etc. which can never become metaphors. They would fall into 'nonsense' if one attempted to metaphorize them, and not be retrievable from such an abyss. Derrida explains:

> Now, only that which claims – or henceforth claims – to have a complete and independent signification, that which is intelligible by itself, outside any syntactic relation can be nominalized. (*Marges* 278; MP 233)

He further insists that the nameable for Aristotle entails a possibility of complete abstraction from a discursive context since the 'name' entails for its meaning a one-to-one correspondence to the thing signified.

It is clear from contemporary work in structural linguistics that the meaning of any term is 'conditioned' by its participation in a particular situation or context. The 'play of difference' between terms, as Saussure says, is that which constitutes the meanings of those 'semantically full' terms as results rather than origins. It is this issue which fundamentally divides Ricoeur from Derrida with respect to the differing notions of discourse, language and articulation in general.[13] For Derrida, it is the syntactical and pre-semantic levels of textuality (discourse) which are the conditions of the possibility of the semantic and are thus not reducible to the latter. With respect to metaphor, according to Aristotle's definition, this level (the syntactic) is *excluded* from the field of metaphorics in general. As Derrida says:

> Articulation has no meaning because it makes no reference by means of a categorematic unity, to an independent unity, the unity of a substance or a being. Thus, it is excluded from the metaphorical field as onomastic field. Henceforth, the anagrammatical, which functions with the aid of parts of names, dismembered names, is foreign to the metaphorical field in general, as is also the *syntactic play* of articulations. (*Marges* 287; MP 240–41: trans. modified, my emphasis)

We thus have the limits of the concept of metaphor, according to Aristotle, described by Derrida. Prior to the articulation of the relation of these 'excluded' aspects to the 'included' in the concepts of metaphor, which as we shall see becomes a law (despite its invisibility as a blind spot), we must turn our attention to the role of authorial intention in the use and production of metaphors.

(d) Intentional Tropes

We should recall that for Aristotle the production of metaphor via an 'eye for resemblance' is no chance event but rather the work of *genius*. Thus we have a level of intention invoked as the origin of metaphor. According to Derrida, however, there is more to metaphorics than, as it were, meets the eye. With respect specifically to philosophic discourse and its usage of metaphor, Derrida suggests the following, since, as we have mentioned, all metaphors therein are 'borrowed terms' from 'other discourses':

> Thus, the criteria for a classification of philosophical metaphors are borrowed from a derivative philosophical discourse. Perhaps this might be legitimate if these figures were governed, consciously and calculatedly, by the identifiable author of a system, or if the issue were to describe a philosophical rhetoric in the service of an autonomous theory constituted before and outside its own language, manipulating its tropes like tools. (*Marges* 266; MP 224)

Not only are the metaphorics found in philosophic discourse not simply under the control of their respective philosopher, Derrida claims, but rather metaphors in each philosophical system extend beyond the range of that system as determined by the proper name of its author. Despite the fact that 'the light' for Descartes does not have precisely the same significance as it does for Hegel or Plato, there is nonetheless a larger system of metaphorics in effect which each of the authors, as philosophers, or writers of philosophic texts, participate in, draw upon as a resource, and sustain as a framework for the future and the past of that discipline. We shall approach the details of this 'larger system' of metaphorics which transcends the will, intent and control of each author in our next section but here we wish only to show that for Derrida the concept of an instituting genius is insufficient to explain the actual interplay of metaphorics within and between philosophic texts.

Derrida also insists that the very 'founding concepts' of philosophy itself are already *metaphorical*. It is these he refers to as 'archaic tropes' which the 'philosopher/genius/producer' of metaphor also *makes use of* as a philosopher but *does not produce or regulate* (at least not since Plato). Hence he aims:

> ... to point out ... when it is a question of 'archaic' tropes which have given to the 'founding' concepts (*theoria*, *eidos*, *logos*, etc.) the determinations of a 'natural' language. And the signs (words/concepts) from which this proposition is made, beginning with those of trope and *archè*, already have their metaphorical charge. (*Marges* 267; MP 224: trans. modified)

One could inspect the principal founding *roots* of philosophy's natural language and indeed find nothing which is *naturally* (originarily) suited to it. For instance:

ground, base, *meta*physics, *in*finity, logos, methodos, etc. It is simply, as Hegel claimed, that philosophic discourse and perhaps philosophy itself is constituted by the *metaphoric transfer* which therefore institutes rather than simply represents; or constitutes rather than simply decorates. We shall return to this.

It seems clear therefore that metaphor as a controlled insight by a genius is simply not a sufficient model of explanation for the play of metaphor within philosophic discourse. Indeed the concept of metaphor itself has been shown to be far from adequate as a description of the role, function and structure of metaphor as it is found and operates within philosophic discourse. One might add also that 'metaphor as such' is never to be found except as embedded in a discourse – be that philosophic, literary, sociological, political, or psychological. Suffice it to say that an analysis of a metaphorics between these discourses is yet to be established or addressed. For the moment then let us return to our subject which is the metaphorics within and yet transcendent of metaphysics.

B. The Metaphor of Metaphor: Constituting Philosophical Discourse

> If one wished to conceive and to class all the metaphorical possibilities of philosophy, one metaphor, at least would always remain excluded, outside the system: the metaphor, at the very least, without which the concept of metaphor could not be constructed . . . *the metaphor of metaphor*. (*Marges* 261; MP 219–20: my emphasis)

We propose in this section to elucidate precisely this notion of 'the metaphor of metaphor' to which Derrida refers here. The role of metaphor and its functioning within philosophic discourse has already been shown to exceed the philosophic (at least Aristotle's) concept of the same. We propose now, in tracing Derrida's deconstruction of that concept, to analyse the conditions of the possibility of both metaphor and philosophy which we shall see partake of that same 'borrowed' structure which at the same time effaces their common origin. To begin, let us return to the idea of the 'proper place' of metaphorical terms – i.e. an original, appropriate discourse and usage – and examine the presuppositions of such a claim.

(a) Proper Tropes

We began with an analysis of the notion of transfer which constitutes metaphor and institutes a doubling of meaning such that an initial 'nonsense' is overcome and a 'correct, figurative' meaning is achieved. In this process a displacement occurs either of a term or name that is shifted from its *appropriate* object of reference to a new and strange one, or as a transfer of discursive specific terms (i.e. biological terms) to another discourse wherein they instantly become metaphoric (i.e. the discourse of psychology).

Now this model of an original, proper sphere no longer works with respect to philosophy's foundational metaphors – or its own *proper tropes*. It is not as if the meaning they institute could be found elsewhere and furthermore the 'founding tropes' of philosophic discourse are located *within* pairs of oppositions rather than single terms which could be isolated and theoretically sent back to their respective proper discourses. As Derrida says:

> The constitution of the fundamental oppositions of the metaphorology (*physis/technè*, *physis/nomos*, sensible/intelligible, space/time, signifier/signified, etc.) has occurred by means of the history of a metaphorical language, or rather by means of 'tropic' movements which, no longer capable of being called by a philosophical name – i.e. metaphors – nevertheless, and for the same reason do not make up a 'proper' language. (*Marges* 272–3; MP 228–9)

Thus we have a 'higher order' metaphorics which grounds philosophy and which is: (a) based on 'metaphors', as Aristotle has defined them with respect to the transfer from their 'proper' places; yet (b) is not reducible to this model since the 'new terms' formed via the oppositional structure *in which* the 'borrowed terms' are set up cannot be localized anywhere else. Their proper place is their improper place or in short, they have no proper place. As Derrida says, the first order metaphors, simple effects of transfer, produce effects in the second order which are radically originary. They are in effect, irreducible tropes and in turn the *founding tropes* of philosophy. This effect Derrida will call *tropology*:

> It is from beyond the difference between the proper and the nonproper that the effects of propriety and nonpropriety have to be accounted for. By definition, thus, there is no properly philosophical category to qualify a certain number of tropes that have conditioned the so-called 'fundamental', 'structuring', 'original' philosophical oppositions: they are so many 'metaphors' that would constitute the rubrics of such a tropology. (*Marges* 273; MP 229)

Furthermore this tropology is not the work of a controlling consciousness that would 'initially decide' or intend to construct such metaphors of metaphors. We have discussed this with respect to the 'limits of the genius' above, but now let us add that the resultant philosophic discourse, produced by the higher order metaphorics (or founding tropes, for Derrida) is powerless to *control* the tropology under the title of a metaphorology. In short, philosophy's own conditions of possibility are necessarily outside the domain of its circumscription of control – as with all systems and their conditions of possibility. Thus we have metaphor, as a concept, within philosophic determination, yet also a process of metaphorization that in turn produces the 'proper' of philosophy which philosophy proper can no longer articulate. Derrida explains:

> It is therefore enveloped in the field that a general metaphorology of philosophy would seek to dominate. Metaphor has been issued from a network of philosophemes which themselves correspond to tropes or to figures, and these

philosophemes are contemporaneous to or in systematic solidarity with those tropes or figures. This stratum of 'instituting' tropes, the layer of 'primary' philosophemes . . . cannot be dominated. It cannot dominate itself, cannot be dominated by what it has itself engendered, has made to grow on its own soil, supported on its own base. (*Marges* 261; MP 219: trans. modified)

Thus we have a ground for the 'ground' which can no longer be called a *ground*, properly speaking. Philosophy, as Derrida says, cannot, within the limits of its conceptual structure, articulate this process. The metaphor of metaphor here is not, however, simply an abyss nor an infinitely regressing or deferred origin but rather that of a *conceptual resource* that philosophy requires but which it did not produce. It is this *resource* that we are attempting to describe here as Derrida portrays it.

(b) The Economy of Metaphor

There is a metaphor, Derrida claims, which recurs in numerous discourses concerning metaphor. This metaphor of metaphor, used to articulate, describe, represent metaphor is that of *usure* – or usury, wearing down, wearing out, usage all in one term. The articulation of this 'metaphor' will show, according to Derrida, that *usure* not only describes and represents the metaphoric process but rather opens the space in which the regional sciences of economics and linguistics (both of which rely on the term *usure*) are possible or founded. Thus the 'metaphor' of *usure* in turn inverts under close scrutiny in order to reveal a more profound 'usury' within metaphor itself, and thus within discourse in general. Derrida's inflation of the centrality of the term will also be closely scrutinized as we proceed here. Derrida claims:

In order to signify the metaphorical process, the paradigms of money, silver and gold are imposed with remarkable insistence. (*Marges* 256; MP 216: trans. modified)

And with this there is an imposition of a relation between *metaphor* and *economy*. Indeed, as we have seen, metaphor is used as a 'sign', a token, a mark (money) to represent the idea of resemblance, analogy or similarity. In fact, we have also shown that metaphor (traditionally understood) is considered a *means* to an end – idealization or meaning – and in turn is *effaced* as a thing-in-itself with any significance of its own (as with money). This process is analogous to the role of language within the discourse of metaphysics. The notion of *economy*, as a system of exchange, is also introduced by Aristotle's own definition of metaphor in the transfer process, from naming one object to another, or the shift in attributes from one thing to another. The metaphor of metaphor fails us here in the comparison of *returns* – or equal exchange – since it is a unidirectional process which metaphor seems to be engaged in. However, this term *usure* – both as usury and wearing away – situates the notion of metaphor firmly within the 'economic' structure which is traditionally used as a linguistic resource for the articulation of metaphor by metaphor, as we have said above. Now Derrida claims, that *usure* is perhaps not a metaphor for metaphor but rather articulates its essence; or at least the concept of metaphor initially:

> This characteristic – the concept of *usure* – belongs not to a narrow historico-theoretical configuration, but more surely to the concept of metaphor itself, and to the long metaphysical sequence that it determines or that determines it. (*Marges* 256; MP 215–16)

Thus the repeated reliance on *usure* is no accident, he claims, but repeats itself or represents itself as something essential. Let us consider the 'concept itself' of *usure* for a moment. *Usury* is the lending of money at high interest, and *usage* entails the wearing away of the original identity of something over time – the progressive effacement of origin. The first articulates the borrowing and transfer process noted earlier and the latter suggests the effacement of 'origin' in the production of the proper. Both of these aspects accurately describe the 'traditional definition' of metaphor, or its 'concept', as Derrida says. Now what allows for the transfer of an economic concept to the domain of language (considering metaphor as a linguistic structure) if not some process of transfer itself which is neither? Hence, the analogy considered *within* language is represented by an analogy situated *between* language and something else: economy. Thus metaphor, as *usure*, is that which is to be described within language yet also that which (as a process) is outside of language and economy as well since it allows for their relation *via* analogy. As Derrida says:

> But that which here seems to 'represent', to figure, is also that which *opens the wider space* of a discourse on figuration and can no longer be contained within a regional or determined science, linguistics or philology. (*Marges* 257; MP 216: my emphasis)

Thus we have a *process* of *usure* prior to both linguistics and philology and 'economics' which Derrida will call *metaphorics*. We return therefore to philosophy for a concept of this metaphorics and once again are driven back to a realm *prior* to the 'concept': 'What could the *usure* properly speaking be of a word, an expression, a signification, a text?' (*Marges* 249; MP 209: trans. modified) As we have shown, philosophical discourse effaces its metaphorical 'non-origin', or the constitutive role that metaphor plays in the production of philosophic discourse, and thus we have the term *usure* in effect here in the second sense of the term – wearing away of the origin. This effacement will presently be our focus as it also describes the metaphor of metaphor for Derrida, but first let us turn to his articulation of the *usure* with respect to philosophy's treatment of its metaphoric origin:

> And the history of metaphysical language is said to be confused with the *erasure* of the efficacy of the sensory figure and the *usure* of its effigy. The word itself is not pronounced, but one may decipher the double import of *usure*:

erasure by rubbing, exhaustion, crumbling away, certainly; but also the *supplementary product* of a capital, the exchange which far from losing the original investment would fructify its initial wealth, would increase its return in the form of revenue, additional interest, linguistic surplus value, the two histories of the meaning of the word remaining indistinguishable. (*Marges* 250; MP 210: my emphases)

(c) Forgetting

Why is metaphor as productive to be effaced, or forgotten? By whom or by what? What is at stake here and how can the 'forgotten', if indeed forgotten, be remembered, brought back, or 'made present' perhaps for the first time? What can 'forgetting' or erasure mean here, for Derrida?

What is forgotten, Derrida claims, is simultaneously the first meaning, or original, non-metaphorical, proper meaning, and in addition, the transfer process itself. This double effacement in turn results in what we take to be *proper* philosophical discourse – as if these terms had their origin there and nowhere else. As we have shown, the 'metaphors' which philosophy uses for its own proper language are not metaphors *until* they are transferred to philosophy and yet are not metaphors either *once* they are effectively transferred; which is to say that they have been adopted by philosophy as its own. The question might well be then *where* are the metaphors? Of course, philosophy in turn relegates metaphor to a merely ornamental and decorative, in short, superfluous role with respect to the transport of a meaning. A poem's meaning can always be said otherwise – in prosaic style. This demarcation of metaphor as essentially superfluous has been shown to be insufficient and inadequate but it does reveal the *essential effacement* performed by philosophy on its own metaphorical origins. That is, since metaphor is defined as an accessory, an *external* addition to meaning and *a fortiori* with respect to truth and its description, metaphor can be excluded from the essence of philosophy. The very attempt of this *exclusion* reveals, Derrida has shown,[14] a more profound *internal* relation which the discourse of philosophy cannot itself articulate or understand. It is this *internal* relation, as irreducible, that Derrida calls 'white mythology' after a French idiom, 'white night' (*nuit blanche*) which represents the forgotten events of a night passed via serious intoxication. It is this 'white night' that the tradition of metaphysics has, in its very structure, sought to forget with respect to its metaphorical origins. As he says:

> *Metaphysics* – the white mythology which reassembles and reflects the culture of the West: the white man takes his own mythology, Indo-European mythology, his own *logos*, that is the *mythos* of his idiom, for the universal form of that he must still wish to call Reason.
> . . .
> [Further:] *White mythology* – metaphysics has erased within itself the fabulous scene that has produced it, the scene that nevertheless remains active and stirring, inscribed in white ink, an invisible design covered over in the palimpsest. (*Marges* 254; MP 213: trans. modified)

It is this palimpsest which we will now begin to decipher which Derrida insists can be revealed via the guiding thread of the father of metaphors and indeed the metaphor of the father for philosophy: the sun.

C. Metaphysics as a Metaphor of Theory: Heliotropes

The 'sun' plays several roles in the discourse of philosophy, according to Derrida. First, it is simply a metaphor and as such entails a system of metaphors, or a metaphorics, which include: light, dark, clarity, visibility, invisibility, etc. Secondly, it is the metaphor for sensibility itself, which is to be overcome with intelligibility. For instance, it is that which never presents itself fully in sensible intuition; that which is always partially absent; that which entails its own eclipse. It represents, in short, an economy of presence and absence that is irreducible and characterizes perception itself. Thirdly, the 'sun' represents, with its metaphorics, the very structure of metaphor itself. The 'turning' of the sun is the turning of metaphor. More precisely, the economy of light and dark, presence and absence, obscurity and clarity replicates precisely that of nonsense to meaning, the literal to the figurative, which as we have shown characterizes metaphor. Thus the 'sun' in this third sense is not simply a metaphor, nor simply a metaphor of metaphor, but rather illustrates the essence of metaphor in the former's own metaphoricity which is indistinguishable here from the literal or the true. Now, fourthly, the 'sun', according to Derrida, is not one metaphor among others for philosophy itself. Further, it is not only a metaphor for sensibility in general, or the concept of sensibility, but rather the structure of philosophy as such. The 'sun' with its metaphorics, *orients* (another heliotropic metaphor) the discourse of philosophy. These 'rhetorical flowers' are what Derrida will call *heliotropes* and it is thus that he characterizes the interdependence of metaphorics and metaphysics ultimately. We propose to analyse each of these notions of the role of the 'sun' for Derrida, in the following sections.

(a) The Literal Metaphor

For Plato, the 'sun' plays the role of the invisible source of all visibility. It is the 'light' that illumines the world but which will blind the envious philosopher if looked at directly. It produces that which we call 'essence' but it is not itself an essence. The 'sun' as metaphor, appears and disappears and with it appear and disappear the truth, the Forms, and indeed the Good. As Derrida explains, for Plato:

> ... the sun appears. In order to disappear. It is there, but as the invisible source of light, in a kind of insistent eclipse, more than essential, producing the essence – being and appearing – of what is. . . . Keeping itself beyond all that which is, it figures the Good of which the sensory sun is the son: the source of life and visibility, of seed and light. (*Marges* 289; MP 242)

Thus the 'sun' is not present for Plato, according to Derrida, but rather presents what is present. It makes presence and absence possible – both literally, sensibly, and metaphorically, intelligibly or philosophically. This is more than 'one metaphor among many', as we shall see.

For Aristotle, the 'sun' plays a similar founding role, specifically in his *Poetics* where it appears as such, by name. He speaks of the 'sun' (metaphorically, of course) as 'seeding a divine light'; that is, the light of truth which thus grounds the possibility of philosophy as such. Since the 'sun' is the name of something that has no substitution, no possibility of *re*presentation, is unique, singular, simple, this metaphor consists in the substitution of *names*, in Aristotle's sense of this term. That is, names are proper for Aristotle, as we have mentioned, when they have but one single referent: univocal. Thus the name 'sun' represents the *propriety* of the proper name itself. As Derrida says:

> Here, the metaphor consists in a substitution of proper names having a fixed meaning and referent, especially when we are dealing with the sun whose referent has the originality of always being original, unique and irreplaceable, at least in the representation we give of it. *There is only one sun in the system.* The proper name, here, is the nonmetaphorical prime mover of metaphor, the father of all figures. Everything turns around it, everything turns toward it. (*Marges* 290; MP 243: my emphasis)

Thus the 'sun' at the most basic descriptive level of literal metaphor, no longer simply plays that role, for Derrida. Instead, the 'sun' represents the *ground* upon which metaphoricity is based and made possible. The 'sun' represents the possibility of the *proper name* – the one, unique, univocal meaning of the term, from which substitution takes place therein producing metaphor, as Aristotle defines it. We have here recovered some of the fruits of deconstruction in that we find Aristotle using a metaphor – ostensibly the 'sun' – in a manner that can no longer simply be called metaphorical by his own definition and articulation of this process. We have instead, Derrida claims, found Aristotle dependent on the 'sun' as metaphorical and as nonmetaphorical in order to ground his own 'theory' of metaphor. In short, Derrida reveals that metaphor in Aristotle (and Plato, for that matter) is surely inhabiting that which the latter terms theory and in such a way that one is tempted to call his 'theory of metaphor' a metaphor of theory, as Derrida actually does (see *Marges* 303; MP 253).

Beyond both Plato and Aristotle, Derrida claims that the metaphorics of the 'sun' (i.e. light/dark, presence/absence, clarity/obscurity) orient the entire history of philosophy. For instance:

> Certainly the metaphors of light and the circle, which are so important in Descartes, are not organized as they are in Plato or Aristotle, in Hegel or Husserl. But if we put ourselves at the most critical and most properly Cartesian point of the critical procedure, at the point of hyperbolic doubt and the hypothesis of the Evil Genius, at the point when doubt strikes not only ideas of

> sensory origin but also 'clear and distinct' ideas and what is mathematically self-evident, we know that what permits the discourse to be picked up again and to be pursued, its ultimate resource, is designated as *lumen naturale*. Natural light, and all the axioms it brings into our field of vision, is never subjected to the most radical doubt. (*Marges* 318; MP 266–7)

Thus on the one hand, we have a specific instance of a specific metaphor of a specific discourse, yet also, and more importantly, Descartes's reliance on *lumen naturale* and the metaphorics therein involved situates his discourse within a *tradition* which relies on that same *metaphorics*. This more general syntax is what Derrida is concerned to articulate as it grounds all philosophic discourse, rather than simply adorns it. Let us now address the 'sun' as a metaphor for sensibility in general, or indeed the concept of sensibility, before approaching the most wide-ranging conclusions Derrida draws on the subject.

(b) The Concept of Sensibility

The concept of the sensible entails an irreducible relation to an economy of presence and absence of its appearance to us. What becomes 'present to us' immediately, for the tradition of philosophy, is truth and that requires a certain use and a certain overcoming of the sensible – this structure of overcoming differing according to various theories. Derrida describes this concept of the sensible in the following way:

> The sensible in general does not limit knowledge for reasons that are intrinsic to the *form of the presence* of the sensible thing; but first of all because the *aistheton* can always *not* present itself, can hide itself, absent itself. (*Marges* 299; MP 250: trans. modified)

Now the model of 'that which can always absent itself' or hide itself, or not reveal itself, in short, disappear behind the clouds, is of course the *sun*. It is in this sense, Derrida claims, that the 'sun' is the paradigm of the 'sensible', or the concept of its concept (its structure) and in addition for the concept of metaphor, as we shall *see* shortly. Further, the 'sun' is the sensible object par excellence since it *reveals* more clearly than any other this essential structure that characterizes *all* sensible objects, for us, or in short, the notion of sensibility itself. As he says: 'the sun in this respect is the sensory signifier of the sensory par excellence, that is the sensory model of the sensory (the Idea, paradigm, or parabola of the sensory), then the turning of the sun always will have been the trajectory of metaphor' (*Marges* 299; MP 251). The implication of an *animate* sensibility, although unaddressed by Derrida, is clearly suggested here. Sensible objects themselves do not 'turn themselves' or 'hide themselves' regularly. Rather, the 'other side', the eclipsed back of the perceived object X is certainly never to be shown to us in an absolute vision of the object as a whole – except of course in its concept, which transcends the properly sensible sphere. The metaphor of the sun here is thus appropriate only if the subject is drawn into the picture which Derrida (significantly perhaps) omits to add. It is certainly the absent subject's relation to object X which more exactly parallels the 'regular eclipsing' of its respective presence and absence. What 'turns' regularly, eclipses regularly the sensible object is the activity of the subject which brings X into view at one time, and forgets it, leaves it, or does not address it at another. It is not simply the 'back' of this cup here that so neatly parallels the absence of the sun that is night. It is not the 'other side' of the sun either that we are referring to here, nor is Derrida, although that too would certainly complicate the 'model par excellence' here of the concept of sensibility. Let us continue however, with Derrida a little further with the third role of the 'sun' which is 'the very structure of *metaphor* itself.'

(c) The Heliotropic Structure of Metaphor

In the discourse of philosophy, Derrida claims:

> . . . the literally, properly named sun, the sensory sun, . . . is itself solely metaphorical. . . . the sun is never properly present in discourse. Each time that there is a metaphor there is doubtless a sun somewhere; but each time that there is sun, metaphor has begun. (*Marges* 300; MP 251)

Why is there necessarily a 'sun' each time we find a metaphor? Let us recall that the 'sun' represents the possibility of light and dark, and that light in turn represents knowing, truth, insight, and awareness whereas darkness *reflects* ignorance, etc. Now in the structure of metaphor as mentioned earlier, we have at least two levels of interpretation to perform in order to reach the light, the clarity, the distinctness, the visibility of meaning 'hidden' therein. The first entails the recognition of *absence*, of nonsense, of darkness that does not enlighten us, seemingly. This is the literal interpretation of a metaphor which, as it were, leads one nowhere. The shift, however, to the so-called figurative or properly metaphorical level of interpretation gives us meaning out of the original nonsense, or light out of what was formerly darkness. In short, in the moment of the *Aufhebung* of the darkness, the sun comes out and we *see* the meaning formerly invisible to us. The structure of metaphor thus, metaphorically perhaps, portrays that structure of the 'sensible object par excellence' which gives us the double possibility of light and dark – the 'sun', of course.

The question is which is a metaphor of which here? Which metaphor or structure is a metaphor and which is that which has been metaphorized? Or, in short, which is the referent and which is the representation; and more precisely, which is the *sign* and which the *signified*? For Derrida, of course, this is a false dichotomy. There is no pure referent that would not already be within a system of signs and thus be itself a sign in order to have meaning at all. Yet, we seem here to indeed have something outside of the system; at least, at the initial level of darkness or nonsense which although transcended in the effective reduction of metaphor nonetheless still inhabits that result. The *Aufhebung* is not an elimination, we should recall, but rather preserves that which it overcomes and relocates in a larger economy. Now, the issue is where has this absence gone in the presence of the 'sun' as the structure of metaphor itself? If the two aspects of the analogy here were precisely homologous, as it seems that Derrida is suggesting, then have we not achieved a pure transcendental light which has no possibility of itself being eclipsed, or turning from day to night, or to return again at a 'regular' interval? Has the absence of light, already preserved in the *Aufhebung*, not itself disappeared here in this blinding perfect homology? Perhaps, the answer entails a different characterization of the relation of metaphor to the metaphor of the sun and 'in turn' to the literal sensible sun, and its concept. If the 'sun' sets up a paradigm for all sensibility, and thus becomes a metaphor and a concept at the same time, have we not reached a ground deeper than simply the metaphorical? That is, the paradigm of the sun can no longer be *called* a metaphor, if this simultaneously allows for the production of metaphor and conceptualization as such. The paradigm of the sun is thus neither a metaphor, nor a concept, nor an example from sensible experience. Let us turn now to this *common ground* which Derrida claims structures the metaphorical space of philosophy; that is, the latter's discursive conditions of possibility.

(d) The Metaphor of Philosophy

> The sun does not just provide an example, even if the most remarkable one, of sensible being such that it can always disappear, keep out of sight, not be present. The very opposition of appearing and disappearing, the entire lexicon of the *phainesthai*, of *aletheia*, etc., of day and night, of the visible and invisible, of the present and the absent – all this is possible only under the sun. Insofar as it structures the *metaphorical space of philosophy*, the sun represents what is natural in philosophical language. (*Marges* 299; MP 251: trans. modified, my emphasis)

We suggested earlier that philosophic discourse has no proper nature except to itself be borrowed from other discourses and that it is the metaphorical transfer of particular terms that transforms them into philosophical concepts. However, now Derrida is suggesting that the structure of philosophic discourse itself is metaphorically grounded from within, as it were, with its own proper metaphorics, the centre of which is the metaphor of the 'sun'. All of this is only possible 'under the sun', as he says. Further, it is this system of metaphors which 'represents the natural language' or proper discourse of philosophy, Derrida claims. It is the metaphorics of the sun – the solar system – which alone is proper to philosophy and not borrowed from astronomy or astrology, contrary to appearances, and not borrowed from optics or biology.

The issue here is not only the 'sun' but its effects which in turn provide the framework for philosophic description and analysis. The most significant of these effects are, we mentioned earlier, the production of presence and absence. Now rather than prohibit the notion of 'presence' as a ground for truth, that is, consciousness as present to itself, pure transparency in the revelation of truth, the constitution of the identity of the proper within presence, and so *a fortiori* the meaning of Being as presence, this 'solar system' instead *institutes these possibilities* and restricts their alternatives. Indeed, it blinds the would-be philosopher from other possible modes of Being or meanings of Being itself. As Heidegger said, the meaning of Being has always been determined as *ousia*, and as we now know, this is no longer sufficient. The very absence that is simultaneously made possible via the metaphorics of the 'sun' is effaced from that same system, or rather, which amounts to the same thing, it is included as a means to an end, as a preliminary stage in the teleology of consciousness 'toward the sunlight', or truth. As Derrida says:

> Everything, in the discourse on metaphor, that passes through the sign *eidos*, with its entire system, is articulated with the analogy between the vision of the *nous* and sensory vision, between the intelligible sun and the visible sun. The determination of the truth of Being in presence passes through the detour of this tropic system. The presence of *ousia* as *eidos* (to be placed before the metaphorical eye) . . . faces the theoretical organ . . . . Philosophy, as a theory of metaphor, first will have been a *metaphor of theory*. *This circulation has not excluded but, on the contrary, has permitted and provoked the transformation of presence into self-presence, into the proximity or properness of subjectivity to and for itself. It is the history of 'proper' meaning*, as we said above, whose *detour* and *return* are to be followed. (*Marges* 303; MP 253–4: my emphases)

The *detour* is of course 'the night in which all cows are black', as Hegel puts it, or the literal nonsense that we initially are confronted with in metaphor. The detour is the momentary, or temporary *eclipse* of the sun which threatens to leave us forever in darkness and ignorance. The return of day which illumines the meaning of the 'proper' metaphor by making it proper, or confirming its propriety, is the *recognition* of meaning therein produced by the metaphorical shift from the proper meaning, to nonsense to proper meaning or the figurative level. With respect to this process within philosophic discourse itself, it operates on at least two levels also. First, as we have mentioned, there is the shift from, as Derrida puts it, the sensible sun, or vision, to the intelligible one, or truth. The move is from appearance to essence, in short. Secondly, there is the 'solar system' itself which allows for the notions of presence and absence and indeed promotes the notion of the teleology of consciousness. Further, this *teleology* is characterized, deterministically to be sure, as *heliotropic*. Meaning and truth and presence and the proper are all taken to be interchangeable, substitutable and hence synonymous terms for philosophic discourse. Thus consciousness is necessarily directed towards 'presence' as truth, since what is 'present' is 'in the light', in the day, visible, clear, distinct, etc., and hence sanctified, ratified, guaranteed as in some sense valid; the true truth. This necessity, this teleology is however also governed by the *metaphorics* of the sun. What determines the privileging of presence over absence, of light over darkness, of visibility over invisibility, of proximity over distance? (We could speculate on the relation of the 'sun' to the father here, but shall leave this for another project.) Further, what necessitates this choice between the privileging of one *side* of this system of oppositions over the other *side*? What sets up presence/absence as an opposition – mutually exclusive – in the first place, if not the mutual exclusion of the presence and absence of the *sun* at one and the same time, if not the mutual exclusion of the simultaneity of day and night for our earthbound experience? And why should, by what rights, according to which principle should the 'sun' dominate our system of conceptuality that we so proudly name philosophy – as a law of wisdom and the search for truth? These questions have only begun to appear and certainly have not yet been answered, let alone seriously considered or addressed except by Derrida.

A possible alternative is the notion of an *economy* of presence and absence, already in operation, albeit clandestinely, within this same system of metaphysics/metaphorics. This economy which Derrida names *différance*, is the process which he aims to articulate as being at work within (and yet in spite of authorial intention) the texts of philosophy as our tradition defines them. We cannot pursue this enormous issue here, but wish only to suggest that there is nothing *essential*, intrinsically, about the 'solar system' that orients metaphysics, nor about the effacement of the metaphorical processes that ground it, limit it, and frame it as a *system* of conceptuality. As a suggestion for any projected analysis of the grammar of metaphors which he has here only begun to reveal, Derrida claims:

> . . . it would doubtless be necessary to make appear, beneath the layer of apparently didactic metaphors, . . . another stratification, one that is less apparent but just as *systematically organized*, and that not only would be beneath the preceding one, but *interwoven* with it. . . . To reconstitute the *grammar* of these metaphors would be to articulate its logic with a discourse that presents itself as nonmetaphorical which here is called the philosophical system. (*Marges* 318; MP 266: trans. modified, my emphases)

D. The Death of Metaphor and the Resurrection of Metaphysics

Metaphor, then, always carries its death within itself. And this death, surely, is also the death of *philosophy*. But the genitive is double. (*Marges* 323; MP 271: my emphases)

The notion of the 'death' of metaphor and of philosophy is surely a metaphor itself here and one that represents the 'end'. This end of philosophy, as having a double meaning possibility, means the end of an *aspect* of philosophy, and secondly, the end of a *type* of philosophy, or philosophizing. The absolute end of philosophy is not something Derrida himself foresees or suggests here or elsewhere.[15] As for the end of metaphor, we have already announced it as the 'overcoming' of metaphor which situates it in the kind of 'no-man's-land' between meaning and nonsense, between truth and falsity, between visibility and invisibility. In its successful production metaphor as we have shown, gives way to (produces, albeit clandestinely) the concept. It also inaugurates the possibility of philosophic discourse as fundamentally non-metaphoric. The 'intelligible' is not simply a metaphor for the sensible, but rather its *truth*. Hence the proper place of metaphor, in philosophy, is as Derrida says, 'between two suns':

> Philosophical discourse – as such – describes a metaphor which is displaced and reabsorbed between two suns. This *end* of metaphor is not interpreted as a death or dislocation, but as an interiorizing anamnesis (*Erinnerung*), a recollection of meaning, a *relève* of living metaphoricity into a living state of properness. (*Marges* 321; MP 269)

In short, the overcoming of metaphor is its own proper end, or *telos*, within the discourse of philosophy and on two levels. First, the figurative aspect of what is produced (i.e. philosophy's proper terminology) is effaced as figurative in order to become properly philosophic. And secondly, metaphor within philosophy, when recognized is effaced as being in any sense productive rather than simply reproductive, or decorative; an unnecessary, inessential, extrinsic appendage that the discourse could just as well do without. An accidental addition. Its role as establishing a structure or a framework, effectively effaced within the concept itself (philosophic, of course) of metaphor thus making 'metaphor itself' no longer a threat to the purity of transcendent philosophic discourse. Just as discourse is itself, and *a fortiori* writing, effaced within philosophy as inessential, merely reproductive, so too is metaphor within philosophic language as such.

Now, what prohibits this total annihilation of metaphor within philosophy is the *syntactical* level of analysis. On the semantic level, metaphor becomes indistinguishable from the concept, paradoxically, to be sure, in its successful overcoming/production of meaning. That which is not reduced however is the syntactical structure that metaphor exhibits – beyond simply the *Aufhebung*. This syntax is that of *metaphorics* which, as we have shown, transcends or extends beyond one authorially inscribed limit of a particular philosopher or philosophy. This larger economy of metaphorics provides the framework in which and by which particular philosophies and philosophers participate in the tradition and in turn distinguish themselves from each other, never altering the fundamental presuppositions and bases of operation – at least not on the syntactical metaphorics level.[16] As Derrida says:

> This time, then, in traversing and doubling the first self-destruction, it passes through a *supplement of syntactical resistance*, through everything . . . that disrupts the opposition of the semantic and the syntactic, and especially the philosophical hierarchy that submits the latter to the former. (*Marges* 323; MP 270: my emphasis)

This 'syntactical supplement' – or metaphorics – as the foundation of philosophy, no longer permits itself to be known simply as syntactical therefore, but rather must be understood prior to the division and separation as an opposition of the semantic and the syntactical. As we have shown, metaphorics opens up the possibility of both levels in philosophy in particular and therefore in all regional discourses in general, including psychology.

Derrida further claims that no ontology can describe this 'supplement of the code', this syntax of all syntaxes, since it does not itself form an object, an entity, or, which is the same thing, completely present itself to the light of philosophical vision as such. As we have discussed earlier, the philosophic concept of metaphor is powerless to describe this process. This metaphorics instead, since it is neither present nor absent, yet both; since neither visible nor invisible, yet both; since neither simply metaphorical nor philosophic, yet both; is what does describe what Derrida calls *différance*. On the other hand, *différance* is a more general process, not itself restricted to a 'syntactical stratum of metaphorics' but it does exhibit the same characteristics in its relation to metaphysics.

Once again, as with *différance*, metaphorics is necessarily overcome, effaced, covered up, hidden, repressed (even if only for a period of time) by what Derrida calls the 'irrepressible philosophic desire' or perhaps, more appropriately – the irrepressible desire for philosophy:

> The irrepressible philosophical desire – to summarize-interiorize-dialecticize-master-*relever* the metaphorical division between the origin and itself, the Oriental difference. (*Marges* 321; MP 269)

Thus it is clear that the death of metaphor in whatever sense this is understood, entails the resurrection, the resumption, the continuity, the history and the tradition of philosophy itself, as if it were its own proper foundation, as if it did not require metaphor, as if it could dispense with the very thing it excludes explicitly, in its own discourse, from its own discourse, as we have shown with the case of Aristotle.

Finally, it is clearly possible that there is a kind of contract, or a grammar, a law or a rule, perhaps even a principle which might articulate the relation between *metaphorics* and *metaphysics*, since the rotation of presence and absence is perhaps, as Derrida himself has suggested within metaphysics, a *regular occurrence*. This is of course work that is yet to be done.

Notes

[1] Jacques Derrida, *Marges de la Philosophie* (Paris: Editions de Minuit, 1972), p. 272 (MP 228).

[2] Derrida claims: '. . . the writer writes *in* a language and *in* a logic whose proper system, laws, and life his discourse by definition cannot dominate. He uses them only by letting himself, after a fashion and up to a point, be governed by the system. And the reading must always aim at a certain relationship, unperceived by the writer, between what he commands and what he does not command of the patterns of the language that he uses. This relationship is not a certain quantitative distribution of shadow and light, of weakness or of force, but a signifying structure that critical reading should *produce*' (OG 158).

[3] Aristotle, *The Poetics* (Cambridge: Harvard University Press, 1973), p. 81.

⁴ Aristotle, *Poetics*, p. 83.
⁵ Aristotle, *Poetics*, p. 91.
⁶ For more on this notion of the sign as 'the carrier of truth' see Derrida's essay entitled: 'Le facteur de la vérité' in *La Carte postale* (Paris: Aubier-Flammarion, 1980), pp. 439–524 (PC 413–96).

⁷ See Ricoeur's text: *La Metaphore vive* (Paris: Editions du Seuil, 1975) and also his brief but succinct discussion of 'Metaphor and Symbol' in *Interpretation Theory* (Fort Worth: The Texas Christian University Press, 1976), pp. 45–69. In particular with respect to this issue of the nonsense, he says: 'The metaphorical interpretation presupposes a literal interpretation which self-destructs in a significant contradiction. It is this process of self-destruction or transformation which imposes a sort of twist on the words, an extension of meaning thanks to which we can *make sense* where a literal interpretation would be *literally nonsensical*' (p. 50).

⁸ Aristotle distinguishes between a riddle and jargon with respect to the proper use of metaphors in the following way: 'By "unfamiliar" I mean a rare word, a metaphor, a lengthening, and anything beyond the ordinary use. But if a poet writes entirely in such words, the result will be either a riddle and if of rare words, jargon. The essence of a riddle consists in describing a fact by any *impossible combination of words. By merely combining the ordinary names of things this cannot be done, but it is made possible by combining metaphors.* For instance, "I saw a man wield bronze upon a man with fire", and so on. *A medley of rare words is jargon. We need a sort of mixture of the two*' (*Poetics*, p. 85).

⁹ See note 7 for Ricoeur's position on this issue and see Carl Hausman's text: *A Discourse on Novelty and Creation* (The Hague: Martinus Nijhoff, 1975). In particular see pp. 99–116 and for his articulation of this moment of 'nonsense' see p. 104 where Hausman says: 'A metaphor, then, calls attention to what, for established concepts, is not the case; and in so doing, it emphasizes a tension between determinate and familiar concepts. From the standpoint of the thinker or experiencing subject, it *disrupts* his conceptualization of the world. From the standpoint of the world already known it negates the past viewed as the *status quo*. And in offering an unprecedented meaning through disclosing a *gap* in a rational pattern: a metaphorical expression manifests itself to us as an instance of novelty.'

¹⁰ See Derrida's essay on Kant's *Third Critique*, 'Parergon' in *La Vérité en peinture* (Paris: Flammarion, 1978), pp. 19–168 (TP 15–147).

¹¹ Derrida makes the point in *Of Grammatology*: 'Heidegger brings it up also when in *Zur Seinsfrage*, for the same reason, he lets the word "being" be read only if it is crossed out (*kreuzweise Durchstreichung*). That mark of deletion is not, however, a "merely negative symbol" . . . . That deletion is the final writing of an epoch. Under its strokes the presence of a transcendental signified is effaced while still remaining legible' (OG 23). This process both Derrida and Heidegger refer to as 'being under erasure'.

¹² Derrida claims that: 'A name is proper when it has but a single sense. Better, it is only in this case that it is properly a name. Univocity is the essence, or better the *telos* of language. No philosophy as such has ever renounced this Aristotelian ideal. This ideal is philosophy' (*Marges* 295; MP 247: trans. modified).

¹³ For more on this debate over the primacy of the syntactical or the semantic see the *Proceedings* from the conference on 'La Communication', at the Université de Montréal – 1971: *La Communication II: Actes du XVe Congrès de l'Association des Sociétés de Philosophie de Langue Française* (Montreal: Editions Montmorency, 1973), pp. 393–431.

¹⁴ For more on the significance of the gesture of exclusion according to Derrida see OG 2, 39 and 31, for example. See also his *La Voix et le phénomène* (Paris: Presses Universitaires de France, 1967), pp. 100 and 102 (SP 90 and 92), for instance.

¹⁵ See Derrida's text, *Positions* (Paris: Editions de Minuit, 1967), p. 14 (P 6).

¹⁶ Derrida claims: 'This metaphorics is of course articulated in a specific syntax; but as a metaphorics it belongs to a *more general syntax*, to a more extended system that equally constrains Platonism [as well as Descartes]; everything is illuminated by this system's sun, the sun of absence and presence, blinding and luminous, dazzling' (*Marges* 319; MP 267: my emphasis).

CHAPTER 8

Time after Time: Temporality, Temporalization

Timothy Clark

This paper attempts two things. First a consideration of the question 'what is time?' through a deconstructive reading of Heidegger's *Being and Time* (1927) and *Time and Being* (1961). The privileging of Heidegger on this question reflects Derrida's consideration of the Heideggerian meditation as uncircumventable and the only 'thought excess of metaphysics as such' (MP 62). Secondly, therefore, the 'relation' of Heidegger and Derrida is to be examined, guided by Rodolphe Gasché's recent discussion of this issue.[1] If Heidegger's thought remains bound by a certain phenomenology then one should attempt to trace the manner in which, through Derrida, something completely *other* than any phenomenon imposes its necessity. Rather than assuming Derrida's break with 'presence' as an act of faith, therefore, this essay is deliberately *slow motion*, following the insistence of this something other as it disrupts received metaphysical accounts of time.

I

The aim of the latter sections of *Being and Time* is to analyse human *Dasein* in such a way as to demonstrate that a non-conceptualized 'primordial' temporality is the condition of existence and of the presencing of any entity in a world. The temporality of *Dasein*, Heidegger believed at this time, would provide the basis for an analysis of the temporality of Being itself. Derrida's description of *Being and Time* as a 'breakthrough' (MP 62) would rest on the insistence that temporality be no longer conceived in an accidental external mode, as a medium 'in which' entities happen to be or into which they have 'fallen'. Being itself, rather, will have to be considered as rendered irreducibly finite through a structure of temporality that produces it. Heidegger demands an interrogation of the 'vulgar' concept of time as set forth in metaphysics from Aristotle to Henri Bergson. Furthermore time can no longer be assumed merely as the *object* of the ontological question 'what is x?'. Rather classical ontology will be shown to be established already on an understanding of the *is* according to a certain mode of time – the present. Metaphysics and a certain conception of time are mutually implicated; consequently, to overthrow the latter through an analysis of *Dasein*'s temporality would be to disrupt ontology at its very basis. This would be, then, what Derrida describes as 'The extraordinary trembling to which classical ontology is subjected in *Sein und Zeit* . . .' (MP 63).

Heidegger's argument that the determination of Being as presence has been decisive in metaphysics is instanced in an account of the Aristotelian notion of substance (*ousia*) as the being of any entity, that which remains in permanent being throughout any process of change it may undergo. *Parousia* or *ousia* signify 'in ontologico-Temporal terms "presence" ("*Anwesenheit*")' (BT, p. 47). The early sections of *Being and Time* thus announce a project of *Destruction* (De-layering):

> . . . we shall show that whenever Dasein tacitly understands and interprets something like Being, it does so with *time* as its standpoint . . . . The Fact remains that time, in the sense of 'being (*sein*) in time', functions as a criterion for distinguishing realms of Being. Hitherto no one has asked or troubled to investigate how time has come to have this distinctive ontological function or with what right anything like time functions as such a criterion . . . . (BT, p. 39)

'Destruction', in *Being and Time* (the term has a slightly different application in later Heidegger) will be an analysis of the manner in which certain notions of Being and time are co-implicated and their origination in a more 'primordial' temporality which they dissimulate even in their derivativeness.

The fundamental trait of the traditional description of time is that it is taken merely as one entity among others. It appears, in Aristotle and later in Hegel, as part of the science of Nature. Its determination, therefore, rests on a preconception of what it means *to be* at all, this being unthinkingly derived from the present. To be is to be present or to endure in this presence. To be 'out' of time would thus mean to be 'perpetually present elsewhere', eternity as the *nunc stans*. As Derrida observes, 'From Parmenides to Husserl, the privilege of the present has never been put into question. It could not have been. It is what is self-evident itself . . .' (MP 34).

Heidegger anticipates an analysis of Aristotle's notion of time in Book IV of the *Physics*, chosen as an exploration of the basis and the constituting (internal) limits of 'the ancient science of Being' (BT, p. 48). It is this destruction that the footnote to section 432 both sketches and anticipates. Derrida's account will supplement Heidegger's in both fulfilling this project *and* delimiting it according to Heidegger's own Aristotelianism. This repetition and delimitation performed in both Aristotle and *Being and Time* will provide Derrida with a '*formal rule*' concerning the relations of any metaphysical text to its limits. This 'formal rule', moreover, 'must be capable of guiding our reading of the entire Heideggerian text itself' (MP 62).

Chapters ten to fourteen of Book IV of the *Physics* are the scene of Aristotle's attempt to *derive* time from the nature of change and ultimately the line (*grammè*) as a spatial model of the path of change. For Aristotle the problems associated with time will be resolved if it is understood that 'time is logically and ontologically dependent on changes' (Hussey, p. 139). The analysis of time thus *follows* the account of change in Books II and III of the *Physics* in both order of analogy and order of the text.

Aristotle's attempt to *derive* time is partly a consequence of the *aporia* in the thought of time which he reproduces in the opening of chapter ten. This is essentially a rehearsal of one of the famous paradoxes of Zeno (see MP 50).² Derrida's account of *Physics IV*, strategically employing this paradox as that which Aristotle essentially repeats in trying to exclude, constitutes the most powerful example of the serious attention devoted to Zeno recently. The *aporia* arises in thinking time on the basis of the now (*nun*), which has the paradoxical consequence of excluding the temporal altogether. For the temporality of time will not inhere in the instant itself, but only in so far as the instant is evanescent, giving way to another now. 'The now is given simultaneously as that which is *no longer* and as that which is *not yet*. It is what it is not, and is not what it is' (MP 39). Time thus cannot be said to *be* in the form of presence. No division of any duration into a series of nows will give time. Zeno's paradox most explicitly relating to time, the 'Arrow', runs as follows. Zeno argues that an arrow in flight is always in fact static. If any instant of the arrow's motion from A to B is taken, the arrow, occupying at that instant a space equal to itself, will be still. No motion can be conceived as occupying the instant, for it would thus encompass duration and cease to be a now. Thus, at no point of its flight path can the arrow be said to move. The motion either does not take place or it takes place somehow *between* one instant and another, i.e. in no time at all. Zeno, as a pupil of Parmenides, is said to have employed this argument to demonstrate that time and change are unreal and all that truly exists is the 'One'.³ Aristotle's problem is to show at which point the argument is false. The specific problem in regard to time is that the paradox follows from the assumption that time is composed of parts, that is, time thought in terms of the priority of the indivisible now.

At this point Derrida cites the Heideggerian argument concerning the 'vulgar' concept of time. The specific aim of Heidegger's footnote, to demonstrate the decisive affiliation between Aristotle's *aporia* and Hegel's deduction of time from the inherent self-contradictoriness of the instant, need not be of concern here. The issue is that time, in this *aporia*, is being determined according to an understanding of Being derived from the temporal *present*. The question, 'what *is* time?' is really the question 'what – of time – is (present)?' Accordingly only the now *is*, leaving time and change in the realm of non-existents. Similarly to assert (as Zeno would) the non-existence of time is possible *only* on the basis of the present as a mode of time. Derrida recapitulates this circle:

> In order to state the no-thingness of time, one already has had to appeal to time, to a precomprehension of time, and within discourse, to the self-evidence and functioning of the verb's tenses . . . . Being has been determined temporally as being-present in order to determine time as nonpresent and nonbeing (MP 50–51).

Later in 'Ousia and *Grammè*', Derrida will suggest that *Being and Time* itself does not escape the consequences of the determination of Being as presence and that Heidegger will be found also going round in circles. At this point therefore, a brief account is necessary of the temporality which Heidegger opposes to the 'vulgar' concept of time.

II

Heidegger argues that the 'vulgar' notion of time is derived from a 'levelling-off' of a more authentic mode of temporality. He thus establishes a dichotomy of the authentic and inauthentic. The latter is the seemingly objective series of successive moments, quantifiable according to a duration whose measure is a regular paradigm change (for Aristotle the motion of celestial bodies). In effect this is the 'public time' measured by the clock and as 'days' and 'years'. The sophistication of the measurement is an irrelevance to the ontological issues at stake. The traditional notion is that of a time which

> – whether conceived mechanically or dynamically or in terms of atomic decay
> – is the dimension of the quantitive or qualitative calculation of duration as a sequential progression.[4]

Two of the more straightforward objections to the 'inauthentic' conception of time appear in *Being and Time* as follows. First, 'public time' seems to be blandly neutral, excluding the themes of finitude and transience usually associated with time – 'Why do we say that time *passes away* when we do not say with *just as much* emphasis that it arises?' (BT, p. 478). Considered as a sequence of quantifiable periods, however, this thought of transience would be indifferent. Second, the time of physics does not give the asymmetry of the temporal – 'it is incomprehensible in itself why this sequence should not present itself in the reverse direction' (BT, p. 478).

In seeking a more 'authentic' time in the temporality of *Dasein*, Heidegger's analysis is above all a refusal to think 'man' or 'consciousness' on the basis of *substance* (the *res cogitans*, for instance, which Descartes affirms with the *res extensa* of space). It is a question of phenomena from which the traditional subject-object opposition is merely derived.[5] 'Existing is always factical' (BT, p. 236). *Dasein* obeys the structure of an *always already thrownness* into a world always previously disclosed to it. Before any thought that might conceive itself as a subject over against an object there is facticity as the already given co-implication of a being with a world (*Da-sein* 'there-being'). Consequently, as David Krell points out, 'It is impossible to envisage a *Dasein* that is wholly present . . .'.[6] It eschews the self-reflexivity that might be ascribed to thought's supposed identity with itself. The temporality that constitutes *Dasein* is *the mode* in which entities are opened to its circumspection as being-there.[7] In effect, the instant is not in any sense simple in the manner of an entity merely present-at-hand, but a complex synthesis (without unification) of movements that could only provisionally be termed 'anticipation' or 'retrospection'. Neither of those could be called in any sense *acts* of *Dasein* as a *subject*, rather they describe the structure of existence itself. Heidegger gives a phenomenological description of this primordial temporality in its mundane obviousness. The 'now' is primarily 'datable' in that it is implicated in a concern whose references are future and past:

> When we use a clock in ascertaining what o'clock it is, *we say* – whether explicitly or not – 'It is *now* such and such an hour and so many minutes; *now* is the time for . . .' or 'there is still time enough *now* until . . .' . . . the 'now' has in each case already been understood and *interpreted* in its full structural content of datability, spannedness, publicness and worldhood. This is so 'obvious' that we take no note of it whatsoever; still less do we know anything about it explicitly. (BT, p. 469)

Heidegger's hermeneutic of *Dasein*, while remaining a phenomenology (see below), nevertheless has the effect of a considerable complication of the instant, the evident itself. This complication should be allowed to make its full impact before moving on to Derrida's demonstration of the necessity of thinking something *other* than phenomenality in any mode. The temporality of *Dasein*, as that which constitutes the evidence of any phenomenon in the context of a world, is the original 'outside-itself'. Time is *ecstatic* in the sense of *ec-stasis* as 'standing-outside-itself'. Temporality has no substantial identity, it is merely an interweaving of the 'future', the 'having been' and the 'present' as *ecstases* of time. 'Temporality "is" not an *entity* at all. It is not, but it temporalizes itself' (BT, p. 377).

Derrida's critique of *Being and Time* would be a deconstruction of the authentic/inauthentic dichotomy. This is largely implied (MP 63). Its implication, however, can be made effective upon Heidegger's account of the relative *priority* to be granted to the temporal ecstases that constitute *Dasein*'s openness to a world. The future 'has a priority in the ecstatical unity of primordial and authentic temporality' (BT, p. 378). Heidegger grants the future to be the *'primary phenomenon'* of temporality (BT, p. 378). A prior disclosedness of the future constitutes 'understanding' as a 'fundamental *existentiale*' (BT, p. 385) of *Dasein*. 'Disclosedness' as the basis for any understanding of a world is thus inseparable from the fact that *Dasein* is always already *thrown* into a world, already *pro*jected in it. Its structure is thus 'ahead-of-itself-in-Being-already-in' (BT, p. 236). This priority of the futural is not just a contingent element in the account that could be either retained or discarded. Rather it sets up the entire project of *Being and Time*. The aim of a more fundamental ontology is based on *Dasein*'s vague *pre*-comprehension of the question of Being. The structure of prior-disclosedness thus allows the method of the entire hermeneutic of *Dasein*'s facticity; without it there could be no movement from the metaphysical determinations of time, space, etc. to the 'authentic' modes described by Heidegger. This *pro*ximity of *Dasein* to the question of what *is*, and its vague *pre*comprehension of Being is claimed to give 'destruction', as a hermeneutic of the everyday, something other than the mere circularity of the so-called hermeneutic circle. ('If we must first define an entity *in its Being*, and if we want to formulate the question of Being only on this basis, what is this but going in a circle?' (BT, p. 27)). The circle however is an open one and need not be circular if it is entered 'in a certain way'.

Derrida's analysis of *Physics IV*, however, in revealing the complicity between Heidegger's delimitation of Aristotle and the 'vulgar' concept of time, will eventually force the issue – is this priority of the future defensible and, if it isn't, can the notion of time be said to have a future at all?

III

Derrida's treatment of Aristotle resembles, at a first reading, little more than a model of scholarly meticulousness – a detailed insistence upon elements in *Physics IV* that Heidegger seems to have overlooked. However, if, as Derrida writes, Aristotle's account of time is *decisive*, in the context of an understanding of metaphysics as a series of *ethico-theoretical decisions*, then no succeeding thought of time, either that of common sense or of *Being and Time*, will be left unaffected by this scholarly close-reading.

'Having recalled why it may be thought that time is not a being, [the *aporia* arising from taking time as the now] Aristotle leaves the question in suspense' (MP 47). In this evasion, Derrida will argue, the metaphysical determination of time is constituted. The question, however, is the manner in which the *aporia* and the metaphysical determination will come to seem inseparable – both *paradoxa* and *doxa* constituted on the underlying privilege of the *circle*.

Having left the *aporia* of chapter ten, Aristotle repudiates the results of considering time along the analogy of a continuous path, divisible into nows, only to reconstitute the analogy with the line (*grammè*) in another manner. Time cannot be taken as identical with movement. Nevertheless, it is only in movement that any apprehension of time is given. Derrida quotes section 219a, 'Therefore it is clear that time neither *is* change nor is apart from change'. Time is thus considered as on the basis of an analogy with motion. *Analogy* is thus discreetly affirmed as that which relates time and space.

At the risk of being overschematic, it can be said that Derrida's analysis interrogates Aristotle on two fronts, the second only of which is concluded here, leaving the first to a later section. The *first* critique is that Aristotle has *given* himself the difference between space and time as if it were already evident. In fact close textual analysis reveals an unconceptualized 'temporalization' already at work in the account of space and time. This temporalization (MP 57) smuggles in a more primordial granting of space/time in a manner in which it is neither yet one nor the other. Derrida specifies the word *hama* at work in the account of the difficulties of time, a word whose meaning is 'together' – indifferently spatial *and* temporal ('together'/'at the same time'). No *aporia* could even be described *without* this prior *co*-implication of space and time *together*. Temporalization is discussed fully in the final section of this paper. For the moment a brief instance of its effects must suffice. Derrida reformulates the *aporia* according to which the nows cannot 'follow each other by immediately destroying one another' (that would give no time), nor can they *not* destroy each other in following (for any delay would be to grant intervallic nows *together/at the same time* as those already in existence), nor can they be all together in the same now for then 'things that occur at intervals of ten thousand years would be *together, at the same time*, which is absurd' (MP 56). Hence the *aporia*, 'denounced in the self-evidence' of the 'at the same time' (MP 56). The term 'follow' is doubtless equally symptomatic. The irreducible nature of temporalization, granting a certain time/space in advance of their metaphysical determination, is also at work in the notion of *analogy* or *co-respondence*. The word Derrida translates as 'correspond', *akolouthein*, is also 'to follow'; it is as 'follow' that *akolouthein* is translated in the recent edition of *Physics III-IV* in the Clarendon Aristotle (see Hussey, pp. 142–6). The irreducible nature of an *accompaniment*, a *with*, a *together*, as both (non) spatial and (non) temporal terms, is *temporalization*: 'the complicity, the common origin of time and space, appearing together (*comparaître*) as the condition for all appearing of Being' (MP 56). This is described in the final section.

Derrida's *second* strategy is to demonstrate the necessary circularity of Aristotle's attempt to derive time from a pre-given model of space. The *aporia* concerning the now is apparently resolved by analogy with the conception of change and motion as *entelecheia*, the transformation of the *potential* into the actual: 'if there is something which is actually x and potentially y, motion is the making actual of its y-ness'.[8] Building, for instance, is the actualization of a house from its brick and mortar. In effect, the process is conceived after, or according to, its *end*. As Heidegger has pointed out, Aristotle's coinage of *entelecheia* was probably directed by its containment of *telos* (EP, p. 6). Motion is *not* conceived as the (impossible) sum of (infinitely) divisible parts, nor time as a series of nows, but on the basis of a completed direction. Derrida's apparently reckless statement that 'time' has, fundamentally, never been conceived in any other mode, is at least borne out by Bergson's resolution of Zeno's problem,[9] in essence the same as Aristotle's:

> To suppose that the moving body *is* at a point of the course is to cut the course in two . . . and to substitute two trajectories for the single trajectory which we were first considering. (p. 64)

The immobile points are only 'potential' (p. 63). The resolution is achieved by insistence on the *unity* of the movement from A to B, not the traversal of an infinite series of intervening points across an infinite series of nows, but 'a single and unique bound' (p. 64). The number 'one' is paramount. A potential division would be 'to distinguish two successive acts where . . . there is only one'. If the bound is singular, however, this is only because it is being viewed from the anticipation of its completion.

Bergson's example makes explicit this inherent teleology in the understanding of time and motion: 'Suppose an elastic (*already*) stretched from A to B, could you divide its extension?' (pp. 63–4). Bertrand Russell's mathematical formulation and 'resolution' of Zeno is equally Aristotelian. The problem arises, Russell insists, only if one wants to *count* each potential fraction in the series $½ + ¼ + ⅛ + 1/16 \ldots$, that is to actualize them. In fact, of course, there is something 'beyond the whole of an infinite series . . . 1 is beyond the whole of the infinite series $½, ¾, ⅞, 15/16, \ldots$'.[10] In effect, in time and motion, all that *actually* exists is the 'one'. In regard to temporalization however, Derrida will bear out the claim that 'says the dyad as the minimum' (MP 56) adding a certain twist to the Aristotelian treatment of *two* as the smallest number (as the first to introduce plurality).

Aristotle's definition of time thus preserves the model of the line, but thought according to the priority of its ends. Time is 'number of movement in respect of the before and after' (220a, 25). In effect, Derrida argues, the underlying model of the continuity of the line is the circle. In motion an entity becomes what it is *actually* from what it was *potentially*. The origin (*arché*) of the movement is thus the same as its end (*telos*). This circularity inheres in the concept of *entelecheia* as 'having-(itself)-in-the-end' (EP, p. 6). As Derrida concludes, the pure *presence* of the point or the now (which necessarily excluded the co-presence of other points/nows) has not been broken but merely re-elaborated in the form of a circle. Moreover the line of time or motion, between *arché* and *telos*, is continuous only on the basis of this 'having-(itself)-in-the-end', its circularity:

> The *gramme* is *comprehended* by metaphysics between the point and the circle, between potentiality and the act (presence), etc.; and all critiques of the spatialization of time, from Aristotle to Bergson, remain within the limits of this comprehension. (MP 60)

Since its hidden basis is a re-elaboration of time as the simple 'now' or space as the indivisible point, one should not be surprised to find the original *aporia* (for which to think time as the 'now' was to exclude temporality) repeating itself in the apparent resolution. The analogy with movement as *entelecheia* has 'a double consequence as regards time' (MP 62). As the number of movement, time is part of 'non-Being, matter, potentiality, incompletion. Being in act, energy [*energeia*], is not time' (MP 62). This conclusion, however, must also *exclude* non-Being from time, for it is clearly *in* time that beings must have begun their existence and 'tend, like every potentiality, toward act and form' (MP 62). Time, then, is both on the side of beings and non-beings, as in the *aporia*. Derrida need not be explicit; this is also a circle. Circularity, therefore, seems to constitute metaphysical thought in this case as both its *doxa* and its *paradoxa*. Each, based on the determination of Being as presence, repeats the other in the same circle. The problem and the resolution of the problem seem the same.

In *Speech and Phenomena* (1967), in a discussion of the disruption which an attempt to conceive time brings to Husserl's phenomenology, Derrida writes: 'The word "time" itself, as it has always been understood in the history of metaphysics, is a metaphor which *at the same time* both indicates and dissimulates the "movement" of . . . auto-affection' (SP 85). Similarly time is both *submitted to* and *subtracted from* the Aristotelian text, 'belonging as much to the de-limitation of metaphysics as the thought of the present, as to the simple overturning of metaphysics' (MP 62). This play of subtraction and addition is suggested as a formal rule for reading metaphysics, a reading to take place within, yet also against, the 'Heideggerian breakthrough, which is the only thought excess of metaphysics as such' (MP 62). The issue of the circle, for instance, would lead to a questioning of 'that circle into which, Heidegger tells us so often, we must learn to enter in *a certain way*' (MP 60).

IV

The dichotomy of the inauthentic and authentic accounts of time, Derrida suggests, is precisely that aspect of *Being and Time* that is least an exit from metaphysics. The following reading might suggest itself. The teleological account of time and motion is a form of the circle to the extent to which its *end* is already effective in the origin. This might be called a priority of the futural in so far as it dictates the motif of a return into a full self-presence. The priority of the 'futural' in the temporal *ecstases* that constitute *Dasein* is similarly the function of a pervading teleology throughout *Being and Time*. (This correlation does not, as might appear, confuse a logical with a merely empirical priority of the future – i.e. *telos* as logically primary yet in experience last; the futural ecstasis, in however remote a sense, experiential. As is clear in regard to Heidegger's accounts of the basis of *logic* on a certain privilege of being as presence, the *existential* analytic would hold the more 'primordial' futurity.) The account of dread and the nothing in *Being and Time* remains sufficient warrant of the determination of *Dasein* and its temporality according, in both senses of the word, to its *end*. The authenticity of the authentic future (as opposed to the inauthentic future that merely waits for a present-to-be) is constituted through the anticipation of death and finitude. Not only is death (as against the mere perishing of an animal) peculiar to *Dasein*, but the awareness of it is a function of *Dasein*'s pre-ontological sense of Being. *Dasein* alone asks the fundamental question: 'Why are there essents, why is there anything at all, rather than nothing?'[11] The thought of death is inseparable from *Dasein*'s guiding sense of Being as distinct from entities. The questioning mode is determined as the proper, the authenticity, of *Dasein*. *Dasein* is 'distinguished by the fact that, in its very Being, that Being is an *issue* for it' (BT, p. 32). As Derrida argues in 'The Ends of Man', this functions as a *telos* in a manner familiar to all humanism – '*The thinking of the end of man . . . is always already prescribed in metaphysics, in the thinking of the truth of man*' (MP 121). The inauthentic/authentic dichotomy supports an account of temporality that remains the quest for an *arché*. Derrida's conclusion in 'The Ends of Man' implies the problem of thinking a future that would in no sense be an end:

> In the thinking and the language of Being, the end of man has been prescribed since always, and this prescription has never done anything but modulate the equivocality of the *end*, in the play of *telos* and death. (MP 134)

In conclusion, then, both Aristotle's account of time and the supposed delimitation of it given by Heidegger, are teleological, i.e. ultimately based on the determination of Being as 'authentic' presence (both as *arché* and *telos*). Not even *Being and Time* is exempt from Derrida's insistence that time is a metaphysical notion through and through:

> Time is that which is thought on the basis of Being as presence, and if something – which bears a relation to time, but is not time – is to be thought beyond the determination of Being as presence, it cannot be a question of something that still could be called *time*. (MP 60)

V

It remains to consider the idea of *temporalization* sketched briefly in '*Ousia* and *Grammè*'. Temporalization is there described as a 'complicity' or 'common origin of time and space, appearing together [*com-paraître*] as the condition for all appearing of Being' (MP 56).

Temporalization, as the condition for presence, must, above all, be distinguished from the notion of 'presencing', as distinct from the 'present', that regulates the later Heidegger, in particular the 1961 lecture, *Time and Being*. In a sense, or rather *to* sense, there *is* no distinction here, as Gasché demonstrates. Nevertheless the play of temporalization incorporates an element that is other to any movement of presencing, and indeed marginalizes it. This element, as a non-existent, escapes any thought of the meaning or being of time. It inheres in the logic that enables one to assert that the distance between Derrida's account of temporalization and the Heidegger of *Time and Being*, is both imperceptible and infinite.

Derrida sets out the structure of Heidegger's account of the distinction of presencing and presence (Being and entities) in the latter sections of 'Differance' (1968: MP 3–27, 23). While the *ontological difference*, the distinction of presencing and presence, regulates *Time and Being*, the play of this *difference* is nevertheless arrested by Heidegger. Heidegger's account of the giving of time/space may be schematized as follows. Being as presencing presents 'itself' *as* the world of entities, across the difference. As presence, the entity is the *withdrawal* of Being/presencing, which is not an existent. Being thus hides in the *a-letheia* or uncovering of its (non)manifestation as an entity. Moreover the difference between Being and entities is not only erasing in this structure but, further, the ontological difference itself is erased in the determinations of metaphysics. Metaphysics, forgetting the difference itself, construes Being only in terms of entities, as the ground of entities, and as an entity itself, the *summum ens* or *causa sui*. Being is thus doubly dissimulated/withdrawn in (*as*) presence.

Playing across the difference (self-)presencing is irreducibly duplex. This doubleness is expressed in *Time and Being* in the structure of a play of giving and the gift. Being, thought *other* than as the ground of entities, is the *es gibt* (*there is* (Being)), which in no sense *is*, as a presence, but rather give (itself) as presence. Being both gives and loses itself together:

> As the gift of this It gives, Being belongs to giving. As a gift, Being is not expelled from giving. Being, presencing is transmuted. As allowing-to-presence, it belongs to unconcealing [of entities], as the gift of unconcealing it is retained in the giving. (TB, p. 6)

The movement is in no sense reflexive in the sense of something simple effecting itself in a structure of auto-affection. It is a dissimulative fold that can never be symmetrical. Being gives and is what it is sent, but, in no sense an entity, it *withdraws* in this movement. Nor, as Gasché points out,[12] can one call this *self-withdrawal*: any entity of 'self' would already be a function of (self-withdrawal). This dissymmetric fold is thus the structure of the presence of any entity. In L.M. Vail's example, 'something comes to be present precisely as a rose. Ensconced in this "as" is the mysterious interplay of Identity and Difference'.[13] The rose *is*, as the luminous ensconcing of a withdrawal.

The account of time in *Time and Being* provides the most explicit instance of Heidegger's subjection of this logic of withdrawal and the gift to a certain *arrestation*. 'Time', as a notion, is a function of the double sense of the present – 'the present understood in terms of the now is not at all identical with the present in the sense in which guests are present' (p. 10). Time cannot be thought on the basis of the present as now since this leads to the familiar *aporia*: 'time cannot be found anywhere in the watch that indicates time' (p. 11). Nevertheless the dimensions of time can be thought in terms of presencing (*as* withdrawal). Neither the future nor the past can be said to be *quite* absent, Heidegger insists, although they are not presently present. The past is not merely a past now – 'even that which is no longer present presences immediately in its absence – in the manner of what has been, and still concerns us' (p. 13). Likewise the future 'never just begins since absence, as the presencing of what is not yet present, always in some way already concerns us' (p. 13). Thus 'Not every presencing is necessarily the present. A curious matter' (p. 13). Finally the present in the sense of now must be determined from the sense of presence as *Anwesen*. The latter, as the medium of the interplay of the three dimensions, is thus a fourth dimension of time, designated 'nearness'. The presencing of time, determined by 'nearness', is through a structure of delay and withholding withdrawal. It constitutes the past ('what has been') 'by denying its advent as present' and similarly 'keeps open the approach coming from the future by withholding the present in the approach'. If the rose *is* (in time) it is through the *knot-like* structure of the reciprocal interplay of the dimensions:

> ... futural approaching brings about what has been, what has been brings about futural approaching, and the reciprocal relation of both brings about the opening up of openness. (p. 15)

Thus the rose comes into its own. This reciprocal interplay is the possibility of any 'where' in general. 'With this presencing there opens up what we call time-space' (p. 14).

Derrida's query of *Time and Being* concerns 'The facility, and also the necessity, of the transition from the near to the proper' (MP 132), the near *as* the proper. This concerns Heidegger's delineation of the *es gibt* as 'the event of Appropriation' – the sending of Being and time into 'what is their own, namely . . . Being as presence and . . . time as the realm of the open'. Appropriation determines both as their essential 'belonging together' (p. 19). Nearness, however structured as withdrawal, determines presence as what is *proper* to it. As Derrida writes in 'The Ends of Man', concerning the movement of the gift, Being, as the *es gibt*, can only (not) manifest itself in the dissimulation of present entities:

> It remains that Being, which is nothing, is not a being, cannot be said, cannot say itself, except in the ontic metaphor. And the choice of one or another group of metaphors is necessarily significant. (MP 131)

The problems in conceiving 'metaphor' without the possibility of a literal (the *es gibt is* not (literal)) need not be the issue here.[14] Heidegger's 'metaphors' of *nearness, homecoming* and the open are all phenomenological. Phenomenality itself remains what Heidegger will not displace in the movement of the dissimulating gift. Withdrawal, and the withdrawal of withdrawal, nevertheless effect a coming into *presence* as the proper of Being's sending of itself. This privilege of the present is enabled by a determination of the proper of man as that entity 'nearest' to Being. This proximity is decisive. The very notion of Phenomenon as *'that-which-shows-itself-in-itself'* (BT, p. 51) already inscribes it. As Vail writes, man's reception of Being is unique in that, in this case, 'the apprehension and the showing form a unity.'[15] This co-propriety of man and Being, Derrida insists with characteristic scholarly care, 'is not to be taken in a metaphysical sense' (MP 133). Certainly, however, *no* metaphysics is imaginable without it. The togetherness of man and what is, in presence, constitutes *the* ethico-theoretical decision of philosophy. Man's authenticity, Heidegger affirms, is to stand in this proximity. The proper of Being, correspondingly, is its destining as the showing of presence to man – 'Propriety, the co-propriety of Being and man, is proximity as inseparability' (MP 133). Authenticity thus governs the lecture, its dichotomy of a false and 'true time' for instance. The notion of Appropriation thus functions as a *proto-telos*, and it arrests the potential dissimulation in the *es gibt* of Being's sending (itself) across the ontological difference. The proper of man and the proper of Being work normatively: 'we do not reside sufficiently where in fact we already are'.[16] We *are* not (yet) but we may become ourselves. How far is this determination of proximity from a thought of the *arché* and *telos*? Moreover, how far is temporality from being the line that is their relation? The proper determines time's dimensions as a convergence or *gathering* through which an entity comes into its own in the open of presence:

> True time ... is the arrival of that which has been. This is not what is past, but rather the gathering of essential being, which precedes all arrival in gathering itself into the shelter of what it was earlier, before the given moment.[17]

A great deal of Derrida's work has concerned a re-elaboration of the 'giving' in *es gibt* (missives, sending, despatches) as a dissimulative structure not halted by the magnetization of any proper (see SNS 117–19). Being as the *es gibt* (i.e., thought as other than as the ground of entities) gives itself across the ontological difference as the gift of Being *qua* presence of entities. Yet the *es gibt* (which *is* not in any sense) does not so become present but, in a movement which escapes classical logic while making it possible, withdraws in its (non)(self) (manifestation). If this movement is conceived without the arrestation of the proper as *telos* it becomes a structure in which presence and phenomenality lose all priority. 'Truth, unveiling, illumination are no longer decided in the appropriation of the truth of being, but are cast into its bottomless abyss as non-truth, veiling and dissimulation' (SNS 119). That the *es gibt* dissimulates is a necessary conclusion if showing as phenomenality is no longer determined as its end. 'Presence' can only become itself by a dissymmetric fold in which manifestation is withdrawal, its gain its loss.[18] This play must always exceed any thought of presence *as such* since it fissures the as such in advance. Nor can any origin be ascribed to this movement; presence can only 'begin' as its dissimulation. In Heidegger the difference between Being (as the *es gibt*) and the Being *of* entities, the ontological difference, is not yet Derrida's differ*a*nce because it is a relation determined by the question of the truth *of* Being – 'the difference *between* presence and the present'. As the passing (without arrival) of one into the other, differ*a*nce, is thus 'older' than Being itself (cf. 'Differance', MP 22) and eschews the possibility of the Heideggerian 'hope' of finding any *Ur-Wort* for Being. Delay and deferral and differentiation are prior to presence. The rose is not even the luminous knot of a withdrawal, but an expenditure that never quite comes into its own. It only *is* in so far as its roseness is a trace of what never was in the sense of essence.

As this last sentence indicates, the copula as a non-reflexive and non-originary fold has a very peculiar temporality. The *es gibt* as the 'giving' of space and time can only be conceived as 'temporalization'. What is called 'time' has the structure of an originary delay. However, both 'originary' and 'delay' must at once be qualified. 'Delay' is inaccurate to the extent that it suggests something 'present' that is held back rather than a 'delay' that, in constituting the present, only appears in so far as it is over. Nor is there anything 'originary' in this retro-action. It is *always already* over and thus both succeeds and precedes itself. In refuting Husserl's (continuous) model of time as the synthesis of protention and retention, Derrida submits the *aporia* of the now to the structure of (originary) deferral:

> It is not a matter of complicating the structure of time while conserving its homogeneity and its fundamental successivity . . . this model of successivity would prohibit a *Now* X from taking the place of *Now* A, for example, and would prohibit that, by a delay that is inadmissible to consciousness, an experience be determined, in its very present, by a present which would not have preceded it immediately but would be considerably 'anterior' to it. (OG 67)

Heidegger's preference for the present perfect tense in his account of 'true time' (the 'has been') constitutes a privileging of the present. Derrida's preferred tense is a displaced future perfect. The present is always already what *it will have been*. It is not (yet), but it also has already been and is no longer. The structure of retro-action (strategically reinscribed from Freud – see 'Differance', MP 21), and the structure of movement without arrival or departure in the *es gibt*, forbid the present ever to be anything but *what will have been*. Only this tense suffices to describe a fold that may never fold back on itself. 'Time' eschews any circular reduction and is that which folds itself (another) onto another (itself). The fold is always *over* in this irreducible contamination of sameness and alterity. Similarly there is no unity in a present, but a 'singular plural, which no simple origin will ever have preceded' (D 304). Thought as any sort of line, 'time' may only have the form of that line described by Philippe Sollers in a passage from *Nombres*: *'The line now no longer closes up into a point or a circle ("science is the circle of circles") and also no longer rejoins its own repetition'* (quoted in D 352–3).

The notion of temporalization limits any thought of permanence as the extension of an unfissured *now*. 'Presence', as the trace of its disappearance, and an opening to an absolute past, forbids any entity the proposition '"*I am immortal*"' (SP 54). In 'Limited Inc' (1977) Derrida insists that 'permanence' must be reinscribed as 'remaining', a notion of the similar that always already includes alteration, rendering 'all absolute permanence impossible' (LI 54).

If the present is possible only on the basis of an *absolute past* (a past that has never been (present)), what of the future? This can no longer be conceived in terms of an *end* or as a present to-come (*l'avenir*). In the brief account of temporalization in *Of Grammatology* Derrida affirms that the 'future' no less divides a present from itself than the past (OG 66). This, however, is a direction not followed in *Grammatology*. It would 'risk' effacing the 'passivity' of 'time', presumably a precautionary move to dissociate the movement of temporalization from any notion of 'intentionality' such as directs Husserl's account of time. The question of a to-come that is not a present coming, or a restitution (presence not yet), is opened in the essay, 'Of an Apocalyptic Tone Recently Adopted in Philosophy' (1984). That which might be despatched towards a present (the missives of an Apocalyptic text for instance) obeys the abyssal structure of all sending as presencing. Destiny as a destining from the future can be considered the summons of a 'come'. Sending is fissured by the dissimulative movement of the gift which, thought without 'proper' arrival *as* presence, renders the 'come' destitute of destination or origin:

> It leaps [*saute*] from one place of emission to the other (and a place is always determined *starting from* the presumed emission); it goes from one destination, one name, and one tone to the other; it always refers to (*renvoie à*) the name and to the tone of the other that is there but as having been there and before yet coming . . . . (OAT 27)

The 'come', never present except as the shuttle of the not-yet and having-been, is not subject to ontological determination. This ontological trembling appears as a tonal instability. 'Come' may be said in any tone – 'imperative', as a 'jussive modality', or 'a performative' (OAT 34): 'Come [*Viens*] beyond being – this comes from beyond being and calls beyond being . . .' to and from *no* proper end, only 'a drift [*une dérive*] underivable from the identity of a determination' (OAT 34). The summons is plural and without destination or origin. It is the end of any *telos*, the 'apocalypse without apocalypse', 'truth' or 'revelation'. Any eschatology could only operate as a function of the greater play of a chance which would disrupt it and which it could never govern.

VI

To conclude, if one determines to use the word 'time' at all it will have to have been thought 1) without the present 2) without permanence and 3) without *telos*, or restitution, or direction. Above all, it must have been thought outside the conjunction with Being (either *Being and Time* or *Time and Being*).

Abbreviations

(Dates of original publication are given in brackets, unless already in the main text).

BT   *Being and Time*, trans. John Macquarrie and Edward Robinson (Oxford: Basil Blackwell, 1980).

EP   *The End of Philosophy* (1961), trans. Joan Stambaugh (London: Souvenir Press, 1975).

Hussey   *Aristotle's Physics: Books III and IV*, trans. with notes Edward Hussey. Clarendon Aristotle Series (Oxford: Clarendon Press, 1983). All references to Aristotle are to this edition.

TB   *Time and Being*, trans. Joan Stambaugh (New York: Harper and Row, 1972).

Notes

[1] Rodolphe Gasché, 'Joining the Text, from Heidegger to Derrida' in Jonathan Arac, Wlad Godzich, Wallace Martin (eds), *The Yale Critics: Deconstruction in America* (Minneapolis: University of Minnesota Press, 1983), pp. 156–75.

[2] See *Zeno's Paradoxes*, ed. Wesley C. Salmon (Indianapolis and New York: The Bobbs-Merrill Company Inc., 1970).

[3] See Plato, *Parmenides*, 128b.

[4] 'Language in the Poem: A Discussion of Georg Trakl's Poetic Work' (1953), in *On the Way to Language*, trans. Peter D. Hertz (New York: Harper and Row, 1971), pp. 159–98, 176.

[5] '*Dasein* is not simply the man of metaphysics' (MP 124).

[6] 'Rapture: The Finitude of Time in Heidegger's Thought', in David Wood and Robert Bernasconi (eds), *Time and Metaphysics* (Coventry: Parousia Press, 1982), pp. 121–60, 123.

[7] As Otto Pöggeler observes, 'Being is no longer revealed by the *intuitus*, which is oriented toward seeing and directed toward the being-present of what is present-at-hand, nor even by Husserl's *intentio*'; 'Being as Appropriation', in Michael Murray (ed.), *Heidegger and Modern Philosophy* (New Haven and London: Yale University Press, 1978), pp. 84–115, 90.

[8] Sir David Ross, *Aristotle* (1923; rpt London: Methuen, 1964), p. 81.

[9] 'The Cinematographic View of Becoming' (1911), in *Zeno's Paradoxes*, ed. Salmon, pp. 59–66.

[10] 'The Problem of Infinity Considered Historically' (1929), in *Zeno's Paradoxes*, ed. Salmon, pp. 45–58, 49.

[11] Martin Heidegger, *An Introduction to Metaphysics* (1935), trans. Ralph Manheim (New Haven and London: Yale University Press, 1959), p. 1.

[12] Gasché, 'Joining the Text', p. 157.

[13] L.M. Vail, *Heidegger and Ontological Difference* (Philadelphia: Pennsylvania State University Press, 1972), p. 115.

[14] For Derrida's elaboration of this problem see 'The *Retrait* of Metaphor', *Enclitic*, 2:2 (1978), 5–34.

[15] Vail, *Heidegger and Ontological Difference*, p. 14.

[16] Martin Heidegger, *Identity and Difference* (1957), trans. Joan Stambaugh (New York: Harper and Row, 1969), p. 33.

[17] 'Language in the Poem', p. 176.

[18] 'The present can only present itself as such by relating back to itself; it can only aver itself by severing itself, only reach itself if it breaches itself, (com)plying with itself in the angle, along a break [*brisure*] (*brisure*: 'crack' and 'joint' created by a hinge in the work of a locksmith. *Littré*); in the release of the latch or the trigger. Presence is never present. The possibility – or the potency – of the present is but its own limit, its inner fold, its impossibility – or its impotence'; 'Dissemination' (1969), in D 289–360, 302–3.

CHAPTER 9

Circumcising Confession: Derrida, Autobiography, Judaism

Jill Robbins

On Jewish Philosophy

At the first Colloquium of French Jewish Intellectuals in 1960, Emmanuel Levinas gave a talk devoted to Franz Rosenzweig entitled 'Between Two Worlds'. He drew attention to Rosenzweig's 'spiritual biography', to the fact that Rosenzweig stood on the threshold of conversion to Christianity before he turned back to Judaism. Rosenzweig said *no* to the inherited prejudices of post-Emancipation Judaism, to the Pauline tropes of literalism and legalism; he persevered in Judaism in the face of Christianity's proselytizing mission. In this way Rosenzweig's itinerary is a distinctively modern Jewish one, which fully acknowledges the facticity of assimilation (BTW 181). Levinas is particularly impressed with 'the force in Rosenzweig that could resist *both* the seductions of Christianity and also the seductions of philosophy' (Franz Rosenzweig 52). In other words, Rosenzweig's achievement is not only that he resisted being a protagonist in a drama of salvation, in a narrative of conversion (and the temptation resisted is, in the terms of one of Levinas's talmudic readings, no less than the Christian structure of temptation in general, or the very structure of philosophical experience), but also that, to mark this certain *return*, Rosenzweig wrote *The Star of Redemption,* a Jewish book and a book that challenged philosophy's totalizing pretensions, or the philosophies of the All. Levinas, who will articulate his own challenge to philosophy's totalizing pretensions in the name of the other, writes in the preface to his first major book, *Totality and Infinity*, 'we were impressed by the opposition to the idea of totality in Franz Rosenzweig's *Stern der Erlösung*, a work too often present in this book to be cited' (TI 28), thus acknowledging a debt so massive that it cannot be acknowledged.

Rosenzweig's near conversion to Christianity and 'turn back' to Judaism deserves further comment, because it is not, ultimately, the story of a conversion. Is it a story at all? Is it not the story of *an event* – however decisive – *that did not happen*? How to think this event? More like an interruption of conversion than a conversion, it is a partial turn (*versio*) rather than a turn all the way around (*conversio*), a circumventing of conversion, of the *circus* of the return to oneself as another. Again, the event (if it is one), related solely in the text of Rosenzweig's correspondence, is marked by the writing of *The Star of Redemption*. He wrote neither a first-person autobiographical account of his experience nor a conversion narrative, the narrative of a self that recounts how it came to be itself, although his commentators can't help writing one for him.[1] Levinas himself is not immune to this temptation: within his essay's third-person narrative account of Rosenzweig's 'spiritual biography' he acknowledges that Rosenzweig's life would 'tempt' a hagiographer (BTW 181). In short, the *storial* character of Rosenzweig's conversion may be a narrative – autobiographical or biographical – exigency.

But this exigency is not merely formal: it is a concrete hermeneutical issue of the access to Judaism, a question with which Levinas's reading of Rosenzweig is preoccupied. For Levinas, the way in which Rosenzweig arrives at Judaism is significant, via a 'double movement' (BTW 182) or a double detour that passes necessarily through the Christian, and which in the process undoes the negative and privative interpretation of Judaism within Christianity and reinscribes it. Modern Jewish philosophies, I contend, cannot think themselves *as* Jewish without this relay through, this going by way of, the Christian. Moreover, the distinctive sense of Judaic religion that Rosenzweig's hermeneutic opens up is significant. As Rosenzweig suggests by his reading of the Jewish liturgical calendar, Judaic religion hides or shelters an originary significance, which is, as Levinas puts it, ontological. It is concerned with the fundamental structures of existence and the irreducible relations or conjunctures between God and the world, God and man, and man and world. The task of *making explicit* this significance, of retrieving the forgotten philosophical (or 'Greek', if you will) dimension of Judaic religion is admittedly enormous, and its consequences will involve no less than a radical putting into question of philosophical systematicity and totalization, the tracing of an alternative intelligibility. All of modern Jewish philosophy can be said to take up this task, and whether we call it a translation from Hebrew into Greek, a hermeneutic, or a certain deconstruction, this project remains singularly indebted – in a debt so measureless that it seems to necessitate a kind of ingratitude – to Rosenzweig.

(Temptation of) Temptation

Levinas's Rosenzweig address was delivered one year before the 1961 publication of *Totality and Infinity*. In 1964 he delivered to the same audience his reading of the talmudic tractate *Shabbath* 88a–88b, entitled 'The Temptation of Temptation'. Both lectures reflect Levinas's professional commitment to Judaism during the postwar years, when he served as Director of the Ecole Normale Israélite Orientale, a branch of the Alliance Israélite Universelle, which sought to train teachers of Jewish education in North Africa. Both were later collected in what Levinas terms his 'confessional' writings, which he keeps separate from his philosophical works.[2] Ultimately, as I have argued elsewhere, this distinction between the philosophical and the confessional writings is not absolute. The philosophical works strongly suggest – by way of allusion to and citation of biblical and talmudic texts – that

Levinas's ethical thought of responsibility to the other finds its precedent in the classical texts of Judaism. Similarly, the confessional works register the ethical preoccupations of his phenomenological texts of the same time period.

Levinas argues that the repression of, or allergy to, 'the other that remains other' (T 346) is manifested not just throughout the tradition of the history of philosophy, but on every level of philosophical conceptuality, where it is called being, totality, self, Same, and even, as Levinas does in the preface to *Totality and Infinity*, 'war'. (Levinas's usage, which intends a technical reference to philosophy's tendency to think in terms of warring oppositions and its concomitant violence also refers necessarily to *the* war.) Levinas seeks to reawaken the thought of the ethical from the torpor into which it has fallen by writing at once within and against the very philosophical idiom that habitually suppresses transcendence.

The ethical relation, as Levinas describes it, is a relation *without* relation. It maintains the distance of infinite separation, 'without this distance destroying this relation and without this relation destroying this distance' (TI 41). Levinas insists on its radical asymmetry. The other is not my equal, at least not on the originary – that is, nonempirical, quasi-transcendental – level at which Levinas's description takes place. Moreover, this encounter with the other is not something that can be thought or spoken about as if one were observing two entities from the outside (an antihypostatizing tendency that can also be seen in Rosenzweig's thinking of relation and conjunction). Levinas rarely speaks of the same *and* the other; his descriptions proceed from me *to* the other, and they enact as well as describe the obligation that ensues.

If, in Levinas's descriptions, the self relates first of all and most of the time to an alterity that is finite – a structure he also describes as 'identification', the I's tendency to absorb otherness into its identity as thinker or possessor – the encounter with the other, the infinite alterity of which Levinas calls *face*, interrupts the self's habitual economy. Its tendency towards possession and power and, ultimately, its murderous tendency are checked. This cessation of the self's habitual tendency is, in positive terms, its becoming gift and discourse, forms of nonadequation in which asymmetry and separation are maintained. The ethical discourse is one that never speaks *about* the other, but only *to* him or her, that relates to the other as interlocutor.

This interruption or calling into question of the self is precisely what Levinas means by *ethics,* and here one should note the remove of Levinas's use of the term from its ordinary senses of right conduct, a set of moral precepts, or any particular morality.[3] Prior to the elaboration of all moral precepts, the interruption *opens* ethics. Moreover, when consciousness is put into question by the face, this is not reducible to a consciousness – or an awareness – *of* being put into question (T 352). This means that ethics, in Levinas's radical sense, is not the result of any kind of cognition; it does not proceed from the initiative of a subject. It ruins the subject.

When the term *religion* is introduced in Levinas's philosophical writings, it is in as mediate and removed a way as his use of the term *ethics*: 'we propose to call religion the bond [*le lien*] that is established between the same and the other without constituting a totality' (TI 40). Levinas thinks religion *as* (nontotalizing) relation, in a manner that draws him close to Rosenzweig. But since the originary or proto-religion that Levinas describes cannot be equivalent to any positive religion, the question arises: what is its relation to positive religions, and specifically to Judaism?

Levinas's 'confessional' writings provide in effect an extended answer to this question when they seek to render explicit the hidden resources of Judaism. These resources are hidden to the extent that they have been covered up by the negative and privative determinations of the Judaic within the dominant conceptuality in the West. There the central achievements of Judaism – such as the law and the Talmud – seem lacking or unintelligible. For example, the law is a yoke, a legalism, a Pharisaical obsession with positive and negative commandments (an interpretation of Judaism that Rosenzweig, on the threshold of conversion to Christianity, knew only too well). The Talmud, with its nonexpository logic, is alien and bewildering. But Levinas detaches the terms for the Judaic from their negative determination and from the dyadic hierarchy in which they are invariably found; he reinscribes the subordinated terms so as to bring out their positive force, even the alternative intelligibility they harbour. For example, the observance of the law in traditional Judaism is not a yoke but an originary ethical orientation, a ceaseless reminder of the obligation towards, in the biblical diction, 'the stranger, the widow, the orphan'. The law does not mean servitude but freedom, although not in the Enlightenment sense of this term: it denotes something as contradictory in its terms as a heteronomous freedom. The Talmud, beneath the aridity of some of its discussions, dissimulates an unwavering preoccupation with the ethical.

For Levinas, the Talmud dissimulates not just an ethical discourse but, more specifically, a 'philosophical' discourse, an alternative intelligibility that is antitotalizing and that goes against the grain of the dominant philosophical conceptuality in the West. This is to say that within Levinas's confessional writings, the Talmud, written in Hebrew, as it were, dissimulates a 'Greek' dimension. Conversely, insofar as Levinas's philosophical writings make reference to 'Hebrew' ethics, they do so necessarily in 'Greek', as Derrida suggests in his 1963 essay 'Violence and Metaphysics'. In short, what Levinas had described in Rosenzweig as a double movement, first towards Christianity, then towards Judaism, that is, as a necessary confrontation with Christian conversion, could be formulated with regard to Levinas's hermeneutic of Judaism as a necessary intrication of 'Hebrew' ethical thought in the 'Greek'. It is as if the very distinction between Hebrew and Greek can only be thought from within the 'Greek'.

Nowhere in the confessional writings is this more evident than in 'The Temptation of Temptation'. The starting point for the talmudic text that Levinas reads is the scriptural verse immediately prior to the giving of the law: 'And the people stood at the foot of [literally, 'under'] the mountain' (Exod. 19:17). After remarking that God held the mountain over the people's heads and threatened to drop it on them if they did not accept the law, the rabbinic commentators point to, as a cross-reference, another scriptural verse that relates the people's words following the donation of the law and affirming their acceptance of it: 'And the people said: all that the Lord has spoken we will do and we will obey [*n'aseh venishmah*; literally, 'hear, hearken']' (Exod. 24:7). As the rabbinic commentators read these words, the syntactical order signifies a temporal order: the people did the law first and then heard it, or understood it.

Levinas comments that this indeed looks like a blind adherence to an authoritarian and violent order. Not only is it against the order of reason – for generally we want to understand what we do, thus to understand before we do – but it seems a denial of freedom. This lack of clear judgment and rational calculation, this naïveté, would be all the more unfortunate because Israel never seems to keep the law well enough.[4] Why, then, is 'doing before understanding' praised throughout the rabbinic reading, even exalted as an angelic secret? Perhaps, Levinas asserts, because this mode of relation to the law is 'older' than naïve spontaneity; perhaps consciousness is not its own precondition; perhaps freedom does not begin in freedom (TT 49). When the people announce at the foot of Mount Sinai, 'we will do and [then] we will understand', they perform a relationship to the law that does not proceed by trial and error, that does not 'try' the law first or subject it to rational examination before adherence to it. Doing before understanding, like the ethical relation to the face that speaks, 'is a movement towards the other which does not come back to its point of origin' (TT 48). In both cases, the obligation is immediate; it does not go by way of comprehension or the theoretical.

To summarize, then: in terms of Levinas's expanded conception of '*tenter*', what tempted Rosenzweig about Christianity, was not any doctrinal content but the structure of temptation itself. What is tempting is not this or that particular pleasure or temptation but the life of temptation that structures Christian existence, even, Levinas remarks, the lives of its very saints. What is tempting is a model for a self that can undergo the extremes of self-alienation and self-loss and still return to itself, as another, as an 'I', identifying itself. The temptation of temptation is the structure not only of personal experience but, as we have seen, of philosophical experience, of a certain conception of knowledge, with its built-in distance, its 'merciless demand to bypass nothing', and its refusal of the 'dangerous generosity' of 'we will do and we will understand' (TT 35). As Levinas's 'Jewish philosophy' formulates it, doing before understanding announces a relation to the law that is *not* tempted by temptation.

How Not to Do Typology

While Jacques Derrida is the author of a number of texts dealing with theological and Jewish matters, including 'Violence and Metaphysics' (1963), 'Of an Apocalyptic Tone Recently Adopted in Philosophy' (1980), 'How Not to Speak' (1987), *Schibboleth* (1986), as well as a number of texts that could be loosely termed autobiographical, such as *The Post Card* (1980) and *Memoirs of the Blind*

(1990), his 1991 text 'Circonfession' may be a first, in that Derrida writes something *like* a Jewish autobiography.[5] It is not exactly a confessional text, although Derrida's text does mimic the style and mode of Augustine's *Confessions*. It acknowledges the necessary 'detours of self-presentation' and the inevitable rhetoricity that make confession anything but a straightforward outpouring of the heart. But Augustine, a former professor of rhetoric who became a preacher of the Word, acknowledged as well the circumlocutions and the tropological circling that haunt every true conversionary turn to God (and ultimately sought to sublate them). Derrida's text is *confessional* neither in Augustine's sense of *confessio* – at once avowal of sin and praise of the grandeur of God – nor in Levinas's, where the term seems to denote a denominational adherence. Derrida's text is *circonfessional* or *circumfessional*, for it is 'about' his childhood experiences of being Jewish in Algeria, his expulsion from school due to anti-Jewish legislation in North Africa in 1942, the question of assimilation, and the death of his mother. It is also a meditation on the significance of the Jewish ritual of *circum*cision.

But the autobiographical project – namely, a self that proposes to speak about its self and the apparent circularity of a narrative that recounts the spiritual experiences that enabled it to come into being as a narrative – would seem to be one of the most egregious examples of literary totalization that one can imagine. Derrida tries to circumvent this problem, one could argue, by letting someone else, a commentator (Geoffrey Bennington), write the text about 'Derrida' and his work, while Derrida appends his 'own' 'autobiographical' text to Bennington's as a bottom column or 'internal margin'. In this way, according to the 'contract' announced at the book's beginning, Derrida proposes to 'destabilize' and 'disconcert' (C 30) what he calls Bennington's theological project of knowledge, Bennington's effort to systematize Derrida's texts, to get on top of Derrida's text; he writes something that will escape the proposed systematization, that will 'surprise' (C 16) Bennington's text. This surprise – which undoes the self-assurance or self-identity of Bennington's exposition – is the surprise of alterity. It is infrastructural as well as ethical. Of course, one could ask – if Derrida's text surprises Bennington's in a way that is anticipatable, does it surprise? But this is the double bind within which the demand for a nontotalizing interpretation must be negotiated.[6]

Suffice it to say that there are other ways in which Derrida's autobiographical text seeks to avoid allegorizing his life in a totalizing autobiographical account. When Derrida follows Augustine's example, he interpolates Latin quotations from Augustine into his text in the same manner that Augustine had interpolated scripture. Consider briefly what was at stake for Augustine in such a gesture: it implied a *typological* relationship to scripture. Not only did Augustine understand the events of his life in accordance with patterns found within scripture; scripture simply overwhelmed his life (and here one should observe that, historically, the practice of early Christian typology has more in common than not with early Jewish interpretive modes). Derrida, like Augustine, to whom he refers as his 'compatriot' (Augustine came from what is modern Souk Ahras in Algeria) recounts the death of his mother, far from her native Africa, on the other side of the Mediterranean. (Augustine's mother died at Ostia; Derrida's in Nice. Both sons wept for their mothers who had so often wept for them.) Thus Derrida establishes a typological relationship to Augustine's text. When he interpolates Augustine into his text, he puts Augustine in the place of scripture, that is, Augustine's is the text that overwhelms his own.

This typological gesture has its risks and its considerable rewards. When Augustine, for example, immediately before his conversion in book 8 of the *Confessions*, finds himself under a certain fig tree, weeping (*ego sub quadam fici arbore stavi me nescio quomodo*: 'I flung myself down under a certain fig tree, I don't know how' (*Conf.* 8: 12)) the fig tree functions as a sign that points back to another tree – the pear tree of Augustine's original sin or episode of perversion in book 2 – and redeems it. John Freccero describes the operative typological structure of promise and fulfilment thus:

> The fig tree was already a scriptural emblem of conversion before Augustine used the image in his *Confessions* to represent the manifestation of the pattern of universal history in his own life . . . [I]n the gospels . . . Christ says to his disciples that they must look to the fig tree if they would read the signs of the Apocalyptic time . . . . Behind that fig tree stands a whole series of anterior images pointing backward to Genesis . . . . In the Old Testament the prophet Micah looks forward to the day when the promise will be fulfilled: 'He shall sit every man under his vine and under his fig tree.' The hope of the Jews . . . is represented by the same tree that in Genesis suggested their estrangement from God. (35–6)

In other words, typology, which proposes correspondences between the two Testaments (a tendency of scripture to mirror itself which is already evident within the 'Old Testament'), makes it possible for Augustine to discover not only correspondences between his own life and scripture but also within his own life. Augustine understood his own conversion as an imitative relationship to previous pious models (of imitation). His spiritual autobiography is organized – rhetorically as well as theologically – around internal correspondences: *per*version, *a*version, *ad*version, *re*version, *e*version. These false turns serve to anticipate or 'type' Augustine's eventual conversion, the decisive turn in the right direction. In short, Augustine's confessional text, which allegorizes his moral and spiritual wrong turns, was always already self-allegorizing, that is, an allegory of his own use and abuse of words and therefore very much concerned with circling of a linguistic kind. (Similarly, in Derrida's 'circumfessional' text, which 'turns around' his own circumcision, the *circum-* series is particularly active.)

Because it is self-allegorizing, the theological genre of confessions has a remarkable degree of aesthetic autonomy. Kenneth Burke calls attention to the stylistic and aesthetic motivation for Augustine's reliance on the psalms, especially since book 1 of *Confessions* is 'built of quotations from Psalms 145 and 147'. There one finds an exemplary crossing of Augustine's motives from classical rhetorician to Christian preacher: 'In praise there is the feel of freedom. . . . Praise "wells up". Augustine thought of it as a power that, coming from God, enabled him to praise God. While the pagan world about him was falling into decay, he nonetheless could praise vigorously, by praising as it were the very Principle of Laudability' (Burke 55). This is where the risk of doing typology might be stated, a risk that will be freely assumed by Petrarch, who is in something like an aesthetic relationship to Augustine's text. Petrarch will go so far as to establish himself as a sinner in order to justify his tropological activity. This might be the theological equivalent of the sin of idolatry, Freccero demonstrates, but it is the price of aesthetic autonomy.

What typology can do for you, however, goes beyond any consequence that one could term aesthetic. It is terribly productive of inner life. With regard to the New Testament's self-imposed hermeneutic detour through the Old, Paul Ricoeur has asked if it would not have been simpler 'to proclaim the [Christ] event in its unity?' His instructive answer – that the event 'receives a temporal density' by being inscribed in a signifying relation of promise to fulfilment (385) – could certainly be applied to typology's relation to existence as well. Typology gives a life 'temporal density'. It con-denses. Freccero, in analysing not just the internal resonance of the fig tree in Augustine's text but also its ability to point simultaneously back to the beginning of time and ahead to the last days, draws attention to the figure of prolepsis, a future event dated past. Like the figure of prosopopeia, which Paul de Man analyses in line with the solar trope of autobiography, this would be a figure by which autobiography seeks to recapture retrospectively a life from the (impossible) perspective of totalization in death (see de Man, 'Autobiography As Defacement'). Conversion narrative, which has a double perspective – the partial view of the sinner, to whom the workings of grace are incompletely understood at the time, and the converted narrator's vantage point of one who has survived his own death – describes, at the moment of conversion, its own constitution, when sinner and narrator coincide. Augustine opens scripture and reads the scriptural verse which reads him. This self-recognition by reading is the narrative's point of maximum closure, its dogmatic foundation, its circular establishing of its origin. In short, the specular self-constitution of the subject is inherent to the (theological) project of autobiography.

'Prens et lis' ('Prens, E-lie')

Derrida's Augustine, the Augustine he interpolates into his circonfessional text, is not the Bishop of Hippo, that is, not the institutional Augustine, nor is he the schoolmasterish author of *On Christian Doctrine*. Derrida's Augustine is the personal Augustine, the proto-Romantic Augustine, the father of interiority, the thinker of inwardness. This is the Augustine who loves wisdom (and indeed, most of the pages from Augustine that Derrida interpolates are from *Confessions*, books

9–11, the philosophical sections which come after the narrative proper). Derrida's Augustine is the Augustine of 'prayers and tears' (C 9):

> And now from my hidden depths my searching thought had dragged up and set before the sight of my heart the whole mass of my misery. Then a huge storm rose up within me bringing with it a huge downpour of tears [*Ubi vero a funda arcano alta consideratio traxit et confessit totam miseriam meam in conspectu cordis mei, oborta est procella ingens ferens ingentem imbrem lacrimarum*]. (*Conf.* 8: 12)

Romano Guardini calls this flood of tears the 'donum lacrimarum' of religious stirrings, which originate in what religion calls the 'heart' (240–41). As André Solignac puts it, in the avowal of sin 'the soul proclaims at once its nothingness, its misery, and the grandeur of God who pardons the sinner' (15; my translation). That is why, in the literary and theological genre of confessions, there are so many tears.

The form of the *Confessions* is a 'dialogue' with God, even though 'Augustine alone speaks, exposits, recounts, questions' (Solignac 12). It has a double address, at once to God and to those Augustine calls his 'brothers' (and the motive is frankly proselytizing): 'Why am I telling these things in your presence [Lord] and to my own kind . . . that both I myself and whoever reads what I have written may think *out of what depths we are to cry out to you* [*de quam profundo clamandum sit ad te*]' (*Conf.* 2: 3). Moreover, in confession, as in the psalmic petition or lament, one does not constate or report something to God; one *does* something with reference to God. Confession arguably has a performative aspect. Augustine tacitly acknowledges this when he speaks not of 'telling the truth' but of 'making the truth', or 'doing the truth' [*volo facere veritas*], a formulation to which Derrida repeatedly refers.

The mode of address of the *Confessions* – interlocutionary, conative, vocative – signals not just its performative but its ethical – in the specifically Levinasian sense – dimension. Here the question arises: does the Augustinian confessional text give to think alterity? Because of the crossing in his work of the project of self-knowledge and the knowledge of God, at times it appears that Augustine's conception of God is not sufficiently other. God gets folded into the specular self-understanding of the subject. Of course, if one emphasizes the apophatic or negative theological dimension of the discourse of self and God in Augustine, it is possible to argue that the discourse does not attempt to bring anything to knowledge (*Cur confitemur Deo scienti*: why bother confessing to God who knows everything already, whose knowledge exceeds, marks the eclipse of, Augustine's self-knowledge?). In other words, confession *performs* a relation which is utterly asymmetrical. To rephrase the question then: does not the proselytizing motive of the *Confessions* – which hegemonically 'universalizes' alterity, as when Augustine passes the book to his friend Alypius and, metonymically, to all of Augustine's future readers – repress the specifically *ethical* alterity of the other? Does not Augustine's text attempt to repress its condition of (im)possibility – whether we call it ethical alterity, self-alteration, or even the Judaic letter (see Robbins, *Prodigal Son/Elder Brother*)? One may answer schematically. To the extent to which it is specular, yes. To the extent to which it is blind – at the level of the condition of possibility of visibility – no. One always prays on the verge of tears, says Derrida in *Memoirs of the Blind*, as if the structure of interlocutionary address to the other that is prayer had always already opened confession to the other (MB 117–29). In Derrida's reading, confession always confesses (to) the other, is shot through with the problem of the other. Suffice it to say, then, that one of the things that Derrida's reading of Augustine does is to insure that there is alterity in the Augustinian genre of confessions. He finds the elements in Augustine that tug against its specular and totalizing theological project of 'absolute knowledge'. Again, I would borrow the style and formulation of the question that Derrida asks with regard to negative theology: how to avoid writing in the mode of Augustine? – a formulation that would have at least two senses: how is it possible to avoid this, and how *must* one avoid this? I am arguing, in short, that Derrida's interpolation of Augustine serves precisely to dramatize the inevitable engulfment of his text in the Augustinian form, or better, the Augustinian language. Call it Latin.

Ecclesia ex circumcisione

Derrida knows that there is something not quite kosher in this. Concerning his own prayer, his address to God, he asks, 'why [do] I talk to him in Christian Latin French when they expelled from the Lycée de Ben Aknoun in 1942 a little black and very Arab Jew who understood nothing about it, to whom no one ever gave the slightest reason' (C 58)? It is as if Derrida is thematizing the reluctance – not to mention the incongruity – of his assent to the necessity of speaking Latin. This assent is not a choice, however. What is Latin?

It is, among other things, the language of philosophy. In 'How Not to Speak' Derrida calls Latin 'one of my foreign languages', within a list that includes 'French, English, German, Greek, the philosophic, metaphilosophic, Christian, etc.' (HAS 31 n. 13). The foreignness of the Latin language does not mean that there would be any proper language. 'My language, an other' (C 3: trans. modified): does one ever 'own' a language? Derrida indicates the absence of a language in which to speak of *another* tradition of negative theology that is 'neither Greek nor Christian' (that is neither the Platonic space of the khora nor the apophatic theology of pseudo-Dionysius). He does not speak about this other tradition of apophatic theology – namely, the 'Jewish and Islamic' (HAS 31). He writes in a footnote:

> Despite this silence, or in fact, *because of it*, one will perhaps permit me to interpret this lecture as the most 'autobiographical' speech I have ever risked. ... But if one day I had to tell my story, nothing in this narrative would start to speak of the thing itself if I did not come up against this fact: for lack of capacity, competence, or self-authorization, I have never yet been able to speak

of what my birth, as one says, should have made closest to me: the Jew, the Arab. (HAS 31 n. 13: my emphasis)

In a manner rigorously consistent with the logic of negative theology, Derrida speaks of the Jewish and Islamic traditions by not speaking about them. He refers to these other traditions as 'an internal desert', an 'immense place [left] empty' (HAS 53), and within his essay, he speaks of Heidegger in place of this place.[7] Derrida tropes on Heidegger's strange conditional: 'if I *were* yet to write a theology . . ., the word "being" ought not to appear there', in which Heidegger writes exactly what he says he wanted to avoid writing. Of himself, of his Jewish and Algerian background, Derrida says nothing. Note the crossing of the autobiographical and the (Judaic) negative theological projects here. For Derrida, there is no proper language – Hebrew? – for an autobiographical writing of the self.

Of course 'language' here refers in the broad sense to the conceptuality we inhabit and the limits of what we can think. This is what necessitated going by way of Augustine to write a Jewish autobiography. With reference to Levinas, Derrida had called it 'Greek'. These usages of 'Greek', 'Latin', 'Christian', 'French', and 'Hebrew' are not primarily historical. As Heidegger puts it: philosophy is Greek to the extent that philosophy 'first appropriated the Greek world, and only it, in order to unfold itself' (28–31).[8] At the same time, this is not to close off the other senses in which these terms *are* historical: the difficult task is to mediate between these nonhistoricist and historicist senses.

Latin, the language of philosophy (and theology) is also, in 'Circumfession', the language that Derrida had begun to learn 'when Vichy had made it, I believe, obligatory in the first form just before booting me out of the school in the Latin name of the *numerus clausus* by withdrawing our French citizenship' (C 211). French, he says, is the 'language made a present to me by its colonization of Algeria in 1830' (C 285). Further, 'French' meant the democratic, secular, and universalistic ideals that had been so significant in the development of Algerian Jewry. The Crémieux decree of 1870 granted the Jews of Algeria full French citizenship (see Chouraqui). (Derrida's mother's grandfather, born in Algiers in 1832, fulfilled the decree's conditions for naturalization.) 'French' meant the modern, secular education from which Algerian Jews benefited enormously and which accelerated the pace of emancipation for them so that their culture and outlook changed rapidly within the space of only a few generations. The Vichy laws of 1940–43 abrogated the Crémieux decree and stripped the Algerian Jews of French citizenship. They were expelled from schools in the name of the *numerus clausus*, the quota system.[9] For the largely middle-class, highly assimilated Algerian Jews, these events were traumatic. Derrida refers to his own expulsion from school (at the age of twelve) as his 'expulsion . . . from Frenchness' (C 248). (After his expulsion, he went, incidentally, to an Alliance School for a year, which he disliked intensely.) No doubt these events belong to what historian Michel Abitbol calls 'the history of the "fringes" of the Holocaust universe'.[10]

I still do not know, today *[12-23-76]* how you say 'circumcision' in pretty much any language other than French, scarcely, obviously, in Hebrew. (C 76-7)

I'm reaching the end without *ever* having read Hebrew, see someone who multiplies dancing and learned circumvolutions in a foreign language for the simple reason that he must turn around his own unknown grammar, Hebrew, the unreadability he knows he comes from, like his home . . . . (C 286-7)

I pretended to learn Hebrew so as to read it without understanding it, . . . just before the *bar-mitzvah*, which they also called the 'communion' . . . and I did my 'communion' by fleeing the prison of all languages, the sacred one they tried to lock me up in without opening me to it, the secular they made clear would never be mine. (C 288-9)

The question of the problem of language in 'Circumfession' – why does Derrida speak Latin? why does Derrida *pray* in Latin? – can be answered in another way: because there is no speaking Hebrew. 'Hebrew' is covered up by the dominant 'Greco-Christian' conceptuality, and it needs to be critically retrieved. Could one ever gain access to it without the relay through 'Greek', 'Latin', 'French', philosophy, theology, and so forth, that is, through all the 'foreign' languages? When we say that there is no speaking Hebrew, we obviously do not refer to an empirical possibility. Derrida meditates on circumcision as 'the language of the proper', and he does not say 'circumcision' only in French. He writes it in Hebrew, *milah*, five times transliterated, once in 'the square letters'.

How to Read Circumcision

CIRCUMCISION (Heb. בְּרִית מִילָה *berit milah*; 'covenant of circumcision') removal of the prepuce, foreskin of a male [Lat. *circum-cido*, to cut around, cut, clip, trim. II *Trop.* to cut off, shorten, diminish, abridge, circumscribe. – of discourse, to lop or cut off, to remove: *curcumcidat, si quid redundabit*, Quint. 10.2.28]

The form of Derrida's 'Circumfession', as indicated in its subtitle, is 'fifty-nine periods and periphrases'. (He will also refer to them, in the course of his text, as fifty-nine compulsions (C 125), respirations, commotions (C 127), widows (C 255), prayer bands (C 260), circumferences (C 281).) He writes:

. . . what I have turned around . . . the strange turn of the event of nothing, what can be got around or not which comes back to me without ever having taken place, I call it circumcision [*ce autour de quoi j'ai tourné, d'une périphrase l'autre, dont je sais que cela eut lieu mais jamais, selon l'étrange tournure de l'événement de rien, le contournable ou non qui se rappelle à moi sans avoir eu lieu, je l'appelle circoncision*]. (C 13-14)

Why 'without ever having taken place'? Because the event is immemorial; it is not accessible to memory either as a past or a modified presence. That which Derrida turns around is 'like an event having taken place only once' (C 27), 'the circumcision of me, the unique one, which I know perfectly well took place, one time' (C 60). Circumcision is singular, it is the event of the singular (see Derrida, *Schibboleth*).

In 'Circumfession' Derrida reproduces photographs of circumcision instruments and customs dating from the sixteenth century; he alludes to the biblical accounts; he reprints (or interpolates) passages from the notebooks preparatory to a book on circumcision that he has kept since 1976; he 're-members' his own circumcision at eight days, and his paternal uncle, Eugène Eliahou Derrida (whom Derrida is named after), 'who must have carried me in his arms at the moment of this event without memory' (C 96). This 're-membering' is compulsive, phantasmagoric, hallucinatory. Everything is referred back to this immemorial event: it is that against which all subsequent events (and traumas) are measured, and interpreted: 'The first event to write itself right on my body' (C 120), 'the proper language of my life' (C 144), 'the original sin against me' (C 74), a 'wound' (C 66, 293).

Circumcision 'explains' Derrida's lifelong preoccupation with writing, the sense of guilt that he can never separate from writing: does one ask for pardon *in* writing, or does one ask for pardon *for* the crime of writing? It anticipates Derrida's desire for self-surgery, to mark himself: 'I am also the *mohel*, my sacrificer, I write with a sharpened blade, if it doesn't bleed the book will be a failure' (C 130). 'I want . . . to stitch myself up again at this time of my life when I have never been more undone, bloody and bleeding: I no longer even have to sustain me through the operation the arms of Elie *who at the worst moment stays there*' (C 196–7: my emphasis). Note the positive – not necessarily traumatic – associations with the event: it is an image of security – uncle Elie, the holder, who, Derrida iterates, 'held [me] in his arms at the moment of circumcision' (C 187), 'held me in his arms the day of my circumcision' (C 185), 'held me on his knees' (C 129). Would that there were an Uncle Elie to hold him now! 'I would like to gather myself in the circle of the *cum*, the circus of the *circum*' (C 197). In short, not only is every subsequent event referred back to circumcision, its referential and explanatory power seems at times absolute: 'circumcision, that's *all* I've ever talked about' (C 70: my emphasis).

We still do not know what circumcision means, and a look at the biblical intertexts does little to allay this confusion. In Genesis 17, circumcision is commanded and explained as the sign of the covenant. God says to Abraham:

> This is my covenant between me and you and your descendants that you shall keep: every male among you is to be circumcised. You shall circumcise the flesh of your foreskin, and this shall be the sign of the covenant between me and you. At the age of eight days every male among you shall be circumcised, generation after generation. . . . An uncircumcised male, everyone who has not had the flesh of his foreskin circumcised, he shall be cut off from his kin. He has broken my covenant. (10–14)

According to Claus Westermann, Genesis 17 reflects the moment when circumcision, which was practised by many cultures (including Israel's neighbours in the ancient Near East) as a puberty rite, a fertility rite, or an initiation into marriage, acquires a religious significance as a covenantal sign (251–67). Genesis 17 also reflects the shift of the practice away from young adulthood to the eighth day after birth and thus again, as Howard Eilberg-Schwartz points out, a shift in significance from the sexual to the spiritual (142). The passage includes a command to circumcise, which is designated as the confirmation of the covenant, a legal prescription about circumcision (not mentioned in any of the Bible document's earlier legal codes), and the punishment for rejecting it. (Derrida knows and cites this passage: the uncut will be 'cut off' [*karet*].) But beyond the *designation* of circumcision as the sign of the covenant, the passage does not 'explain' its meaning.

The passage in Exodus 4:24–26, a mere three verses, is even more ambiguous:

> Then it happened, at an encampment on the way, the Lord met him and sought to kill him. Then Zipporah took a piece of flint and cut off her son's foreskin and touched his feet with it saying 'A bridegroom of blood you are to me'. So he let him alone. At that time she said 'a bridegroom of blood' in reference to circumcision.

Brevard Childs summarizes the numerous problems and questions this passage poses. Why should Yahweh suddenly seek to kill his chosen messenger? How did Zipporah know what to do? Moreover, the pronominal antecedents in the second half of verse 25 are uncertain: 'she touched his feet . . . saying "A bridegroom of blood are you to me".' Whose feet? (Were they 'feet'?) Verses 24 and 26 share in the indeterminacy generated by the personal pronouns: who was under attack? 'Finally, the meaning of the phrase "bridegroom of blood" is highly unclear', not to mention 'the irrational, almost demonic atmosphere of the passage in which the blood seems to play an apotropaic role' (Childs 95–6). The traditional interpretation connects the incident with Moses' failure to circumcise his child and sees it as an *etiological* explanation of how circumcision, originally a puberty rite, was transferred from adulthood to childhood in Israel. But according to Childs, even this traditional explanation is lacking:

> It seems evident that even when the story was edited, the phrase 'blood-bridegroom' already presented problems. The comment does not attempt to paraphrase the terms in order to illuminate its meaning. Nor does it offer any explanation as to whom the phrase was addressed. Rather it serves only to relate the enigmatic expression to the rite of circumcision. . . . From the redactor's point of view; the story does not explain the origin of circumcision, but rather circumcision explains the meaning of Zipporah's action. This interpretation is of course, the exact opposite of the etiological. (100)

It is as if we know that circumcision is a sign, but the explanation for this sign has been lost. Derrida refers to himself as 'someone . . . who would be capable of inventing circumcision all alone', adding, 'as I am doing here' (C 222).

When Paul reads circumcision, in Romans 2:25–9 and 3:30, Galatians 5:6, and I Corinthians 7:19, he necessarily assumes that he knows what circumcision means when he idealizes it, metaphorizes it. The passage in Romans 2 is especially instructive:

> Circumcision indeed is of value if you obey the law, but if you break the law, your circumcision becomes uncircumcision. So if a man who is uncircumcised keeps the precepts of the law, will not his uncircumcision be regarded as circumcision? Then those who are physically uncircumcised but keep the law will condemn you who have the written code and circumcision but break the law. For he is not a real Jew who is one outwardly, nor is true circumcision something external and physical. He is a Jew who is one inwardly, and real circumcision is a matter of the heart, spiritual and not literal. (25–9)

This reading conceives of the difference between the literal and the figurative as homologous with the difference between carnal and spiritual, sensible and intelligible. Daniel Boyarin has shown that within the homologies of the Pauline discourse – flesh/spirit, works/faith, literal/figurative, carnal/spiritual, earthly Jerusalem/heavenly Jerusalem – circumcision is typed with baptism, as the difference between an allegorical genealogy and a literal one: 'Baptism is figured as the putting off of the garment, namely the physical body . . . and a recladding in the spiritual body of the risen Christ' (*Radical Jew* 27). (Note that Augustine's oracle, 'Not in rioting and drunkenness . . . but put ye on the Lord Jesus Christ' (Rom. 13:13), as well as the reading procedure it presupposes, is based on the same homologies; thus even Augustine's conversion is 'traced' by circumcision.)

Circumcision was already figural in the 'Old Testament' biblical diction: 'the word describes the lips of a person whose speech is not fluent (Exod. 6:12,30) or the heart and ear of a person who will not listen to reason (Jer. 6:10; 9:25)' (*Encyclopaedia Judaica*). For Eilberg-Schwartz, these turns of phrase show that the priestly writers 'equated the lack of circumcision with the improper functioning of a human organ' (149). No doubt this is what authorizes all subsequent 'metaphorical' usages of circumcision (including Derrida's when he refers to 'the internal circumcision of "my life"' (C 229)).

But more important here, when Paul in his metaphorical usage proposes that the difference between literal and figurative, proper and improper be understood specifically as homologous with the difference between carnal and spiritual, 'Old' Testament and New Testament, one of the terms of his analogy, namely, circumcision, serves as both the literal and that which makes possible the difference between the literal and the figurative. Within Paul's discourse, not only is this sense of the literal – as a vacillation between the literal and the figural, as a *figure* for the literal, as a disappearing condition for the difference between the literal and the figural – excessive. Insofar as it threatens to disarticulate the governing oppositions on which his discourse rests, it needs to be 'shed', to be, as it were, circumcised again.

It is as if there is an excess of literality when it comes to circumcision. No doubt the circumcision of Christ (Luke 2:21) is especially troubling in this regard. It would seem to describe the last circumcision, the circumcision that 'circumcises' circumcision, but in so doing, is it not also one circumcision too many? Circumcision is 'the proper', but arguably it troubles the relationship between the proper and the improper, especially as that is understood in terms of the difference between carnal and spiritual. It is carnal certainly, as Boyarin puts it, 'the embodied sign' of 'the sign Israel', a mark of genealogy and ethnicity, although for male Jews only.[11] In sum, it is as if the excessive literality of the event of circumcision as Derrida revisits it were a reversal (and a reinscription) of the prophetic diction that applied uncircumcision to the rebellious heart or obdurate ear, and that Paul takes up from the older scripture in order to discredit that very scripture, a certain literalization of the metaphor.

Under the Sign of Spinoza

'Among the Algerian Jews, one scarcely ever said "circumcision" but "baptism", not Bar Mitzvah but "communion"' (C 72). Yirmiyahu Yovel has demonstrated the significance of Marrano culture (that of former Jews in Spain and Portugal who had been forcibly converted to Christianity, many of whom retained Jewish rites in secret), for the understanding of Spinoza and, implicitly, for an understanding of the problems of language and identity, including 'Jewish secularism', which open up within modern Jewish philosophy. Within Marrano culture, not only was Judaism guarded in a 'fragmentary and distorted manner', but information about Judaism was often gleaned from 'polemical works against it, the Latin Vulgate and other Christian sources' (20). Yovel argues that 'the very experience of Marranism created a tendency to prefer the inner heart to external works', and he characterizes the residual Judaism of Marranism as a hybrid mixture of religions, 'fraught with Christian symbols and categories', making it appear both Christian and Jewish, and neither (15–39).

At issue here is not the adequacy of Yovel's grid for a reading of Spinoza's texts, but the way in which Derrida in 'Circumfession' poses Spinoza as a spiritual ancestor of his own Sephardic experience. 'If I am a sort of Marrano of French Catholic culture', writes Derrida, wondering in effect if he is not practising Judaism in secret, that is, through a necessary double detour, 'I also have my Christian body, inherited from SA in a more or less twisted line' (C 170). He speaks of 'this young man, an ancestor on your mother's side, who, your cousin tells you, one day at the dawn of the last century, arrived from Portugal, I'm sure you look like him' (C 253).

Names are especially significant in this respect in 'Circumfession'. Derrida's mother's Hebrew name is Esther (the 'patron saint' of the Marranos) (Yovel 21). Derrida's Hebrew name is Elie (like his holder, uncle Eugène Eliahou Derrida), but it was never inscribed on his birth certificate, as were the Hebrew names of his family; thus it is hidden, secret. Elijah is the prophet of the last things, associated with the messianic days. He is also said to be the guardian of circumcision; he is said to be present at every circumcision. But unlike Elijah, Derrida does not guard circumcision, as he attests by his references to 'my noncircumcised sons' (C 62, 95, 143, 202, 221, 297). That and his 'endogamous marriage' (C 95) make him refer to himself as 'the last of the Jews' (C 190). 'I shall always have been eschatological. ... I am the last of the eschatologists' (C 75), that is, the most eschatological of the eschatologists.

No doubt Derrida's experience of Judaism is largely a response to anti-Semitism ('The "alliance" was first of all for the 13-year-old child the name of the place one had to go to, a school really, a year after the exclusion' (C 175); 'The "alliance" for me will always be a Jewish building on the rue Bab Azoun' (C 176).) He has sometimes suggested this in interviews. At times it seems as if Derrida reduces all of Judaism to circumcision. But in the terms of 'Circumfession', one could just as rigorously speak of a reduction of circumcision to Judaism. In either case, do we indeed know what we mean when we say 'Judaism', especially after the double detour through the Greco-Christian and its reinscription? In Maurice Blanchot's phrase, it is a matter of 'a singularity which can be called Jewish and which *waits*, to keep on being thought [*qui* attend *d'être encore pensée*]. Prophetic in this respect' (25 n. 8).

Like a Marrano of French Catholic culture, Derrida gets his Hebrew Bible largely through Saint Augustine. Is his finally a Judaism of what Levinas calls 'family memories', and not enough study of the classical Jewish texts (How Is Judaism Possible? 247)? Perhaps. Derrida does not claim to a knowledge of these texts: 'this ignorance remained the chance of my faith' (C 289). For Derrida, the experience of Judaism is circumcision, and ultimately circumcision, the mark of the covenant, *is* precisely that, a mark. It is inseparable from a certain theoretical notion of writing that Derrida gives us to think and that he calls variously 'mark', 'trace', and so on. 'The desire for literature is circumcision' (C 78), he writes. In sum, Derrida's 'circumcising' of confession would seem to mark not only its Judaization, and its ethicization, if you will, but also its circumventing, that is, a certain 'literary' or 'fictional' dimension that has to be thought together with the ethical. It is this that decisively marks Derrida's place within a textual history of what might be called 'Jewish philosophy'. This crossing of the projects of the literary and ethical was already implied in the formulation 'making truth' (*volo facere veritatem*), at once the fictional or literary dimension of confession and its ethical performativity.[12]

Works Cited

Abitbol, Michel. *The Jews of North Africa during the Second World War.* Trans. Catherine Tihanyi Zentelis. Detroit: Wayne State University Press, 1989.
Aouate, Yves-Claude. 'Les mesures d'exclusion antijuives dans l'enseignement public en Algérie (1940–1943)'. *Pardès*, 8 (1988), 109–28.

Augustine, *The Confessions*. Trans. Rex Warner. New York: New American Library, 1963.
———. *Les Confessions*. Ed. André Solignac. *Oeuvres de Saint Augustin*. Vols. 13–14. Paris: Desclée de Brouwer, 1962.
Blanchot, Maurice. *The Writing of the Disaster*. Trans. Ann Smock. Lincoln: University of Nebraska Press, 1986.
Boyarin, Daniel. *Carnal Israel: Reading Sex in Talmudic Culture*. Berkeley: University of California Press, 1993.
———. *A Radical Jew: Paul and the Politics of Identity*. Berkeley: University of California Press, 1994.
Burke, Kenneth. *The Rhetoric of Religion*. 1961. Berkeley: University of California Press, 1970.
Childs, Brevard S. *The Book of Exodus: A Critical and Theological Commentary*. Philadelphia: Westminster, 1974.
Chouraqui, André. *Between East and West: A History of the Jews in North Africa*. Trans. Michael M. Bernet. Philadelphia: Jewish Publication Society, 1968.
Cohen. Richard A., ed. *Face to Face with Levinas*. Albany: State University of New York Press, 1986.
de Man, Paul. 'Autobiography As Defacement'. *The Rhetoric of Romanticism*. New York: Columbia University Press, 1984, pp. 67–81.
Derrida, Jacques. 'Circonfession'. *Jacques Derrida*. By Geoffrey Bennington and Jacques Derrida. Paris: Seuil, 1991.
———. *Schibboleth*. Paris: Galilée, 1986.
Eilberg-Schwartz, Howard. *The Savage in Judaism*. Bloomington: Indiana University Press, 1990.
Encyclopaedia Judaica. Jerusalem: Keter, 1972.
Fackenheim, Emil L. Review of *Franz Rosenzweig: His Life and Thought*, by Nahum N. Glatzer. *Judaism*, 2 (1953), 367–72.
Friedlander, Judith. *Vilna on the Seine*. New Haven, CT: Yale University Press, 1990.
Freccero, John. 'The Fig Tree and the Laurel'. *Diacritics*, 5, 1 (1975), 35–6.
Glatzer, Nahum N. 'Franz Rosenzweig: The Story of a Conversion'. *Essays in Jewish Thought*. Alabama: University of Alabama Press, 1978, pp. 230–42.
Guardini, Romano. *The Conversion of Augustine*. Trans. Elinor Briefs. Westminster, MD: Newman, 1960.
Heidegger, Martin. *What Is Philosophy?* Trans. William Kluback and Jean T. Wilde. New Haven, CT: College and University Press, 1956.
Levinas, Emmanuel. 'Between Two Worlds'. 1960. *Difficult Freedom*, pp. 181–201. (BTW)
———. *Difficult Freedom*. 1963. Trans. Seán Hand. Baltimore: Johns Hopkins University Press, 1990.
———. 'Franz Rosenzweig: A Modern Jewish Thinker'. 1965. Trans. Michael B. Smith. *Outside the Subject*. Stanford, CA: Stanford University Press, 1994.

———. 'How Is Judaism Possible?' 1959. *Difficult Freedom*, pp. 245–54.
———. 'The Temptation of Temptation'. 1964. *Nine Talmudic Lectures*. Trans. Annette Aronowicz. Bloomington: Indiana University Press, 1990, pp. 30–50. (TT)
———. *Totality and Infinity*. 1961. Trans. Alphonso Lingis. Pittsburgh: Duquesne University Press, 1969. (TI)
———. 'The Trace of the Other'. 1963. Trans. Alphonso Lingis. *Deconstruction in Context*. Ed. Mark C. Taylor. Chicago: University of Chicago Press, 1986, pp. 345–59. (T)
Ricoeur, Paul. 'Preface to Bultmann'. Trans. Peter McCormick. *The Conflict of Interpretations*. Evanston, IL: Northwestern University Press, 1974.
Robbins, Jill. *Prodigal Son/Elder Brother: Interpretation and Alterity in Augustine, Petrarch, Kafka, Levinas*. Chicago: University of Chicago Press, 1991.
Solignac, André. Introduction. *Les Confessions*. Vols. 13–14. *Oeuvres de Saint Augustin*. Paris: Desclée de Brouwer, 1962.
Taylor, Mark C. 'Non-negative Negative Atheology'. *Diacritics*, 20, 4 (1990), 2–16.
Westermann, Claus. *Genesis 1–11: A Commentary*. Trans. John J. Scullion. Minneapolis: Augsburg, 1984.
Yovel, Yirmiyahu. *Spinoza and Other Heretics: The Marrano of Reason*. Princeton, NJ: Princeton University Press, 1989.
Zarader, Marlène. *La Dette impensée*. Paris: Seuil, 1990.

Notes

[1] Nahum Glatzer, who, through his editions and selections has largely determined the presentation of Rosenzweig to the English-speaking world, even wrote an article entitled 'Franz Rosenzweig: The Story of a Conversion'. Emil Fackenheim laments this tendency to give an existential presentation of Rosenzweig's thought at the expense of his technical philosophy.

[2] 'I always make a clear distinction in what I write, between philosophical and confessional texts. . . . I would never, for example, introduce a talmudic or biblical verse into one of my philosophical texts to try to prove or justify a phenomenological argument', he states in an interview with Richard Kearney (Cohen 18).

[3] 'We name this calling into question of my spontaneity by the presence of the other, ethics' (TI 43).

[4] The talmudic text *Shabbath* (88a–88b) ends with a dramatized polemic between Jew and Christian (coded in the text as a Sadducee); 'A Sadducee saw Raba studying a tradition. . . . He said to him: "Ye rash people, for whom the mouth passes before the ears. You should have listened in order to know whether you were able to accept, and if you were not able to accept, you should not have accepted."'

[5] He prefigured this in 'How Not to Speak' by not writing what he promised not to write, as Mark C. Taylor establishes in 'Non-negative Negative Atheology'. But one could say that, in contrast to the *via negativa* of autobiography in 'How Not to Speak', the autobiographical 'Circumfession' is written otherwise. [Ed. note: Robbins prefers a more literal translation of the title 'Comment ne pas parler: dénégations', published in English as 'How to Avoid Speaking: Denials' (HAS).]

[6] In his 1980 essay on Levinas, Derrida formulates the double bind thus: 'Suppose I want to *give* to him, to E. L. Not to return something to him, an homage for example . . . but to give him something that escapes from the circle of restitution. . . . It would thus be necessary that, beyond all possible restitution,

my gesture operates beyond debt, in absolute ingratitude. . . . It would however be necessary to do that in conformity to what his Work says of the work. I would still be caught in the circle of debt and restitution' (ATM 13–14).

[7] In *La Dette impensée*, Marlène Zarader explores the significance of Heidegger's forgetting of the Hebraic tradition, within the context and according to the logic of Heidegger's retrieval of the question of Being from its occlusion within ontotheology. See also Taylor's 'Non-negative Negative Atheology' (9–15).

[8] Derrida discusses this passage in 'Violence and Metaphysics' (WD 311–12 n. 4).

[9] Derrida's use of the term *Décremieux* (C 288) would seem to refer at once to the repealing of the Crémieux decree and also to express the criticism of the universalistic Enlightenment ideals of Adolphe Crémieux (founder of the Alliance Israélite Universelle) by the generation of 1968 (see Friedlander, *Vilna on the Seine*).

[10] On the 'heavily threatening atmosphere permeating N. African Jewish communities', Michel Abitbol writes that the situation of North African Jews was in no way comparable to the situation of European Jewry during he same period. He continues: 'But never had persecution in N. Africa been prepared with so great an effort of ideological mobilization, nor with so much juridical "care". Taking inspiration from anti-Semitic "models" totally alien to the Maghreb, Vichy made use of the vocabulary and of the methods that, on the other side of the Rhine, were to stake out the path to the final solution' (12–13). See also Aouate.

[11] Eilberg-Schwartz remarks: 'Since circumcision binds together men within and across generations [the priestly writers' genealogies generally list only the names of men], it also establishes an opposition between men and women. Women cannot bear the symbol of the covenant. Only the bodies of men can commemorate the promise of God to Abraham' (171).

The rabbinic discourse is alert to this problem when it asks (in *Leviticus Rabbah* 25:6 and elsewhere): why does scripture specify 'uncircumcised male' in Genesis 17, since there is no such thing as an uncircumcised female? Daniel Boyarin has shown that within rabbinic discourse even rejected minoritarian opinions have a life of their own within the 'dialogism' of its phrase universe. He would therefore regard the very fact of this question as significant (*Carnal Israel* 26–9, 174).

Suffice it to add that, insofar as the discourse of circumcision represses the question of woman entirely, it is necessarily relayed through this question. This forgotten question is the unthought, the hidden ground of the discourse of circumcision.

[12] I would like to thank Geoffrey Hartman, Carol Jacobs, Henry Sussman, and Cathy Caruth for their comments during various stages of the essay's composition. A condensed version of this essay was first given at a seminar, 'The State of Jewish Studies', Humanities Research Institute, University of California at Irvine, 18–24 June 1994.

CHAPTER 10

Memento Mori

Robert Smith

Philosopher, c'est apprendre à mourir.
Montaigne

Being – we have no idea of it other than 'living'. – How can anything dead 'be'?
Nietzsche

What, then, is it to cross the ultimate border? . . . Is it possible? Who has ever done it and who can testify to it?
Derrida

'Once is never' – this phrase, according to Peter Szondi, encapsulates the golden rule of science and all verifiable knowledge in general. What occurs only once poses something intolerable and indeed impossible for scientific thinking: it cannot be verified and so escapes the order of knowledge as the ground of certainty. How can we be certain of what happens only once? *Einmal ist keinmal* – scientific thinking views the particular only as a specimen, a species implicitly or explicitly belonging to a genus. Knowledge is derived by inference from specific cases in respect of a general order. In the essay from 1962 entitled 'On Textual Understanding' it is literary criticism which Szondi charges with too readily embracing this scientific code of practice when on the contrary it should pause to consider the extreme possibility raised by the way in which tropes work in literary texts, that of existing at random and in relation to no other figural or literal moment, eluding verifiability and thus breaching scientific decorum.[1] I will come back to this but mainly I want to follow a different set of implications provoked by Szondi's insight into science's repression of the singular, its sidelining or denial of it. They concern our knowledge about death. Paul de Man in a later essay (1979) perhaps influenced by Szondi develops this notion of the absolute contingency of the literary trope and associates it with what he thinks of as the random power of death.[2] I read this random power of death, its absolute contingency, its sheer unrelatedness and saturated specificity, in terms of the requirement that it happen to us only once. Death can be experienced only once by definition for death is the death of experience *überhaupt*. On the surface one might say, what could be more particular, more 'real' and thus more choice for a scientific materialism than an event so specific that it happens just once and which therefore cannot in principle belong to an idealizing, totalizing scheme of history? Its particularity could not be gainsaid and no idealist historicism could assimilate it. At the same time, however, such an opportunity brings on a crisis for scientific materialism which thereby reaches its own limit, for it finds an object, an event so specific or singular that it may be unthinkable, no apparatus may comprehend it; and thus an aporia between materialism and the scientific credibility it aspires to is lit up. This singularity of death, its particularity and one-offness, constitutes one of at least two essential characteristics, the other being that insisted on by Heidegger, namely that no-one can die my death in my place – it is unavoidable – which would be a second form of death's uniqueness. 'Death', Heidegger writes, 'is Dasein's *ownmost* possibility.'[3] This is not to be confused with cases of sacrifice in which someone dies for another. The phrase 'to die for another' misleads us for the sacrificial victim will still die his or her own death in dying for another, and only metaphorically or by elision can they be said to die someone else's death. I shall examine such specificity. The question that emerges is, 'if death happens to us only once how can we have any knowledge of it?' Can the golden rule be applied here? Surely science wouldn't say, because death can be experienced only once that it therefore never happens? What does it mean for something to have to happen only once – both *to have to happen* only once and to have to happen *only once* –, to be intrinsically unrepeatable, and what are the consequences for our knowledge about it? What follows is a brief enquiry into the status of our knowledge about death in the light not only of this 'onceness' and specificity but also of other aspects, for example, whether death can be known as certain or if not as certain then as fictional, rhetorical or speculative; whether we can be absolutely certain of it and yet forget it; and how it conditions human experience. In short, how can we *think* death?

Three Responses to Pascal

I would like to begin with two excerpts from a letter of Pascal:[4]

> You do not need a greatly elevated soul to realize that in this life there is no true and firm satisfaction, that all our pleasures are simple vanity, that our afflictions are infinite, and lastly that death, which threatens us at every moment, must in a few years infallibly present us with the appalling necessity of being either annihilated or wretched for all eternity.

And a few paragraphs later:

> Nothing is so important to man as his condition. Nothing is so frightening to him as eternity. And so the fact that there are men indifferent to the loss of their being and to the peril of an eternity of wretchedness is not natural. They are quite different with regard to everything else: they fear even the most insignificant things, they foresee them, feel them, and the same man who spends so many days and nights in rage and despair over the loss of some office or over some imaginary affront to his honour is the very one who, without anxiety or emotion, knows he is going to lose everything through death. It is a monstrous

thing to see in the same heart and at the same time both this sensitivity to the slightest things, and this strange insensitivity to the greatest.

It is 'monstrous', in Pascal's eyes, to be so negligent of the fact of death, our 'condition'. In order to contemplate and respond to his righteous indignation we need to make a distinction between forgetting death and forgetting about the fact that we are going to die. Clearly Pascal has his mind on this second form. After all one will never be able to remember one's own death. That is something that death brings, an end to memory, the impossibility of remembering anything ever again including the death which imposed the impossibility. Rilke in the first of the *Duino Elegies* says that in death you lose even your own first name.[5] Death cannot be remembered. Rather, one remembers or ought to remember *that* one will die. One is called to a 'that', a direction or attribute; a grammar routes the thought, adjusting it towards a determinate content, that one will die. However, this determinate content turns out to be empty. Because it happens only once we cannot know what this 'that' points towards in saying that we will die. In this regard the thought is meaningless. This determinate and absolutely certain thought that we will die subsists undetermined. The thought of death presents itself as thoroughly unique in this regard. No other thought in the world manages absolute certainty and complete indeterminacy at the same time. The price paid for abundant certainty is lack of content. I am certain of something I absolutely do not know. Only the 'that' of death can ever be invoked and precisely because death occurs only once and precludes any subsequent reflection on it; death precludes all subsequence, or more succinctly still, *death precludes*. 'We are a sign', as Hölderlin says, 'meaningless'. There is a sense but there is no meaning; there is direction but no horizon.

And yet, *given* its certainty, how is it possible to ignore or even forget *about* death? If Pascal rankles at the indifference of those who do not ruminate upon it, there must be a prior possibility that death can indeed be forgotten. The stately fact of death in all its gravity and relevance for the human condition may be set aside, overlooked or, what's worse for Pascal, relegated in favour of more immediate worldly concerns.

Is it not strange to have to *remember* that one must die? That one has to be *reminded* of *this*, the most crucial and determining condition of one's existence? For insofar as death can be forgotten it forfeits its pre-eminence as a fact; in its forgettability it stands on a par with all else that may be forgotten; I can forget about death just as I might forget my umbrella. It could well be proved an epistemological or psychological law that nothing exists which cannot in principle be forgotten, but the forgettability of *death* – is that not a scandal of some sort? Ought that not to be a special case when it comes to remembering and forgetting? Isn't there something hubristic or at least irreverent in forgetting about death, some failure to salute an absolute authority? Is it not simply too important to forget even for a moment? St Paul writes in his letter to the Thessalonians of the requirement to pray without ceasing: isn't something equal to that required for the thought of death? Socrates in the *Phaedo* (80c–81) even speaks of the soul as that which emerges through meditation on death. The soul comes into its own through a separation from the body, growing thereby into its condition as 'wisdom' or thought which is nothing but an apprehension of the soul's final separation from corporeality, the intimation of its own being-towards-death. For Socrates all thought, as a form of 'practising death' (80e), should be directed towards this end. The soul *becomes* itself, identifies itself, through this meditation on death. As the epigraph from Montaigne echoed, *'philosopher, c'est apprendre à mourir'*. And one could go further and conclude from Socrates that if death is the most appropriate state for the soul because it is the most noncorporeal and the most intellectual state, then such a death cannot be told apart from the pure exercise of the intellect, that is, wisdom or philosophy.[6]

And yet this solemn task of thought may be forgotten. I can think of three responses to this bizarre opportunity which humans possess of forgetting about the one thing of which they are certain, the fact that we shall die. The first response comes by turning the question round to make it not 'how would it be possible to forget about death?', but 'how would it be possible to *have to remember* it?' What would it mean for something that it would *absolutely have to be* remembered, to the extent that it absolutely would be remembered for certain? For if something *must* be remembered absolutely – with an absoluteness not to be circumscribed – and therefore *will be* remembered in each case, then the notion of memory, paradoxically, no longer makes sense and falls away. The certainty that death would for sure be remembered because it absolutely had to be, would do away with the responsibility at the heart of memory, the responsibility which counts simultaneously as memory's possible failure and its only chance. It would no longer be necessary to remember death because death would *absolutely have to be* remembered. Under an absolute injunction there can be no question of its being forgotten; we need no reminding to remember it. An *absolute* injunction to remember amounts to an invitation to forget. A responsibility conditions memory, injects it with a kind of free will, making it real by giving it the chance to select and to default on what it collects and recollects. Which is as much as to say that memory *qua* memory can never be absolute. If not structured by the possibility of forgetting the experience of memory would become mere programmatic, unreflective, irresponsible retention that would involve no *remembering* as such at all.

This would be the first response to Pascal. How is it possible to forget about death? Because it is impossible absolutely to remember it. The possibility that I forget it furnishes the condition of my remembering. Only insofar as I might forget it does my remembering death become meaningful.

This paradox may be transposed onto an ethical plane to produce a second response. It may look like hubris or disrespect that from time to time I forget about death in its absoluteness, its sovereignty, its authority, but that's just how memory works. Thus I remember-and-forget, respect death and disrespect it. This reveals something about the ethics of respect. The call to respect death, such as Pascal's, unfortunately cannot be answered in a straightforward way. To respect death faithfully, to acknowledge its precedence and incontrovertibility, requires two irreconcilable gestures simultaneously, and this applies to all forms of respect. The practice of respect demands on the one hand that I concern myself with its object (in this case death), that I take it to myself, dwell on it, incorporate it and as it were watch over it, care for it, my respectful concern drawing me to an appropriation of it, a becoming busy with it, an allowing of it to fill me up, to study it, to know it, become instructed in it and give myself over to it in its difference and otherness from me; but on the other hand and owing precisely to that difference and otherness, my respect for death enjoins on me the contrary gesture, of letting it go, respecting it as other, as different and distinct from me, needing to be released, never to suffer the injury and inappropriateness of my appropriation of it, my intentions for it, my crude assimilation which would turn its otherness into my sameness and thus no longer respect it as *it*. Respect in general and the respect for death in particular necessitates this ambiguous intention both to know and not to know, to solicit and to relinquish, and thus my forgetting about death contains an ethical rightness in performing one half of the divided gesture that respect demands, that of letting go, of the movement towards not knowing at all about death, giving up any rights over it, as a sign of my respect for it. Risk, rather than truth, informs the concept of respect, for not to incorporate and not to know death in the respecting of it runs the risk of disregarding, abandoning and thus disrespecting it altogether. It is within this horizon of risk that the *ethics* of respect emerges. What would an ethics be which didn't involve some responsibility and therefore risk, imperfect knowledge, prior hesitation and the freedom that derives from having no certain, prescribed course of action to pursue? The decorum of respect entails an essential anxiety in the perpetual struggle between an apprehension of its object (death in this case) and a nonapprehension, one that could be said to be matched by the interfusing and undecided movement between remembering and forgetting. To know death as death, through the figure of absolute respect which it imposes, is also to abjure the knowing of it. Just as I remember-and-forget death, having no choice but to switch back and forth, so also I acknowledge it carefully, anxiously, through knowing and not knowing, approaching and withdrawing, respecting it thereby at the risk of disrespect and unobservance, this being the very risk by which my respect achieves validity.

As for the third response as to how it is possible to forget death, we can elaborate on the absolute injunction from the first response and with it raise the question of *force*. The phrase '*memento mori*' which I have taken as a title means 'remember you must die'. You must die, of course, but there are two kinds of 'must', two orders of obligation at issue. First, the order of 'you must because you are ordered to', 'you must because I tell you', 'you must do this or else'. Some empirical stricture binds you, and this stricture belongs to the realm of positive law, of force as enforcement where a 'must' must be enforced because it could go unheeded. Thus the force in this first case is a symptom of a basic weakness. If necessary to prescribe that you stop at a red light, it is because it is always possible for you not to, and this possibility has to be countered positively by a law which says you must stop. Obviously this is not the kind of 'must' involved in death. The phrase 'remember you must die' does not stipulate that we must die because without such a stipulation we might not. It pertains to a difference category of must. You must die because you will die, order or no order. No-one could give the order to die more strongly, more forcefully than it is already given. Try it. This is a law that does not need to express itself as an order, and requires no enforcement. It could be called force without force. So forceful that it needs no forcing, the force of mortality thus differs from the gratuity pertaining to the first kind. And this throws up the question of the ambiguity of force in general: force is both essentially gratuitous – where force is required, there has been some lack of force prior to it for which it is making up – but at the same time force achieves an immanence within itself, a perfect entelechy whose force lies in exactly such self-sufficiency and containment.

The phrase 'remember you must die' belongs to the second category of obligation. As such it requires no recollection, unlike in the first where every time I stop at a red light I am in a sense reminded of a law (which could in principle be forgotten). From this perspective the phrase becomes redundant. There is no need for me to remember I must die; it will come about regardless of my remembering it; it is simply the case and dispenses with any need to be recalled or invoked, sublimely indifferent to human apprehension of it. As a third and final response to 'how is it possible to forget about death?' we can therefore say that to remember it in any case is irrelevant. A human remembering makes no difference to it; that we must die is so unassailably true that it has no need of being sheltered in and by our memories. And so equally we can forget it without any consequence.

In this last aspect death becomes that which deprives us of any meaningful psychic relation to it. We might wonder what the consequences of this would be for psychologies of death, and specifically any psychoanalysis of it. What possible ground could there be for the death drive, for example? The psychic pursuit of death as suggested by Freud, the exercise of the death instincts, in a sense implies that death must indeed be pursued as if it were not the inevitability it is. What need a death instinct? No instinct for it is required. If the death instinct is a *drive* as Freud's German word *Todestrieb* indicates, this drive *qua* drive appears supererogatory, gratuitous, for death requires no driving towards. Pre-emptingly it outstrips all psychic relation to it, conscious or unconscious.[7]

Where, then, and how can death be apprehended? I would now like to bridge from Pascal to Heidegger. We have begun to see some of the difficulties in conceptualizing death. Heidegger will suggest that our mistake is in viewing death as actual rather than as possible, which I shall try to explain in a moment. In general a move that might be made is one that takes us away from an epistemology of death, away from the language of apprehension, away from the dimension of consciousness, which includes unconsciousness. In relation to the last point, for example, about psychoanalysis, there are already resources for thinking in a new direction. The *Todestrieb* finds its motor not only in the psyche. The drive of the death drive, according to Freud, that which urges the psychic drive in a particular direction, lodges in the organic determinations of psychic development, prior even to the formation of the unconscious. If the psyche tends towards its own death, it may owe to a phylogenetic link with its pre-psychical past as simple organism. The death drive comprises an a-psychic element, a purely organic or biological compulsion to return to a state of absolute simplicity that can be called death. The point is that the psychic relation to death can be conceived in a way that includes an a-psychic component. Psychoanalysis moves in this direction, as does the fundamental ontology of Heidegger. Both gesture towards a structural, prepsychological relation to death of the human being, though of the two it is Heidegger we shall pursue.

The Possibility of Death

Towards the very end of *A la recherche du temps perdu*, the narrator muses on his time running out, how age caps artistic endeavour:

> For the fundamental fact was that I had a body, and this meant that I was perpetually threatened by a double danger, internal and external, though to speak thus was merely a matter of linguistic convenience, the truth being that the internal danger – the risk, for example, of a cerebral haemorrhage – is also external, since it is the body that it threatens. Indeed it is the possession of a body that is the great danger to the mind, to our human and thinking life, which it is surely less correct to describe as a miraculous entelechy of animal and physical life than as an imperfect essay – as rudimentary in this sphere as the communal existence of protozoa attached to their polyparies or as the body of the whale – in the organization of the spiritual life. The body immures the mind within a fortress; presently on all sides the fortress is besieged and in the end, inevitably, the mind has to surrender.[8]

We arrived at this juncture from a third response to Pascal which said that death needed no remembering, thus frustrating psychic relation to it. A mind–body dualism underlies the point for we are implying that because the *body* is going to die anyway there is no need for the mind to accommodate the fact of death in any fashion. Proust writes pointedly of this disjunction, what could be called the 'dyschronic' link between the two systems that human beings consist in. Death discloses this dualism between the apparent and illusory immortality of the mind and the certain, felt mortality of the body. The mind would not necessarily surrender were not its bodily ramparts eroding.

True, death actually happens and it happens 'to' the body while the mind plausibly might survive indefinitely; similarly, the body is caught up absolutely in time's forward movement while the mind can skip about over the surface of time, recalling, anticipating, imagining, not shackled to the present. In these simple terms, death appears as an event, that which comes, that which happens. The body arrives at death, or death arrives at the body, and once the body falls the mind must fall too; it goes down like a captain with his ship. It is an event. We think death in terms of actual event-time. If we think of it as happening it is because we think of its taking place in the course of such time. But in so thinking, Heidegger warns us, 'death gets passed off as always something "actual"; its character as a possibility gets concealed.' Let us examine this character of possibility that death has.

Pascal's vexation depended on the *actuality* of death, whose actuality as actual *allows for* psychological cognizance of it albeit in the impeded manner we have sketched. What, by contrast, is death's *possibility*? What kind of a possibility is death? Heidegger answers that 'death is the possibility of the absolute impossibility of Dasein'. What kind of possibility is this? Two orders of possibility open up, one at the centre of Heideggerian thought, and another which will take us away from Heidegger through Derrida and back to de Man. The first kind of possibility, the Heideggerian kind, also bears a kind of force. We have already enumerated two kinds of force: that of positive law which requires enforcement and that of actual death which requires no enforcement but which in flagging death as a *factum brutum* depends on a rather unrefined materialism of the body, a biologism. Heideggerian possibility too represents a force in that it signals power. Possibility is strong because it gestures to its own ability, capacity, faculty, to do or to make. The Latin *'posse'* from which the English 'possibility' comes abbreviates the phrase *'potis esse'*, which is having the power and the *pot*ency and the 'can' as the force to do something. The German *'Möglichkeit'* which Heidegger uses for 'possibility' relates to *'Macht'* for 'power'. And death, for Heidegger, marks some kind of possibility though its power, as I shall try to show, is nothing more or less than rhetorical.

In a very general sense the force of possibility constitutes the strongest force conceivable. It makes something possible; it claims some worldly change; it envisions an adjustment of the very future; it forces open a virtual space where nothing had existed. But one should not conflate this idea with the notion that anything is possible. Virtual space, one could say, gives the easiest space of all to open. It takes no force to open, just a little imagination, for any possibility may be conceived – there is no resistance, at one level, in the realm of the imagination. This does not amount to creating the conditions for the possibility of something, however. There is a difference between the received idea of the possible as that which might become actual in the future and already exists in the realm of virtual actuality, on the one hand, what we could call 'soft' possibility; and the possible as a transcendental condition, on the other – 'hard' possibility perhaps. Death is a hard possibility.

How does Heidegger conceive it? It is death itself which allows us to conceive it for, to put it baldly, death annihilates actuality *per se*. He writes:

> *The closest closeness which one may have in Being towards death as a possibility, is as far as possible from anything actual.* The more unveiledly this

possibility gets understood, the more purely does the understanding penetrate into it *as the possibility of the impossibility of any existence at all*. Death, as possibility, gives Dasein nothing to be 'actualized', nothing which Dasein, as actual, could itself *be* . . . . Being-towards-death, as anticipation of possibility, is what first *makes* this possibility *possible*, and sets it free as possibility.⁹

Since actuality vanishes at death, destroyed *by* death, the only character available to death can be that of possibility. Death bears the force of the entirely nonactual – '*Death, as possibility, gives Dasein nothing to be "actualized"*'. It bears the force of possibility which, *qua* possibility, calls for a concept of anticipation in regard to it – with the proviso that anticipation anticipates nothing actual, belonging rather to a structure of time that opens elsewhere than into the actual, and thus once more pre-empts any *psychological* apprehension thereof. Onceness again – death never happens not so much because it *never* happens but because it never *happens*. It *is* unhappening. In this sense death cannot even be experienced. Death is an 'event' without beginning or end. There is no 'death'; there is only the stopping of life, the notion of 'death' a mere personification of that stopping. As such its possibility will have withdrawn from the realm of the actual and of empirical time, becoming even harder than 'hard'; it is hypertranscendental. It holds the status of something entirely structural, preceding all empiricism, all psychism, and if this possibility has power it is the power or force of that which can never become vulnerable because it never 'exists', never comes into time. Death does not die in time. I would suggest that the deathliness of death – its sheer incontestability – resides precisely in this, its having already been constituted as possibility. On account of never being actualized the possibility of death is effectively a *perpetual* possibility; but insofar as it is also the perpetual possibility of *death*, the last thing it can be is perpetual for it must die. We are forced to think the possibility of death as perpetual and finite at the same time.

There are one or two comments relating to what has already been said that may be made about this structure. Firstly, where we spoke about the forgettability of death we can apply a new filter to our thoughts. If we forget about death it is not only because remembering it creates problems in the ways suggested but also because of a more stringent reason. There is no forgetting or remembering of death to be had for, according to Heidegger at least, its deep character is one of possibility which pre-empts and remains absolutely foreign – not just indifferent – to apprehension of it. How is it possible, other than through some mystificatory theory of anamnesis, to remember or forget something which entirely outflanks the actual? True, one can remember things that are not 'actual', such as fictional narratives or lies, but even these are subtended by a virtual actuality. Secondly, the notion of forgetting and remembering we have been using has been rather naïve, suggestive of a simple consciousness at work. What about unconscious forgetting or repression? But even here we can say that death's possibility remains intact for it does not appear in any form whatsoever, harbouring its structurality, thus offering nothing of itself, no matter, to repress. If there is repression at large it pertains to possibility *as* repression, as that which will never become actualized. Which means too that death 'is' repression; is the object of that possibility as the impossibility of any actualization – an impossibility which perhaps may be called absolute repression. What more effective repression could be envisaged than one which precludes actualization in general?

We commonly use the word 'possible' to refer to something which may or may not happen; it might happen precisely to the extent it also might not. Heidegger's notion, by contrast, has the sense that the possible *certainly will not happen*, death forcing the paradox, it being '*the possibility of the impossibility of any existence at all*'. Why does he not use the word 'necessity' for this condition? Why does he not write that death is the *necessity* of the impossibility of any existence at all? One could venture answers such as 'because necessity belongs to the order of actuality whereas death is nothing actual', but there is a more fruitful line. In our quotation Heidegger said that 'Being-towards-death, as anticipation of possibility, is what first *makes* this possibility *possible*, and sets it free as possibility'. As such the possibility of death is created, not given, *made by* Being-towards-death, and to this extent 'contingent'.

But isn't that preposterous? Can death really be contingent? Can *it* (death!) lack transcendental force? Let's read Heidegger's sentence again: 'Being-towards-death, as anticipation of possibility, is what first *makes* this possibility *possible*, and sets it free as possibility.' We could object that there will have had to be death before its being made possible by Being-towards-death if only because the latter is just that, Being-towards-*death*, aiming at the death it purports to make possible. Yet Being-towards-death, as *Being*-towards-death must indeed precede death, for there must be Being in some form in order for there to be death (and in this sense also death is contingent – on the existence of living things which, *as* living, *can* die; there would be no *death* if there were no life, this suggesting an important respect in which death differs from nothingness which must be absolutely uncontingent). There is a contingency of death, then, in that its possibility must be made, created rather than received, but a contingency not to be confused with the contingency of what might have been otherwise, with the optional. It was not possible for this possibility of death *not* to be made for it inheres in Being as Being-towards-death, but all this does not quite add up to a necessity, and it is in the space that the spectrality and rhetoric of death opens up.

Death Persuades me with an Image

In deference to the work of Nietzsche, Ricoeur, de Man and Derrida on it, I elect the term 'promise' to indicate this space where necessity and contingency overlap and where possibility is perpetual yet finite. Death may be inevitable but not so inevitable and not so transcendentally forceful that its possibility exists prior to being made; it necessarily will happen, but rather *a fortiori* than a priori, its necessity depleted by the fact that its happening is not an actuality but a possibility;

and as possibility – one which, moreover, requires being *made* – it also *depends*. It is simultaneously necessary and contingent and to capture the internal energy of this aporetic link the notion of the promise appears helpful. A promise also is both necessary and contingent, assuring an outcome while risking exposure to all that precedes it. Death appears both necessary and contingent and can only be possible because it will have done away with actuality, so all it can *ever* do is promise itself. There will never be an actuality of fulfilment for it.

This promissory structure of death represents the other kind of possibility mentioned above. The first was of a more orthodox Heideggerian kind, shall we say, of the possibility of death as something structural. While not opposing Heidegger in this new view we are nonetheless finding room in his account for thought of a distinctly post-Heideggerian kind. As promise death begins to appear both speculative and rhetorical. It therefore continues to defy any epistemic certainty we might have about it, remaining without determinate content. In this respect we truly are departing from Heidegger who contrasts the being certain with regard to one's death with cases in which one merely has a view about something or another. In the same section as quoted of *Being and Time* he talks of the kind of certainty that applies 'in any arbitrary fiction or in merely having some "view" ["*Ansicht*"]': in such cases, he says, the kind of certainty one has about death 'is lacking'.[10] There exist in other words two distinct and even opposite types of certainty, one exclusively to do with death, the other with having a view about arbitrary things in general. But from what we have seen very little difference obtains in fact between our supposed certainty about death and the relation we might have to something arbitrary or fictional. For if death, bearing nothing that could be actualized yet sustaining possibility, is structured like a promise, and thus has a character that is both rhetorical and speculative, then we can be certain about it only in the mode of the kind of trust or credulousness we bring to the reception of just such arbitrary fictions. And all the more so in that the promise does not pertain to real time, to the time of actuality. A *transcendental* promise engages us, one which does not bind itself to an empirical future but which, like a fiction, takes place in the realm of pure possibility. Indeed the arbitrariness is crucial.

In terms of force this means that although absolutely certain, death can never be stronger than a promise. It is both absolutely certain and not absolutely certain, for the mode of its certainty, taking place outside actuality, thereby renders the certainty inaccessible. It becomes absolutely certain precisely because not subject to that actuality which would always maintain some threat, no matter how small, to certainty, in that it could vary events unpredictably; but in becoming so very certain, the certainty of death becomes impossible to establish. Hence the force of death interrupts itself in making itself absolute. It has to weaken itself to be as forceful as it is. It has become so forceful that it has absconded from and even done away with the realm in which its force can be expressed, for it has obliterated actuality. It has reached the level of a hyperabsoluteness in which mere absoluteness has been superseded with the both weaker and stronger quasi-absoluteness of a promise; and so on and so forth. Having become slightly 'weaker' through its absolute strength, it must resort to a kind of sublime rhetoric to affirm its force.

In terms of 'being', however, things appear simpler at first sight. Nothing in the transcendental workings of the promise disturbs the being to which it appends. Yes, its relation to death in Being-towards-death gets complexified by the promise, but 'being' stays in place as the promise's transcendental referent or counterweight. To this extent our analysis remains soundly metaphysical, upholding a tradition of thinking about the promise as a kind of stabilizing element in concepts of being. In another de Man essay, for example, the author says in a footnote that Nietzsche derives the transcendental referent, 'man', from the promise:[11] man is distinguished from animals by his capacity to synthesize his identity forcefully over time and making promises affords a pre-eminent modality of such continuity; man outfaces the contingency of history, wilfully positing his promise and thus himself as what will override the future. I shall come back to this, the point for now being that the promise offers a means of configuring the future according to one's will, thus in a sense anthropomorphizing time, assuring the ontological power of the one animal capable of making promises – man, who achieves a transcendental continuity, a self-necessity in the face of the accidents otherwise looming. Paul Ricoeur makes a similar point though with an emphasis more on the duty to the future than the mastery over it of the promising animal. For Ricoeur the promise binds its maker to the future in an ethical way which enjoins responsibilities on him or her – and again an ontological substrate forms.[12]

But surely the transcendental promise as we have introduced it would fail to support an ontology? Not only does it not pertain to an actual time in which being could be sustained but it promises the nonactualization of being *per se*. And besides, the promise of death is not made by anyone, is not the object of an intention, thus one could not derive a subjective agent for it with ontological properties. The promise of death must indeed concern the death of being or of a being – for as we said, only being can die – and to this extent we cannot simply deny or bypass the ontological dimension; but at the same time we are obliged to consider a more enigmatic kind of death which radiates at the limit of ontology. We must try to think this very difficult aspect of death.

As promised death is coming but not as anything actual. In this sense it does not come at all; it cannot come for there is no actuality for it to penetrate. Its coming conforms rather to an already-here. What is promised has already been given for though only ever promised it cannot be deferred since no actuality exists into which to project it. It will have already insinuated itself. This would be the structure raised by the transcendental or rather quasi- or hyper-transcendental promise. Death consigns us not only to an actual death to come but also to a being already dead; contained in the 'towards' of Being-towards-death is an echo of the death that has preceded it, thus one travels towards the thing one has departed from.

In this respect actual death, the common-sense version of death, might look like the typological fulfilment or the prophetic completion of the death that has taken place surreptitiously beforehand. In dying one is catching up with death as in a kind of delayed effect, and in saying this I have in mind not only theoretical work on this subject – by Freud, of course, in terms of *Nachträglichkeit* and by Žižek in not dissimilar terms[13] – but also a couple of fictions. There is Tolstoy's *Death of Ivan Ilyich* (to which Heidegger devotes a footnote in *Being and Time*[14]) for example, and a later fiction by Don DeLillo called *Mao II* which seems tacitly to invoke Tolstoy's story. Ivan, having suffered the vicissitudes of a civil service career in Russia, eventually secures a prestigious post in St Petersburg. Full of pride he buys a house in the city for his family and sets about decorating it:

> He was so taken up with it all that he often did things himself, rearranging the furniture or the hangings. Once when mounting a step-ladder to show a workman, who did not understand, how he wanted some material draped, he made a false step and slipped, but being a strong and agile person he clung on and only knocked his side against the knob of the window frame. The bruise was painful but it soon passed off. All this time, indeed Ivan Ilyich felt particularly alert and well. 'I feel fifteen years younger', he wrote.[15]

That trivial knock to his side turns out to be fatal and it works like a *memento mori*. The story is written so as to suggest the prior necessity of the death, with implications for the vanity of human ambition. The long remainder of the story details the time-lag, so to speak, of the stay of execution, the gap between Ivan's having already died in the knock, his actual death at the end of the tale, and the background sense of the knock on the side marking the irruption of an already-deadness of the man. In DeLillo's story the hero, a writer, on a trip to Israel, receives a slight knock to his side from a car as he steps off a pavement. According to a similar, even identical, structure, the knock turns out to be fatal as if some malign promise has been awakened.[16]

This 'promise', this strangely contingent but indubitable necessity which cannot be proved because never actualized, this promise of being already dead entombs its subject, gives it over even in the midst of its actual life to a kind of mourning. If already dead by this promise the living being has a kind of monumentality conferred upon him or her. In other words the mourning process begins with the beginning of life for life is already a kind of death, the being which lives it promised to a death anterior to it. Life begins and continues with a protest against this constant monumentalization, against the ceaseless becoming-dead and sclerosis which makes every image of it a death-mask. In terms of the forgettability of death we could therefore offer a fourth response to Pascal. There can be no forgetting of death at all, transcendentally speaking, for every image I have of myself or anyone becomes a remembering of them as dead even while alive, a precocious mourning. My very self-consciousness becomes posthumous. Every image I have of every animate thing arrives as an object of mourning; though I may forget about death I cannot forget the deathliness of the dead who live around me. And in turn I am subject to the uncontrollable reproduction of myself as 'dead' in the images of me carried by others. Hardened into an image object, my deathly being proliferates irregularly in these fissiparous, sculptural, pseudoaesthetic forms.

One of a number of inferences derived by Derrida from this situation reveals a sheer forcelessness on the part of actual death (see MPDM). Actual death fails to register, it makes no difference: I can be remembered as dead before dying; actual death does not alter the mode of my being remembered. Rather it is the transcendental promise of death which has power over me, and a hyperbolic power to boot for the promise delivers me over to the other who will have begun mourning for me – not just to a singular other, either, but to the possibility of an endless division and dissemination of my image among every other in general. This is power or force as sheer reproduction and augmentation, reiteration, regeneration, repetition and so on, which is in principle infinite. The promise speaks with a rhetoric that affirms the fission of my self, thus my self-identity and my very being, firing it into a myriad specular structure where I am trapped behind glass so to speak, imaged in the other a million times over. I describe it as rhetoric not only on account of its force, that of identity explosion, but also because – as we must never forget – it remains without a basis in actuality, with all the rhetorical uncertainty of the unprovable – for this is where rhetoric springs up, in the absence of an apodictic truth. Meanwhile the force of being for its part must consist in resistance to this promise which saturates it but cannot be confronted, the promise that it is already dead, already mourned for, already turned into an icon and thus, before being even begins, already appropriated by the other. And Derrida makes another inference from *this*, namely that the a priori confusion of myself with the other means that the being I have and which dies will not be entirely my own, that the other always dies my death with me and the 'mineness' of my death fails to soak it all up. Which would fly in the face of one of the essential characteristics of death mentioned at the beginning of this discussion, viz, that my death is always my own and none can die it for me.

Once Again: Such Celerity in Dying

We have looked with reference to Pascal at some of the problems in conceptualizing actual death. We then, at Heidegger's prompting, changed the discussion to the level of possibility at which death, though necessary, gives nothing to be actualized, thus creating for itself the character of a perpetual promise. This promise, rather than projecting an actual future, lay in a possibility which as such inhabited a space of the already. The already of the promise of death led in turn to the being-mourned-by-the-other which affects all 'living' things. But our enquiry began, and here and there referred back to, the 'onceness' of death. This onceness reappears at the juncture we have reached and I shall conclude with some remarks about it.

It transpires that rather than dying once I die again and again through the other, in the other's image of me. My self-identity such as it is gets posited outside myself in unconnected acts deriving from the rhetoric of a promise. And it is not just rhetoric but fiction which springs up, for these images of me abound from my death or absence and are thus not controlled by veracity. They begin with my absence or death, my removal from actuality, thus apocryphal by nature; they can be multiplied or distorted without reference back to a living me, without ratification from anything actual. Derrida says the origin of fiction lies in mourning, in just such 'apocryphal figuration' as he calls it (MPDM 34). This generative figuration makes me die over and over in different, distorted non-self-identical versions, makes me die even as it preserves me in multifarious forms.

It is perhaps little wonder then that Paul de Man associates rhetoric with death, as we said back in the first paragraph. De Man wants to stress the true force of both rhetoric and death as stemming from their violent randomness, their absolute disruptiveness and discontinuity. In the essay referred to earlier, for example, he writes that:

> [Shelley's] *The Triumph of Life* warns us that nothing, whether deed, word, thought, or text, ever happens in relation, positive or negative, to anything that precedes, follows, or exists elsewhere, but only as a random event whose power, like the power of death, is due to the randomness of its occurrence.[17]

It is what makes him also deconstruct the Nietzschean concept of the promise we referred to, as that which sustains over time and thus idealizes the identity of its wilful, forceful maker. For de Man there would be a force of the promise greater than that of the person who makes it in that the promise *fails*, precisely, to sustain the identity of its maker over time. It would be an act of violent positing without recuperation somewhat along the lines we have laid out. The promise of death such as we have described it allows for an absolute randomness in the imaging of me by the other who can make images, posit figurations of me in an arbitrary and fictive manner. Thus I am indeed posited, but posited only in the de Manian, rhetorical sense, as a series of linguistic acts which bear no ideal relation to one another and no transcendental relation to the referent, the me, they 'derive' from. For I begin, begin to be, only within the possibility of this prior distortion and appropriation. A rhetorical machine will have begun to randomly posit my being outside myself owing to the fact that this being is promised to the possibility, rather than the actuality, of death. In this light death appears as the radical intermission of my being *per se*.

This allows us to conclude that death may indeed remain unknowable in its happening only once. But it happens only once again and again in these severely truncated rhetorical acts that ought not be humanized into a meaningful chain. Each time, each toll of death, is a one-off in that I am fictively distorted in each case, thus bearing only accidental and not essential similarity to myself from one time to the next. A principle of confusion is at work, therefore, allowing me also to be mistaken and misprised. The distortion of my image operates by such a principle of confusion, allowing for mistaken identity, projection, prosopagnosia and the dreams of others' deaths.

Notes

¹ Peter Szondi, 'On Textual Understanding', *On Textual Understanding and Other Essays*, trans. Harvey Mendelsohn (Manchester: Manchester University Press, 1986), pp. 13ff.

² Paul de Man, 'Shelley Disfigured', *The Rhetoric of Romanticism* (New York: Columbia University Press, 1984), p. 122. See below for quotation.

³ Martin Heidegger, *Being and Time*, trans. John Macquarrie and Edward Robinson (Oxford: Blackwell, 1962), p. 307.

⁴ Blaise Pascal, 'A Letter to Further the Search for God', *Pensées and Other Writings*, trans. Honor Levi (Oxford: Oxford University Press, 1995), pp. 160–62.

⁵ Rainer Maria Rilke, *The Selected Poetry of Rainer Maria Rilke*, trans. Stephen Mitchell (London: Picador, 1980), p. 155.

> Of course, it is strange to inhabit the earth no longer,
> to give up customs one barely had time to learn,
> not see roses and other promising Things
> in terms of a human future; no longer to be
> what one was in infinitely anxious hands; to leave
> even one's own first name behind, forgetting it
> as easily as a child abandons a broken toy.

⁶ Plato, *The Collected Dialogues*, ed. Edith Hamilton and Huntington Cairns (Princeton: Princeton University Press, 1961), pp. 63–6.

⁷ See in particular Freud's 'Beyond the Pleasure Principle', in vol. 11 of The Pelican Freud Library, *On Metapsychology: The Theory of Psychoanalysis*, trans. James Strachey (Harmondsworth: Penguin, 1984), pp. 269–338.

⁸ Marcel Proust, *Remembrance of Things Past*, vol. 3, trans. Terence Kilmartin, Andreas Mayor and C.K. Scott Moncrieff (Harmondsworth: Penguin, 1981), p. 1092.

⁹ Heidegger, *Being and Time*, pp. 306–7.

¹⁰ Heidegger, *Being and Time*, p. 300.

¹¹ Paul de Man, *Allegories of Reading: Figural Language in Rousseau, Nietzsche, Rilke, and Proust* (New Haven and London: Yale University Press, 1979), p. 273.

¹² See Paul Ricoeur, 'Self as *Ipse*', *Freedom and Interpretation: The Oxford Amnesty Lectures 1992*, ed. Barbara Johnson (New York: Basic, 1993), pp. 103–19.

¹³ For references to Freud's use of this term see J. Laplanche and J.-B. Pontalis, *The Language of Psychoanalysis*, trans. Donald Nicholson-Smith (London: Karnac, 1988), pp. 111–14; Slavoj Žižek, 'You Only Die Twice', *The Sublime Object of Ideology* (London: Verso, 1989), pp. 131–49.

¹⁴ An essay on Heidegger's footnote by Robert Bernasconi, 'Literary Attestation in Philosophy: Heidegger's Footnote on Tolstoy's "The Death of Ivan Ilyich"', appears in *Philosophers' Poets*, ed. David Wood (London: Routledge, 1990), pp. 7–36.

¹⁵ Leo Tolstoy, *The Death of Ivan Ilyich and Other Stories*, trans. Rosemary Edmonds (Harmondsworth: Penguin, 1960), p. 121.

¹⁶ Don DeLillo, *Mao II* (London: Vintage, 1991).

¹⁷ See note 2 above.

Index

Abitbol, Michel 136, 145 n.10
Abraham, Nicolas 32–3, 35 n.19
Adorno, Theodor 29
Algeria 131, 136, 141–2
alterity 24, 29, 123, 128, 131, 134–5, 150; *see also* other
Altieri, Charles 38
antonomasia 72–82
Aouate, Yves-Charles 145 n.10
aporia 4, 112, 115–16; *see also* indeterminacy; undecidability
Aristotle 22 n.11, 23 n.15, 25, 38–9, 49, 62, 86–108, 110–13, 115–18
Artaud, Antonin 9
Attridge, Derek 12 n.17
Augustine, St 131–5, 140
Austin, J.L. 40, 43–4, 50–58
autobiography 67–82, 126–7, 131–42, 144 n.5

Bacon, Francis 24
Bass, Alan vii–viii, 12 n.15
Bataille, Georges 9, 22 n.12
Beardsworth, Richard 12 n.9
Being 105, 110–12, 114–15, 116, 117, 118–22, 124, 155, 157
Bennington, Geoffrey 2, 11 n.1, 11 n.2, 12 n.9, 13 n.22, 131
Bergson, Henri 110, 116–17
Bernasconi, Robert 161 n.14
Bible 21, 131, 132, 133, 138–42
blanc 20
Blanchot, Maurice 9, 11, 13 n.25, 24, 142
Bloom, Harold 27–9
Boyarin, Daniel 140, 141, 145 n.11
Bruss, Elizabeth 68, 82
Burke, Kenneth 132–3

Cantor, Jay 36, 40
Cascardi, A.J. 11 n.4, 12 n.11
Cavell, Stanley 36, 37–8, 42, 43, 44, 46, 48 n.15
Celan, Paul 9
chiasmus 76–7, 82

Childs, Brevard 139
Christ 141
Christianity 126–7, 129–30, 135–6, 141–2
Chouraqui, André 136
circumcision 131, 132, 137–42
citation 20, 29, 54
Clark, Timothy 13 n.19, 13 n.25
cogito 6, 39–41, 45–6
Cohen, L. Jonathan 64 n.2
'come' 13 n.25, 124
confession 127–8, 129, 131–5, 141–2
Crémieux decree 136, 145 n.9
critique 1–5, 12 n.8, 29
Culler, Jonathan 51, 58

Danto, Arthur 49
Dasein 110–11, 113–15, 118, 147, 153–4
death viii, 70, 78–81, 118–19, 133, 146–60; *see also* mourning
death drive 27, 151–2
decision 4–6; *see also* undecidability
deconstruction 1–11, 29, 31–2, 36–47, 87, 101, 127
DeLillo, Don 158
de Man, Paul 30, 38, 40, 83 n.7, 133, 146, 153, 155, 157, 160
Derrida, Eugène Eliahou 138, 141
Derrida, Jacques, works by:
  'Of an Apocalyptic Tone Recently Adopted in Philosophy' 123–4, 130; *Aporias* viii, 13 n.24; 'At This Very Moment in This Work Here I Am' 144 n.6; 'Before the Law' 12 n.18; 'Circumfession' 131–42; 'Cogito and the History of Madness' 6, 39, 44–6; 'Coming into One's Own' 33–4; 'Différance' 22 n.7, 119, 122, 123; *Dissemination* 2, 8, 14, 21 n.3, 21 n.5, 22 n.8, 22 n.9, 22 n.10, 22 n.13, 23 n.14, 23 n.15, 23 n.16, 23 n.17, 23 n.18, 23 n.19, 46, 123, 125 n.18; 'The Double Session' 7, 41; 'The Ends of Man' 118–19, 121; 'Force and Signification' 7; 'Force of Law'

Derrida, Jacques, works by (contd.)
4–5; 'Fors' 24; *Glas* 8, 39, 67–82; *Of Grammatology* 16–17, 22 n.7, 23 n.17, 31, 35 n.20, 108 n.2, 109 n.11, 109 n.14, 123; 'How Not to Speak' 130, 135–6, 144 n.5; 'The Law of Genre' 13 n.19; 'Letter to a Japanese Friend' 1, 5; *Limited Inc* 30, 47 n.6, 53, 55, 56–8, 61, 66 n.36, 123; 'Living On: Border Lines' 30, 31, 32; *Margins of Philosophy* 22 n.10, 22 n.11, 29, 48 n.11, 50; *Mémoires: for Paul de Man* 159, 160; *Memoirs of the Blind* 130, 135; 'Me — Psychoanalysis' 32–3; '*Ousia* and *Grammè*' 110–19; *Parages* 11, 13 n.25; 'Parergon' 12 n.8, 109 n.10; 'Perhaps or Maybe' 5–6; 'Plato's Pharmacy' 69; *Points* 4, 8–9; *Positions* 12 n.15, 28–9, 35 n.19, 59–60, 65 n.20, 109 n.15; *The Post Card* 130; 'The Principle of Reason' 6; 'Psyche: Inventions of the Other' 10; 'Remarks on Deconstruction and Pragmatism' 2; 'The *Retrait* of Metaphor' 125 n.14; *Schibboleth* 130, 138; 'Signature Event Context' 12 n.13, 29–30, 48 n.9, 53–5, 63–4, 66 n.36; 'Some Statements and Truisms' 12 n.16; *Specters of Marx* viii n.1, 3; *Speech and Phenomena* 109 n.14, 117–18, 123; *Spurs: Nietzsche's Styles* 122; '"This Strange Institution Called Literature"' 8, 9, 10; 'The Time is Out of Joint' 10; 'The Time of a Thesis: Punctuations' 8; 'Violence and Metaphysics' 129, 130, 145 n.8; 'White Mythology' 86–108; *Writing and Difference* 21 n.2, 21 n.5, 22 n.9, 22 n.12, 23 n.17, 25, 29, 31, 65 n.23
Descartes, René 6, 37, 38, 39–41, 42–3, 44–6, 94, 101–2, 127
différance 7, 17, 20, 106, 108, 122
dissemination 23 n.15, 28–9, 54
'double science' 19, 21
Dummett, Michael 64 n.2
Du Val, Guillaume 49

Eco, Umberto 51
Eilberg-Schwartz, Howard 139, 140, 145 n.11

Eliot, T.S. 25–7
Elijah 141–2
epistemology 37–8, 41–5
es gibt 120–23
ethics 128–30, 134–5, 142, 149–50, 157
event 11, 138, 152–3, 154, 159–60

face 128, 130
Fackenheim, Emil 144 n.1
feminism vii, viii n.1
Feyerabend, Paul 38
figuration 27, 70–82, 133, 140–41, 146, 153, 155, 156, 157, 158–60; *see also* metaphor
filiation 33–4, 69, 74–5, 78–81
force 31, 150–51, 153–4, 156–7, 159, 160
forgetting, *see* remembering
formalism 7, 19, 31
Foucault, Michel 6, 39, 44–5, 46
Freccero, John 132, 133
Frege, Gottlob 49, 61, 64 n.2, 65 n.15
French 136–7
Freud, Sigmund 22 n.8, 22 n.10, 22 n.13, 23 n.15, 25–9, 32–4, 80, 123, 151–2, 158
Friedlander, Judith 145 n.9
Frye, Northrop 68
Fuller, Steven 40, 48 n.18

Gadamer, Hans-Georg 47
Gasché, Rodolphe 11 n.2, 110, 119, 120
Gelley, Alexander 23 n.14
genealogy, *see* filiation
Genet, Jean 67, 69–82
genre 67–9, 82
Glatzer, Nahum 144 n.1
Greek 127, 129, 135–7
Guardini, Romano 134

Hartman, Geoffrey 24
Harvey, Irene 2, 11 n.2, 12 n.12
Hausman, Carl 91, 109 n.9
Hebrew 127, 129, 136–7, 141
Hegel, G.W.F. 21 n.2, 22 n.10, 22 n.12, 22 n.13, 23 n.14, 46, 49, 67, 70–73, 89, 94, 95, 101, 105, 111, 112
Heidegger, Martin 23 n.14, 29, 47, 58, 59, 92, 105, 109 n.11, 110–24, 136, 145 n.7, 147, 151–6, 158, 159
Hill, Geoffrey 24
Hirsch, E.D. 63, 66 n.25

Hölderlin, Friedrich 148
Husserl, Edmund 41, 48 n.11, 49, 53, 55, 59, 101, 111, 117, 123
hymen 7, 20

imagination 21 n.5
indeterminacy 37–9, 62–3, 148; *see also* aporia; undecidability
infinity of language 58, 62–3
institution 8–9, 12 n.8, 68, 74
intention 29, 51, 53–4, 56, 67, 94–5
Islam 135–6
iterability 12 n.13, 29–30, 55, 56, 57, 61

Jakobson, Roman 10, 28
Johnson, Barbara 2, 48 n.10
Jones, Ernest 25–6, 33
Joyce, James 9
Judaism 126–42

Kant, Immanuel 1–2, 21 n.5, 37, 45–6, 49
Kierkegaard, Søren 39
Krell, David Farrell 113
Kripke, Saul 36
Kuhn, Thomas 38

Lacan, Jacques 26–7, 28–9, 33
language 10, 15, 30–31, 33, 38–9, 40–41, 50
Latin 131, 135–7
law 51, 129–30, 150–51
Lejeune, Philippe 67–8
Levinas, Emmanuel 126–31, 134, 136, 142, 144 n.6
literary criticism 7–8, 19–20, 25–7, 31–2, 34, 40, 67–9, 146
literature viii, 8–11, 14–21, 67, 70, 72, 82, 142
logocentrism 16
Lyotard, Jean-François 48 n.11

Maclean, Ian 12 n.13, 65 n.19
Mallarmé, Stéphane 7, 9, 20
Marin, Louis 47 n.7
Marranism 141–2
Marx, Karl 2
Marxism vii, 2–4, 12 n.9
meaning 19–20, 52, 54, 57, 63, 90–92, 103, 105
memory, *see* remembering

messianic 3, 142
metaphor 22 n.11, 86–108, 121; *see also* figuration
metaphysics 2, 16, 58, 87, 89, 95, 97, 99, 100, 106, 108, 110–11, 115, 117, 118, 120, 121
mimesis 21
Montaigne, Michel de 40, 146, 149
Morgan, Augustus de 63
mother 131–2, 141; *see also* filiation
mourning 70, 78–9, 80, 158–60

name 67–82, 87–8, 92–3, 94, 101, 138, 141–2
negative theology 134, 135–6
Nietzsche, Friedrich 29, 36, 38–9, 47, 58, 146, 155, 157, 160
nihilism 47
Norris, Christopher 11 n.2, 12 n.5

ontology 8, 110–11, 114, 124, 152, 157; *see also* Being
other 128, 130, 159–60; *see also* alterity

painting 28
Parmenides 111, 112
Pascal, Blaise 147–8, 149, 151, 152, 153, 158, 159
Paul, St 140, 141, 148
Peirce, C.S. 59
Perelman, Chaim 52
performative 10–11, 39, 134, 142; *see also* speech act theory
Petrarch 133
pharmakon 23 n.15
phenomenology 55, 59, 61, 62, 64, 110, 114, 121
philosophy 14–15, 18, 29, 36–7, 46–7, 49–50, 51, 70, 86–108, 126–8, 136, 149
Plato 15, 17–18, 21 n.3, 23 n.15, 69, 94, 100–101, 135
play 59, 70, 93, 124
pleasure 25, 26, 32
Poe, Edgar Allan 67
  The Purloined Letter 28
poetry 27–8, 72
Pöggeler, Otto 125 n.7
Poirier, René 52, 63
possibility 153–6, 159, 160
pragmatism 7, 12 n.5

Pratt, Mary L. 65 n.13
presence 14, 15–17, 53, 54–5, 57, 59–60, 100–101, 104–6, 108, 110–12, 117, 118–19, 120–22, 125 n.18
promise 3–4, 155–60
proper name, *see* name
Proust, Marcel 152
psychoanalysis 24–34, 151–2

quasi-transcendental 2, 128, 157
quotation, *see* citation

Racine, Jean
   Athalie 64
reading 8, 11, 30–32, 71–2, 76–7, 78–9, 82, 108 n.2
reflexivity 9–10
religion 128–9; *see also* Christianity; Islam; Judaism
re-mark 9, 13 n.19
Rembrandt 77
remembering 148–51, 152, 154, 158–9
repetition 18
repression 154–5
respect 149–50
responsibility 149, 150
rhetoric, *see* figuration; metaphor
Richard, Jean-Pierre 7, 21 n.5
Ricoeur, Paul 61, 62, 63, 66 n.25, 90, 91, 93, 109 n.7, 133, 155, 157
Rilke, Rainer Maria 148
Robbins, Jill 13 n.20, 135
Rorty, Richard 12 n.5, 36, 47, 49
Rosen, Stanley 48 n.16
Rosenzweig, Franz 126–30
Rousseau, Jean-Jacques 18, 21
Rousset, Jean 21 n.5, 23 n.17, 31
Russell, Bertrand 117
Ryan, Michael 12 n.9

sacrifice 147
Saussure, Ferdinand de 15, 17, 22 n.6, 22 n.7, 57, 62, 93
science 14, 21, 146
Searle John R. 30, 47 n.6, 49–50, 52–3, 55–64
Shakespeare, William
   Hamlet 25–7, 28, 33
sign 15–17, 19, 59–60, 88–90, 92, 103, 139, 141
signature 9, 13 n.20, 54, 55, 67–82

singularity 9, 138, 146–7
skepticism 36–47
Smith, Barbara Herrnstein 68–9
Smith, Robert viii, 13 n.24
Socrates 36–7, 148–9
Solignac, André 134
Sollers, Philippe 123
Sophism 37
speech act theory 50–64; *see also* performative
Spinoza, Baruch de 141
Strawson, P.F. 37, 66 n.27
structuralism 31, 59, 61
subject 5–6, 15–16, 25, 53–4, 67–8
sun 17–18, 71–3, 100–106
supplement 18, 20
syntax 18, 20
Szondi, Peter 146

Talmud 127, 129
Tarski, Alfred 61
Taylor Mark C. 144 n.5, 145 n.7
temporality, *see* time
Tennyson, Alfred
   Maud 25
text 8, 9, 14–15, 19–21, 68–70, 71, 76, 80, 82
thought 6–7
time 110–24, 153, 154, 156, 157
Todd, Jane Marie 13 n.20
Tolstoy, Leo 158
trace 16–17, 24, 30
translation 32
Trilling, Lionel 27, 35 n.19
truth 14–15, 18, 51–2, 63–4, 89, 91–2, 104–5, 134, 142
type/token 55–6, 58–61, 66 n.25
typology 131–3

Unamuno, Miguel de 63
unconscious 12 n.10, 24–34
undecidability 4–6, 10–11, 19–20; *see also* aporia; indeterminacy
use/mention 55–6, 58–9, 61–2
usure 23 n.15, 97–9

Vail, L.M. 120, 121
Valéry, Paul 50
Vichy 136, 145 n.10

Westermann, Claus 139

Wittgenstein, Ludwig 36, 41, 44, 45, 46, 48 n.11
Wordsworth, Ann 12 n.10
writing 15–18, 28–34, 54–5, 138, 142

Yovel, Yirmiyahu 141
Zarader, Marlène 145 n.7
Zeno 112, 116–17
Žižek, Slavoj 158

For Product Safety Concerns and Information please contact our EU
representative GPSR@taylorandfrancis.com
Taylor & Francis Verlag GmbH, Kaufingerstraße 24, 80331 München, Germany